AF680642

Advances in Data Science-Driven Technologies

(Volume 4)

Generative AI and Wireless Sensor Networks: Opportunities and Challenges

Edited by

Shelly Gupta
CSE (AI) Department, KIET Group of Institutions
Ghaziabad, UP, India

Sapna Juneja
CSE (AI) Department, KIET Group of Institutions
Ghaziabad, UP, India

&

Sandeep Kautish
Institute of Innovation, PhysicsWallah Limited
Noida, India

Generative AI and Wireless Sensor Networks: Opportunities and Challenges

(Volume 4)

Advances in Data Science-Driven Technologies

Editors: Shelly Gupta, Sapna Juneja & Sandeep Kautish

ISSN (Online): 2972-3450

ISSN (Print): 2972-3442

ISBN (Online): 978-981-5324-69-3

ISBN (Print): 978-981-5324-70-9

ISBN (Paperback): 978-981-5324-71-6

© 2025, Bentham Books imprint.

Published by Bentham Science Publishers Pte. Ltd. Singapore. All Rights Reserved.

First published in 2025.

BENTHAM SCIENCE PUBLISHERS LTD.

End User License Agreement (for non-institutional, personal use)

This is an agreement between you and Bentham Science Publishers Ltd. Please read this License Agreement carefully before using the ebook/echapter/ejournal (**"Work"**). Your use of the Work constitutes your agreement to the terms and conditions set forth in this License Agreement. If you do not agree to these terms and conditions then you should not use the Work.

Bentham Science Publishers agrees to grant you a non-exclusive, non-transferable limited license to use the Work subject to and in accordance with the following terms and conditions. This License Agreement is for non-library, personal use only. For a library / institutional / multi user license in respect of the Work, please contact: permission@benthamscience.org.

Usage Rules:

1. All rights reserved: The Work is the subject of copyright and Bentham Science Publishers either owns the Work (and the copyright in it) or is licensed to distribute the Work. You shall not copy, reproduce, modify, remove, delete, augment, add to, publish, transmit, sell, resell, create derivative works from, or in any way exploit the Work or make the Work available for others to do any of the same, in any form or by any means, in whole or in part, in each case without the prior written permission of Bentham Science Publishers, unless stated otherwise in this License Agreement.
2. You may download a copy of the Work on one occasion to one personal computer (including tablet, laptop, desktop, or other such devices). You may make one back-up copy of the Work to avoid losing it.
3. The unauthorised use or distribution of copyrighted or other proprietary content is illegal and could subject you to liability for substantial money damages. You will be liable for any damage resulting from your misuse of the Work or any violation of this License Agreement, including any infringement by you of copyrights or proprietary rights.

Disclaimer:

Bentham Science Publishers does not guarantee that the information in the Work is error-free, or warrant that it will meet your requirements or that access to the Work will be uninterrupted or error-free. The Work is provided "as is" without warranty of any kind, either express or implied or statutory, including, without limitation, implied warranties of merchantability and fitness for a particular purpose. The entire risk as to the results and performance of the Work is assumed by you. No responsibility is assumed by Bentham Science Publishers, its staff, editors and/or authors for any injury and/or damage to persons or property as a matter of products liability, negligence or otherwise, or from any use or operation of any methods, products instruction, advertisements or ideas contained in the Work.

Limitation of Liability:

In no event will Bentham Science Publishers, its staff, editors and/or authors, be liable for any damages, including, without limitation, special, incidental and/or consequential damages and/or damages for lost data and/or profits arising out of (whether directly or indirectly) the use or inability to use the Work. The entire liability of Bentham Science Publishers shall be limited to the amount actually paid by you for the Work.

General:

1. Any dispute or claim arising out of or in connection with this License Agreement or the Work (including non-contractual disputes or claims) will be governed by and construed in accordance with the laws of Singapore. Each party agrees that the courts of the state of Singapore shall have exclusive jurisdiction to settle any dispute or claim arising out of or in connection with this License Agreement or the Work (including non-contractual disputes or claims).
2. Your rights under this License Agreement will automatically terminate without notice and without the

need for a court order if at any point you breach any terms of this License Agreement. In no event will any delay or failure by Bentham Science Publishers in enforcing your compliance with this License Agreement constitute a waiver of any of its rights.

3. You acknowledge that you have read this License Agreement, and agree to be bound by its terms and conditions. To the extent that any other terms and conditions presented on any website of Bentham Science Publishers conflict with, or are inconsistent with, the terms and conditions set out in this License Agreement, you acknowledge that the terms and conditions set out in this License Agreement shall prevail.

Bentham Science Publishers Pte. Ltd.
No. 9 Raffles Place
Office No. 26-01
Singapore 048619
Singapore
Email: subscriptions@benthamscience.net

BENTHAM SCIENCE

CONTENTS

FOREWORD

This book provides a comprehensive overview of both Generative Artificial Intelligence (AI) and Wireless Sensor Networks (WSNs), describing the features, capabilities, and uses of each technology. It looks at how generative AI could enhance data analysis, anomaly detection, predictive modeling, and WSN optimization. Additionally, it focusses on the security risks and weaknesses brought about by the usage of generative AI in wireless sensor networks. It addresses practical examples that demonstrated the implementation of generative AI and wireless sensor networks.

In this book, Chapter 1 gives an overview of GAI, along with its gradual evolution and various application areas. This chapter specially discusses its application in the field of programming. Programming jobs have the potential to revolutionise software development procedures. The advantages and drawbacks of using GAI to automate code generation, intelligent debugging support, Natural Language Processing (NLP) interfaces, code completion, and documentation generation are examined in this study. This study attempts to offer insights into how GAI might be used to enhance programming techniques and increase the performance and reliability of WSNs through a thorough analysis. Chapter 2 presents the concept of automated agriculture. The authors have provided information regarding the Advanced Crop Management System, how it has empowered farmers to the extent they are today and and how can they perceive events occurring in the future. In this chapter, a comprehensive study of methods for agriculture enhancement from machine learning to deep learning is provided. Chapter 3 discusses digital technologies to enhance the quality of traveling for commuters by integrating wireless sensors in IoT and AI. It gives an idea about how AI Algorithms form a vital part in most effectively handling traffic flow by collecting and integrating data from various sources such as Traffic Sensors, GPS Devices, Weather forecasts, and historical traffic patterns. The further study presented in Chapter 4 discusses the Generative AI-based methods to handle challenges in WSN-based data dissemination systems. The book also provides a study in chapter 5 that examines how big data analytics and Artificial Intelligence (AI) might progress the industrial supply chain's sustainability as manufacturing supply chains are realizing the necessity for eco-friendly operations due to rising healthcare costs and environmental concerns. Keeping this in consideration an Automatic Number Plate Recognition System in Real-time (ANPRS) is an essential component of modern vehicle surveillance and management. In Chapter 6, a Generative AI-based novel framework for real-time Automatic Number Plate Detection is proposed and implemented. Also, a framework for optimizing energy conversation based on Meta-heuristic Algorithms is discussed in Chapter 7. A study in Chapter 8 is presented to investigate the possible advantages and security concerns of incorporating generative AI into communication systems by examining the overlap between GAI and communication engineering. At last, Chapter 9 of this book discusses and explores different generative AI models and their recent trends present in communication engineering in the spectrum of network optimization, resource allocation, *etc*. The potential applications of these models are also discussed, along with security concerns.

This book showcases effective deployments, lessons learned, and best practices. By meeting the stated objective and dimension, this book promises to be a helpful resource for academics, practitioners, and students interested in understanding the potential and security risks related to the integration of wireless sensor networks and generative AI.

Ali Wagdy Mohamed
Operations Research Department
Faculty of Graduate Studies for Statistical Research
Cairo University
Giza 12613, Egypt

PREFACE

The combination of Wireless Sensor Networks (WSNs) with generative Artificial Intelligence (AI) represents the cutting edge of technical advancement as we navigate the digital age. This synergy has important obstacles that must be overcome in order for it to be widely adopted and effective, even though it also promises to improve data processing and decision-making capacities.

This book addresses the constantly changing relationship along with a thorough analysis of how generative AI might improve WSN capabilities in a range of fields, including smart cities, healthcare, environmental monitoring, and industrial applications. There is a rising need for improved analytical tools due to the exponential expansion of data collected by sensors. A strong foundation for deriving significant insights, permitting predictive modelling, and enhancing system performance is offered by generative AI.

This book explores the various aspects of generative AI integration with WSNs, such as data quality, privacy issues, energy consumption, and the resilience of AI models in practical settings. Every chapter offers an integrated perspective of the current state of affairs and lays the groundwork for further investigation and innovation by fusing theoretical underpinnings with real-world case studies.

We encourage you to think about the significant effects of this convergence on communities, businesses, and society at large as you peruse this book. Our mission is to provide the knowledge necessary for academics, practitioners, and policymakers to fully realize the promise of generative AI while addressing its many obstacles.

We would like to thank all of the contributors who helped in making this book a team effort by sharing their knowledge and vision. Our joint goal is to shed light on the way forward, paving the way for a time when wireless sensor networks and generative AI will collaborate to build smarter, more effective surroundings.

Shelly Gupta
CSE (AI) Department
KIET Group of Institutions
Ghaziabad, UP, India

Sapna Juneja
CSE (AI) Department
KIET Group of Institutions
Ghaziabad, UP, India

&

Sandeep Kautish
Institute of Innovation
PhysicsWallah Limited
Noida, India

List of Contributors

Ayasha Malik	Department of Computer Science and Engineering, IIMT College of Engineering, Greater Noida, India
Arunima Sengupta	Department of Computer Science and Engineering, SGT University, Gurugram, Haryana, India
Amena Mahmoud	Department of Information and Communication Sciences, Faculty of Science and Technology, Sophia University, Tokya, Japan
Ankita Sharma	Department of Computer Science and Engineering, SGT University, Gurugram, Haryana, India
Bhawna	Department of CSE(AIML), KIET Group of Institutions, Delhi-NCR, Ghaziabad, India
Charvi	Department of Computer Science and Engineering, SGT University, Gurugram, Haryana, India
Dheerdhwaj Barak	Department of Computer Science and Engineering, Vaish College of Engineering, Rohtak, India
Hemant K. Upadhyay	Department of Mechanical Engineering, Research & Development Cell, Poornima University, Jaipur, India
K.C. Tripathi	Department of Information Technology, MAIT, Delhi, India
Khushwant Singh	Department of Computer Science and Engineering, University Institute of Engineering & Technology, Maharshi Dayanand University, Rohtak, India
M. Nalini	Department of Electronics and Instrumentaion Engineering, Sri Sairam Engineering College, Chennai, India
Manisha Sharma	Department of Applied Sciences, Mathematics, KIET Group of institutions, Delhi NCR, Muradnagar, Ghaziabad, Uttar Pradesh, 201206, India
Mohit Yadav	Department of Mathematics, University Institute of Sciences, Chandigarh University, Mohali, India
Md Arif Hussain	Department of Computer Science and Information Technology, KIET Group of Institutions, Delhi-NCR, India
Muthmainnah	Teacher Training and Education Faculty, Universitas Al Asyariah Mandar, West Sulawesi, Indonesia
Manoj Kumar	Department of Information Sciences, University of Wollongong, Dubai, UAE
Neetu Agarwal	Department of Computer Science and Technology, Manav Rachna University, Faridabad, India
Neelu Chaudhary	Department of Computer Science and Technology, Manav Rachna University, Faridabad, India
P. Harikumaran	Department of Electronics and Instrumentaion Engineering, Sri Sairam Engineering College, Chennai, India
Priyanshu Verma	Department of Computer Science and Information Technology, KIET Group of Institutions, Delhi-NCR, India

Piyush Sharma	Department of Computer Science and Information Technology, KIET Group of Institutions, Delhi-NCR, India
Prachi Dahiya	Department of Computer Science and Technology CST, Maharaja Agrasen Institute of Technology, New Delhi, India
Rohit Khushi	Department of Computer Science and Information Technology, KIET Group of Institutions, Delhi-NCR, India
Rohit Vashisht	Department of Computer Science and Information Technology, KIET Group of Institutions, Delhi-NCR, India
Rohit Priyadarshi	Department of Design, Delhi Technological University, New Delhi, India
Veena Parihar	Department of Data Science and Spatial Analysis, Symbiosis Institute of Geo-informatics, Symbiosis International (Deemed University), Pune, India
Umang Kant	Department of CSE (AI), KIET Group of Institutions, Ghaziabad, India
Yonis Gulzar	Department of Management Information Systems, College of Business Administration, King Faisal University, Al-Ahsa, 31982, Saudi Arabia

CHAPTER 1

Harnessing Generative AI for Enhanced Programming and Wireless Sensor Networks: Benefits, Limitations, and Applications

Veena Parihar[1,*], **Bhawna**[2] and **Ayasha Malik**[3]

[1] *Department of Data Science and Spatial Analysis, Symbiosis Institute of Geo-informatics, Symbiosis International (Deemed University) Pune, India*

[2] *Department of CSE(AIML), KIET Group of Institutions, Delhi- NCR, Ghaziabad, India*

[3] *Department of Computer Science and Engineering, IIMT College of Engineering, Greater Noida, India*

Abstract: The use of Generative AI (GAI) in various fields is proliferating at the current time. This term is related to generating any content that resembles human-generated content to a high extent. This feature of it makes it appropriate to be applied to various application areas. This chapter gives an overview of GAI along with its gradual evolution and various application areas. This chapter especially discusses its application in the field of programming. The advantages and drawbacks of using GAI to automate code generation, intelligent debugging support, Natural Language Processing (NLP) interfaces, code completion, and documentation generation are examined in this study. The time and effort required for development can be greatly decreased by using GAI, which can produce syntactically valid and contextually relevant code snippets. AI-powered enhanced code completion can predict the demands of developers and provide more precise recommendations, increasing coding efficiency. This study also explores the use of GAI in Wireless Sensor Networks (WSNs) and highlights its applications in data production, anomaly detection, network optimisation, and other important domains. To improve the resilience of WSNs, GAI can create realistic sensor data for training and testing. With the use of its anomaly detection features, one can discern peculiar trends that might point to system flaws or security breaches. WSN operating lifespans can be extended through more effective resource allocation and energy management brought about by network optimisation *via* AI. This study attempts to offer insights into how GAI might be used to enhance programming techniques and increase the performance and reliability of WSNs through a thorough analysis.

Keywords: GPT architecture, Generative AI, NLP, Programming, WSN.

* **Corresponding author Veena Parihar:** Department of Data Science and Spatial Analysis, Symbiosis Institute of Geo-informatics, Symbiosis International (Deemed University), Pune, India; E-mail: veena2parihar@gmail.com

Shelly Gupta, Sapna Juneja & Sandeep Kautish (Eds.)
All rights reserved-© 2025 Bentham Science Publishers

INTRODUCTION

Over the past few years, there has been substantial progress in the field of NLP, primarily driven by the emergence of advanced language models like GAI. These state-of-the-art models have played a pivotal role in pushing the boundaries of NLP research and applications. GAI is a sub-area of AI technology that can generate various types of content including text, images, audio, or video. This technology named GAI is not so new technology [1 - 3]. It has its roots in the past research. This technology was introduced in 1960 when the chatbots were developed. This newly generated technology is very useful for better movie dubbing and generating rich educational content. On the other hand, it uncovered the concerns related to deepfakes. With the advent of GAI, two advances come into the picture *i.e.* transformer and language models which will be discussed further thoroughly. These language models undergo extensive training using vast amounts of data, enabling them to generate text that exhibits coherence, contextual appropriateness, and a natural flow. The following Figs. (**1** and **2**) explain the evolution of GAI [4, 5].

Year	Innovation
1932	Georges Artsrouni invented a machine called "mechanical brain" to translate between languages on a mechanical computer encoded onto punch cards.
1957	Linguist Noam Chomsky published "Syntactic Structures" which describes grammatical rules for parsing and generating natural language sentences.
1966	MIT professor Joseph Weizenbaum created the first chatbot, Eliza, which simulates conversations with a psychotherapist.
1968	Computer science professor Terry Winograd created SHRDLU, the first multimodal AI that can manipulate and reason out a world of blocks according to instructions from a user.
1980	Michael Toy and Glenn Wichman develop the Unix-based game Rogue, which uses procedural content generation to dynamically generate new game levels.
1986	Michael Irwin Jordan lays the foundation for the modem use of Recurrent Neural Networks (RNNs) with the publication of "Serial order: a parallel distributed processing approach".
1989	Yann LeCun, Yoshua Bengio and Patrick Haffner demonstrate how Convolutional Neural Networks (CNN) can be used to recognize images.

Fig. (1). Evolution of GAI before 90's [6].

Thus, the GAI is an outcome of this continuous development. GAI, specifically, is a transformer-based language model that has been trained on an extensive dataset exceeding 40 GB of textual data. With its ability to generate text that closely resembles human-written content, the model has become a highly influential and versatile tool applicable across various domains [7, 8]. ChatGPT, a product based on GAI is the language model under discussion, was developed by OpenAI, a research company established in December 2015 by a team of visionaries including Elon Musk, Sam Altman, Greg Brockman, Ilya Sutskever, Wojciech Zaremba, and John Schulman. OpenAI's overarching mission is to ensure the ethical and beneficial use of AI while prioritizing safety. Initially, the company focused on the development and advocacy of AI systems that are friendly and advantageous to humanity as a whole [9]. The inception of the ChatGPT project dates back to 2018, marked by the release of GPT-1 by OpenAI. GPT-1 was a language model trained over 40 GB of text data to generate text which is closely similar to the humanized text [10, 11]. So, it was very useful in various domains and applications. This model lacked the understanding of the actual meaning of the text. OpenAI improved this model and it released the enhanced model in 2019 named GPT-2. This model was trained on a vast amount of data *i.e.* 570 GB text data. It is noteworthy that GPT-2 was the improved version that had the ability to generate text that closely resembled human-written content. Finally, in 2020, OpenAI released ChatGPT, which is a conversational version of GPT-2. ChatGPT is fine-tuned on a conversational dataset that makes it able to understand context, generate human-like responses, and engage in conversations [12]. The ChatGPT project is overall a continuation of OpenAI's efforts to develop advanced language models that are capable of generating human-like text. The company's ultimate goal is to develop AI that can be used for the benefit of all, and the ChatGPT project is an important step towards achieving this goal. OpenAI, the company that developed ChatGPT, has several partnerships and collaborations with other companies and organizations [13, 14]. Some of the key partners and collaborators of the ChatGPT project include the following as shown in Fig. (**3**).

- **IBM:** OpenAI and IBM have formed a collaboration to jointly develop and deploy AI models within the IBM Cloud infrastructure [15].
- **Microsoft:** OpenAI and Microsoft have established a long-term collaboration, aimed at advancing AI technologies and facilitating their successful integration into the market. As part of this partnership, OpenAI and Microsoft have worked together to develop GPT-3 [16].
- **AWS:** OpenAI has a partnership with Amazon Web Services (AWS) to make OpenAI's GPT-3 model available on the AWS Marketplace [17].
- **NVIDIA**: OpenAI has a partnership with NVIDIA to develop and optimize AI models on NVIDIA's GPUs [18].
- **Stanford University:** OpenAI has a collaboration with Stanford University to develop new AI models and methods. Moreover, the user interface of ChatGPT is shown in Fig. (**4**).

Year	Innovation
2000	University of Montreal researchers publish " A Neural Probabilistic Language Model" which suggests a method to model language using feed- forward neural networks.
2006	Data scientists Fei- Fei Li sets up the Image Net database, which provides the foundation for visual object recognition.
2011	Apple releases Siri, a voice -powered personal assistant that can generate responses and take actions in response to voice requests.
2012	Alex Krizhevsky designs the Alex Net CNN architecture, pioneering a new way of automatically training neural networks that take advantage of recent GPU advances.
2013	Google researcher Tomas Mikolov and colleagues introduce word2vec to identify semantic relationships between words automatically.
2014	Research scientist Ian Good follow develops generative adversarial networks (GANs), which pit two neural networks against each other to generate increasingly realistic content. Diederik Kingma and Max Welling introduce variational autoencoders to generate images, videos and text.
2015	Stanford researchers publish work on diffusion models in the paper "Deep Unsupervised Learning using Nonequilibrium Thermodynamics ". The technique provides a way to reverse - engineer the process of adding noise to a final image.
2017	Google researchers develop the concept of transformers in the paper "Attention is all you need", inspiring subsequent research into tools that could automatically parse unlabelled text into LLMs.
2018	Google researchers implement transformers into BERT, which is trained on more than 3.3 billion words and can automatically learn the relationship between words in sentences, paragraphs and even books to predict the meaning of text. It has 110 million parameters. Google DeepMind researchers develop AlphaFold for predicting protein structures, laying the foundation for GAI applications in medical research, drug development and chemistry. OpenAI releases GPT, trained on about 40 GB of data and consisting of 117 million parameters, GPT paves the way for subsequent LLMs in content generation, chatbots and language transformation.
2021	OpenAI introduces Dall -E which can generate images from text prompts. The name is a combination of WALL-E, the name of a fictional robot and the artist Salvador Dali.
2022	Researchers from Runway Research, Stability AI and Comp Vis LMU release Stable Diffusion as open-source code that can automatically generate image content from a text prompt. Open. Al releases ChatGPT in November to provide a chat-based interface to its GPT 3.5 LLM. It attracts over 100 million users within two months, representing the fastest ever consumer adoption of a service.
2023	Getty Images and a group of artists separately sue several companies that implemented Stable Diffusion for copyright infringement. Microsoft integrates a version of ChatGPT into its Bing search engine, google quickly follows with plans to release the Bard chat service based on its Lamba engine. And the controversy over detecting Al - generated content heats up.

Fig. (2). Evolution of GAI after 90's [6].

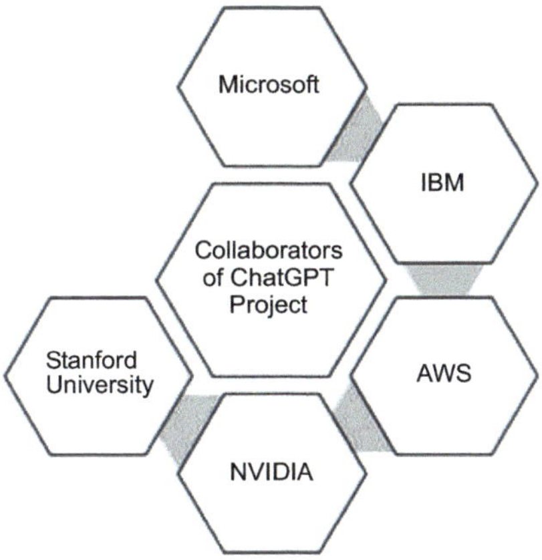

Fig. (3). Collaborators of the ChatGPT project.

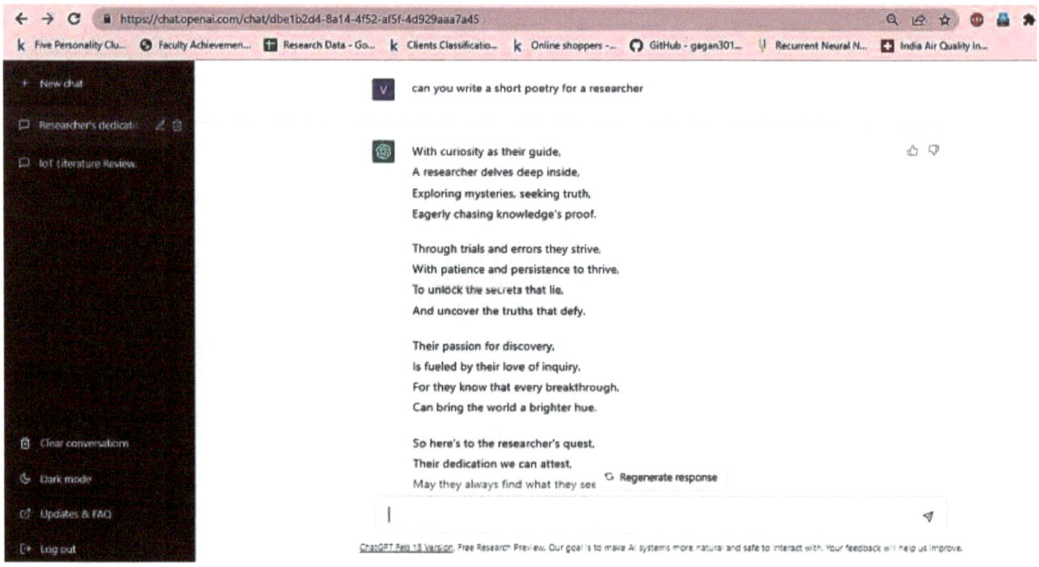

Fig. (4). The user interface of the ChatGPT platform.

The GAI also has its potential in the field of WSNs. It has shown the potential to improve data processing and decision-making in WSNs. The indoor localization that determines the device or person's position inside a building or apartment is useful where the GPS signals are generally not reliable or unavailable at the moment. Wi-Fi fingerprinting is generally used for this purpose. This task is challenging as it requires huge labelled datasets, which are expensive. For this purpose, GANs can be very helpful in producing synthetic data resembling realistic data. GANs can be useful in simulating real Wi-Fi fingerprints, which can make indoor localization less expensive. This technology is useful in navigation, asset tracking, and smart homes [19]. GAI also has its significance in enhancing the resilience and efficiency of WSNs along with advanced technologies such as IoTs. GAI is also impactful in the Multi-Functional Reconfigurable Intelligent Surfaces (MFRIS) for the integration of sensing, communication, and wireless power transfer. GAI is capable of learning with limited real-time data for generating adaptive channel models. GAI can also improve the signal quality with the reconstruction of noisy signals. This is how the GAI can be applicable in multiple applications related to WSNs [20].

This chapter aims to discuss the applications of GAI, which is extremely useful in various fields such as programming, healthcare, WSNs, and many more. It gives an overview of GAI along with its significance in NLP and its continuous evolution from GPT-1 [21, 22]. The chapter is organised in the following manner. Section 2 explores the GAI architecture thoroughly. It discusses the transformer architecture and its modified version which is used in GPT. The section discusses the utilization of GAI for programming purposes. It explains how it is used for generating the codes and what are the possible limitations. Section 3 discusses the testing of GAI. Section 4 is about the application of GAI in the field of WSNs. It discusses how GAI can be useful in improving the efficiency of WSNs. Section 5 talks about the possible impacts of GAI in the coming future whether they are positive or negative. Finally, section 6 concludes the whole study and emphasizes the need for further research and development to optimize GAI's integration into programming workflows.

Generative AI Architecture

The architecture of GAI consists of deep neural networks that specifically involve Generative Adversarial Networks (GAN) and Variational Autoencoders (VAE) [23, 24]. The GANs involve a generator and a discriminator architecture, which is responsible for adversarial training. It creates realistic data. VAEs are responsible for learning the underlying formulation of the provided input data and to generate new samples out of it. Both of them collectively form the GAI architecture. The following Fig. (**5**) illustrates the various layers of GAI architecture [25].

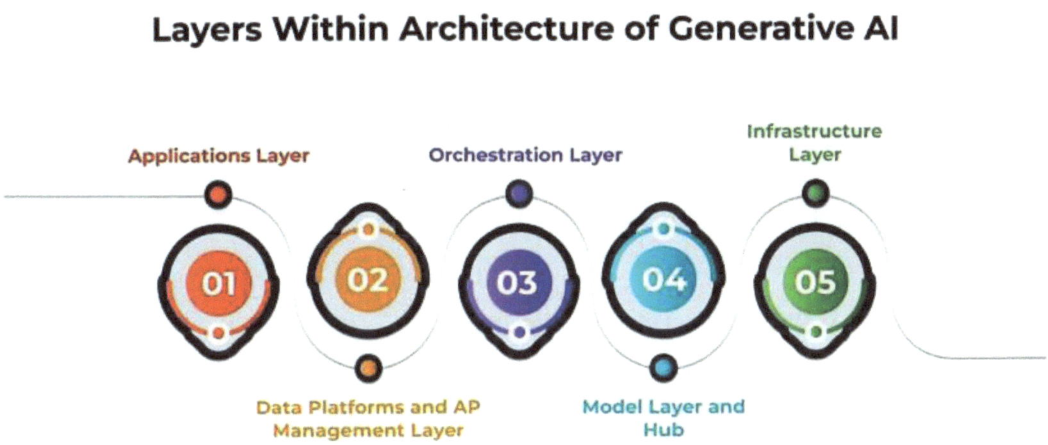

Fig. (5). Basic architecture of GAI [26].

Generally, the architecture of GAI consists of these basic layers shown in the above figure but these may be slightly different for different applications. These layers have the following tasks to be taken care of as shown in Fig. (**6**) [27].

Layer	Functionar
Application Layer	Facilitates human-machine collaboration. Includes applications without proprietary models (using open - source tools) and end-to-end apps with proprietary models for specific domains.
Data Platforms and Management	Ensures data quality for generative AI through vectorization, quality checks, cleaning, and storage. Requires plans for both structured and unstructured data.
Orchestration Layer (LLMOps)	Provides tools and practices for model customization, testing, deployment, and monitoring. Involves prompt engineering and fine-tuning. Includes end-to-end and specific LLMOps tools.
Model Layer and Hub	Contains foundation models and a model hub for access and storage. Foundation models are pre-trained and require expertise in architecture, training, and tuning.
Infrastructure Layer	Comprises cloud platforms and specialized hardware (GPUs/TPUs) for handling large data volumes and training workloads. Major providers include NVIDIA, Google, and TSMC.

Fig. (6). Various layers of GAI architecture.

GPT, a GAI system, developed by OpenAI, implements a variety of language models. These language models are based on transformer architecture. GPT has a series of models released sequentially *i.e.* GPT-1, GPT-2, and GPT-3 [28, 29]. These models use huge datasets for training which enables them to generate the exact human generated context that is appropriate contextually. The core of GPT architecture consists of transformer architecture which is responsible for generating appropriate output sequences. The self-attention mechanism of such architectures enables the model to focus on various parts of input for generating the output sequence [30]. Furthermore, the basic difference between all GPT models is shown in Table **1**.

Table 1. Comparison of ChatGPT and other GPT models.

Model [8]	Release Year	Dataset Size	Fine-tuning	Parameters	Performance Metrics	Key Features
GPT-1	2018	40 GB	Required	117 million	Limited context length	First GPT model, introduced unsupervised pre-training
GPT-2	2019	570 GB	Required	1.5 billion	Better text coherence and fluency	Larger model, focused on unsupervised pre training and text generation

(Table 1) cont.....

Model [8]	Release Year	Dataset Size	Fine-tuning	Parameters	Performance Metrics	Key Features
GPT-3	2020	570 GB	Not Required	175 billion	State-of-the-art on many NLP tasks.	Zero-shot, one-shot, and few-shot capabilities
ChatGPT (GPT-4)	2022	570 GB	Required	Estimated >175 billion	Improved reasoning and contexuality.	Multi-model (text and image inputs); fine-tuned for dialogue.

All the GPT models including ChatGPT are made based on the transformer architecture. This architecture was introduced in the research paper titled "Attention is All You Need" published by Google-Brain in the year 2017. This architecture made a revolution in the field of NLP by introducing self-attention mechanisms. These mechanisms can work on different parts of the inputs in a prioritized manner. The transformer architecture mainly has two components. One is the encoder and another is the decoder. Multiple layers of feed-forward and self-attention neural networks are there in both the encoder and decoder. The transformer architecture is illustrated in the following Fig. (7) [31, 32].

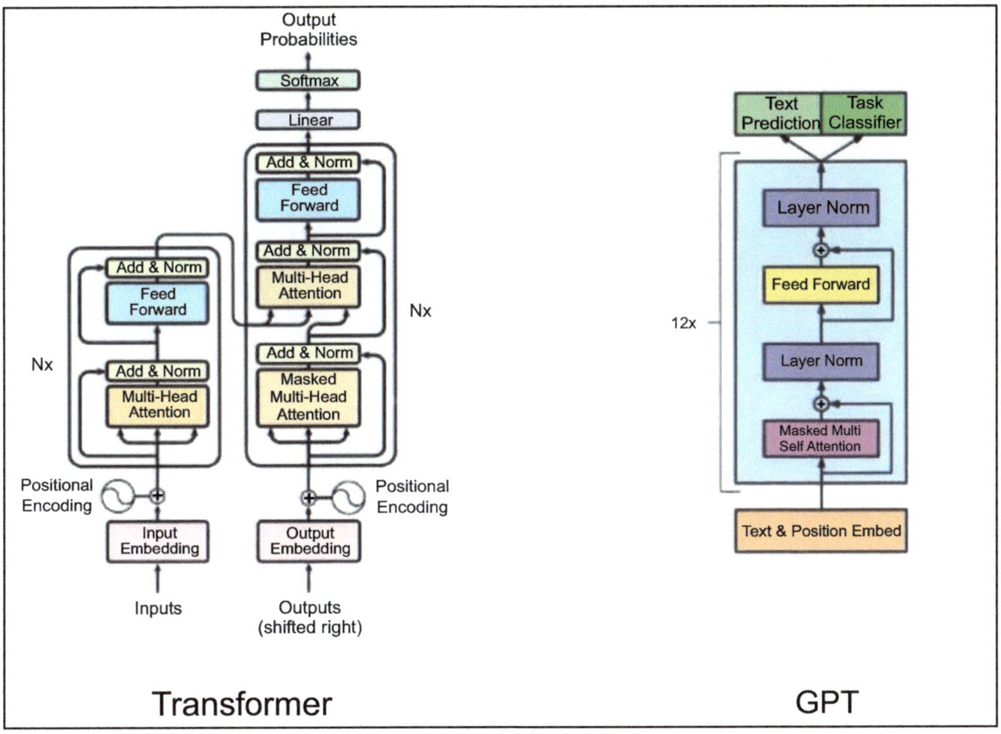

Fig. (7). Transformer and GPT architecture.

The input is initially passed to the encoder during model implementation. The encoder generated some hidden sets of states that identify the input representation. Then the decoder is provided with these hidden state sets for generating the final result. All the GPT models follow a unidirectional approach for training, unlike BERT which follows a bi-directional approach. In the unidirectional method, the model can use only previous tokens of the input sequence whereas in the bi-directional approach, the model can access previous as well as subsequent tokens of the input. The GPT models only use the decoder part of the transformer architecture as illustrated in the above Figure. There are also other models such as T5, Claude, and BLOOM. T5 is based on encoder-decoder architecture specifically used for summarization, translation, and question-answer. Claude uses transformer-based architecture specifically applicable to dialogue, reasoning, and virtual agents. BLOOM is based on the decoder only and is responsible for research and diverse NLP tasks. The vast amount of data around 570 GB is used for training the ChatGPT model to learn the diversity of language patterns. The datasets utilized for training these GPT models belong to various diverse sources. The commonly used data sources are web-crawled data, books and literature (both publically available and licenced books), Wikipedia, news and articles, scientific papers as well as open datasets. These models can also be fine-tuned for performing specific tasks [33 - 35]. The most common features of GAI are shown in Fig. (**8**).

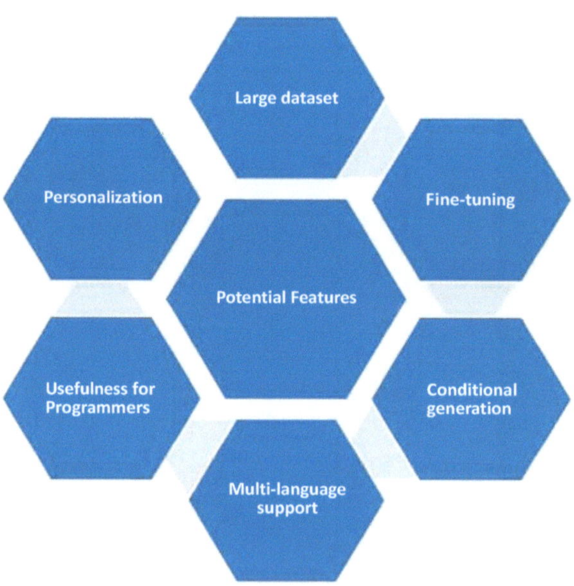

Fig. (8). Features of GAI.

The feature of GAI involves various aspects such as using a huge volume of data to train its model for best performance. These models can be fine-tuned according to the application or task. The model can support multiple languages such as Hindi, English, and many more [36]. It is also useful for programmers as they can generate code in any programming language according to their tasks. They can even find the types of errors and debug their codes. It is helpful to that extent. There are also other GPT architectures which are discussed in the upcoming section 4.

Other GPT Architectures

The ChatGPT model is very useful and popular in the NLP field because of its ability for generating high-quality human-like text. Other than ChatGPT, there are also some other architectures that use this architecture. These architectures are discussed in the following Fig. (**9**) [37].

Platform	Description
CLIPDraw	CLIPDraw is a platform that uses the OpenAI CLIP (Constructive Language - Image Pre-training) model to generate images from text descriptions. It allows users to specify the desired image size, background color, and other parameters to generate images.
VQGAN + CLIP	VQGAN + CLIP combines, the VQGAN (Vector Quantized Generative Adversarial Network) model with the Open AI CLIP model to generate images from text descriptions, allowing users to specify image size, aspect ratio, and other parameters.
Image-GPT	Image - GPT uses the GPT architecture to generate images from text descriptions, similar to DALL-E but with a smaller version of the GPT model (6 layers instead of DALL-E's 32 layers)
GPT-2	GPT - 2, released by OpenAI in 2019, is an enhanced iteration of the GPT architecture with 1.5 billion parameters, known for generating high quality text that often blurs the line between machine and human writing.
GPT-3	GPT-3, unveiled by OpenAI in 2020, is the expansive iteration of the GPT architecture, with 175 billion parameters, excelling in various NLP tasks like text completion, language translation, and question answering.
XLNet	XLNet, crafted by google researchers in 2019, is similar to GPT architecture but uses a different pre - training method that allows it to model bidirectional contexts more effectively.
CTRL	CTRL (Conditional Transformer Language Model), developed by Salesforce Research in 2019, is similar to GPT-2 but designed to generate text conditioned on a specific prompt or context.
T5	T5, also known as Text - to-Text Transfer Transformer, is a language model introduced by Google in 2020. It excels in various NLP tasks using a text-to-text approach where both input and output are in text format.

Fig. (9). Various GPT architectures.

These models have their own specified applications. In this sequence, the next section explores how GAI is useful for programming purposes.

GAI for Programming

In the present time, ChatGPT and some other GAI tools have proven that they can be helpful for the tasks of software developers too. They can actually boost the ability of developers and make their tasks easy. These tools use LLMs for generating, finding errors, and debugging the codes. It is important to keep in mind that these tools are still evolving and are not 100% accurate [38, 39]. These tools are just for the help of developers, they can't replace engineers. These various tools are discussed in below Fig. (**10**). These tools are capable of performing the following tasks.

Tool	Description	Key Features	Languages	Integration
ChatGPT	Free app by OpenAI, known for generative AI capabilities. Generates boilerplate code, translates/refactors code, and automates tasks.	Free with optional Plus version ($20/month), no installation required, no access to codebase needed. Good for exploration but not the best for coding tasks.	Multiple	Web-based
Google Gemini	Google's AI coding assistant (formerly Bard). Leverages transformer architecture.	Can code in 20 programming languages, generates code from prompts, explains and refactors code.	Python, Java, C++, JavaScript, and more	Web-based
Auto-GPT	Tool that uses GPT to oversee additional GPT instances, breaking tasks into subtasks.	Can create and iterate through complex jobs, open-source version on GitHub, or use AgentGPT web app.	Multiple	Web-based, GitHub
GitHub Copilot	AI pair programmer using OpenAI Codex. Designed for writing functional code.	Generates specific code suggestions based on project context, integrates with IDES.	Python, JavaScript, Go, PHP, Ruby, Swift	Neovim, Visual Studio
Amazon CodeWhisperer	Amazon's coding assistant, optimized for AWS APIs.	Suggests complete functions based on prompts and project code, optimized for AWS services.	Python, Java, and more	IDE integration
Tabnine	AI coding assistant using OpenAI Codex.	Auto-completes lines or functions, matches codebase style and conventions.	Multiple	Sublime, Emacs, Vim, Android Studio
Code WP	AI tool for generating code compatible with WordPress.	Generates PHP, JavaScript, and jQuery for WordPress and plugins.	PHP, JavaScript, jQuery	WordPress-based
CodeSquire	AI coding assistant using Chrome Extension for data science apps.	Turns comments into code, writes SQL from natural language prompts, completes lines and functions.	SQL	Google Colab, BigQuery, JupyterLab
What the Diff	Tool for code review and documentation.	Integrates with GitHub/GitLab, summarizes code changes, creates documentation, refactors code, and generates weekly reports.	Multiple	GitHub, GitLab
AI Query	Generates SQL queries from plain English and translates SQL to English.	Supports multiple database engines, defines database structure for specific code generation.	SQL	PostgreSQL, MySQL, MariaDB, Microsoft SQL

Fig. (10). GAI-based programming tools.

- **Generation of Code:** GAI tools can be utilized for generating shortcodes or even complete programs. It takes natural language commands as input and provides us with the required output. We can provide some detailed descriptions for the better outcome. It can also generate multiple alternative solutions; we just need to provide the descriptions of the required task.
- **Code Debugging:** Sometimes, it is not easy to identify even the common errors in the code. In this, GAI can help us. It can help us by identifying the common errors. Also, it can assist in solving and debugging those errors. The GAI potential can also be used by integrating it with the existing debugging tools for better assistance.
- **Programming with Natural Language Support:** GAI has the potential to revolutionize programming interfaces with natural language interactions enabled. This facility can be proven useful for non-technical users or domain experts to interact with programming environments. Humans can provide instructions in natural language and the GAI can execute the commands accordingly to generate or debug the codes. This facility eases the task of programming for non-technical persons also [40 - 42].
- **Code Completion:** The integration of GAI tools into the existing IDE can actually be helpful for providing code completion assistance and making intelligent suggestions. GAI can analyse the existing code and can complete this code accordingly by analyzing the pattern in that code. This feature is useful in enhancing the capability of the developer by reducing the time for writing the common code. The developers can actually focus on writing the new logic [43].
- **Documentation Generation:** GAI tools can also be utilized for generating detailed documents related to the projects or APIs, which is a lengthy task. This automation can save the time of developers and also there is no chance of human errors in the documentation [44].

Practical Case Study

A practical case study was also conducted for the practical demonstration of the usefulness of GAI in programming. Through this study, insights were gained about the practical scenario of benefits, challenges, and real outcomes of the GAI integration for coding purposes. The case study named "**GAI powered code completion and suggestion in IDEs**" is conducted to see the impacts of integration of GAI into the popular IDEs for providing code completion capabilities to the users [45]. This case study followed an experimental set which included the following:

- **Evaluation Metrics**: Code quality, development time, user satisfaction.
- **Qualitative and quantitative measures**.

- **Data Collection**: User feedback, developer surveys, comparative analysis against existing tools.

The findings of the case study presented useful insights related to the practical implementation of GAI. The outcomes revealed the following:

- **Enhanced Productivity**: Automated repetitive coding tasks, relevant code snippets, and rapid prototyping.
- **Limitations**: Potential for semantically incorrect code, dependence on large datasets.
- **Analysis**: Identified areas for improvement, and emphasized GAI as a complementary tool.

However, GAI has good possibilities for programmers but its limitations are also important to be taken into consideration. Although GAI is good for initial programming purposes, it still lacks a deep understanding of programming concepts and optimized programming constructs. The produced code is not completely correct, it needs to be reviewed by humans. The GAI tools still need human considerations and need to be used as helping tools. It cannot be used as a replacement for developers [46 - 48]. There are some coding examples and scenarios where GAI has not performed well.

- **Unable to Understand Complex programming -** In this example, we have considered the code for sorting an array of integer values in ascending order. This task can be considered easy for a human programmer. Although GAI has generated a code for this task, it is unable to generate an optimal solution or code [49]. The generated code is not an efficient code as shown in Fig. (**11**).

```
python                                              Copy code

def sort_array(arr):
    n = len(arr)
    for i in range(n):
        for j in range(0, n-i-1):
            if arr[j] > arr[j+1] :
                arr[j], arr[j+1] = arr[j+1], arr[j]
    return arr
```

Fig. (11). Generated code for array sorting.

A human programmer may have generated a good solution as GAI does not have deep knowledge of algorithms and underlying structures [50].

- **Possibility of Generating Incorrect Code:** The GAI is able to generate syntactically correct codes but there may be some scenarios where code may be semantically incorrect. It means that the program may get compiled successfully but may generate inappropriate results or generate logical errors. Consider the following programming example where we need to write a function to the maximum in an array of integer values [51, 52]. The following code snippet in Fig. (**12**) is generated by GAI, which seems correct but it is logically incorrect.

python Copy code

```python
def find_max(arr):
    max_num = 0
    for i in range(len(arr)):
        if arr[i] > max_num:
            max_num = arr[i]
    return max_num
```

Fig. (12). Generated logically incorrect code.

In the above code, max_num is initialized to 0. However, it may give incorrect results if the array contains any negative value. Only a human programmer can identify this error and make the corrections [53]. The GAI does not have an appropriate understanding of such scenarios. These situations indicate that GAI tools can only be used as supportive tools. We cannot rely completely on it. The GAI systems are automated systems that are completely dependent on their training data. It can perform only to that extent. GAI cannot completely understand the context. It will always be one step behind human understanding. Humans are capable of critical thinking and judging the real context. They may have better domain knowledge whereas GAI will only have the knowledge to some limited extent.

Testing of Generative AI

Testing of traditional AI systems is easy and straightforward in comparison to GAI systems. The reason is that traditional AI systems generate fixed or predefined outcomes whereas the results of GAI systems are not predetermined [54, 55]. Testing GAI systems is a crucial and important task whether it is ChatGPT, DALL-E, or any other product due to their variable nature. OpenAI collaborated with various different companies or organizations such as Google, IBM, *etc.* These collaborations are useful as they provide additional resources for advancing the field of NLP. This partnership helps in continuously improving the performance of models.

The traditional AI systems also do not require red teaming as there are negligible chances of data leaking [56]. The red team is a group of experts that pretends to be the enemy of the system to detect possible attacks. These teams report back to the company to improve the security based on testing. The GAI systems are more prone to these attacks and leakage of sensitive data because these systems are able to generate new content. The non-deterministic behavior of GAI systems creates challenges for testing these systems. The red teaming for GAI provokes the model to do the things or behave it was not trained for [57]. This task is done purposely to check whether the model can perform unethical practices in certain scenarios or not. The other challenge is also there that these systems are less transparent as we don't know how these systems are trained [58, 59]. These systems generate new data. That data needs the judgment of humans to check its authenticity and usefulness. Since these are AI-based systems generating novel data, the ethical aspects should also be taken into consideration, so that they may prove useful instead of harmful to society. The GAI project also has a variety of methods on which it is being tested like any other ML model. The primary testing methods are illustrated in the following Fig. (**13**).

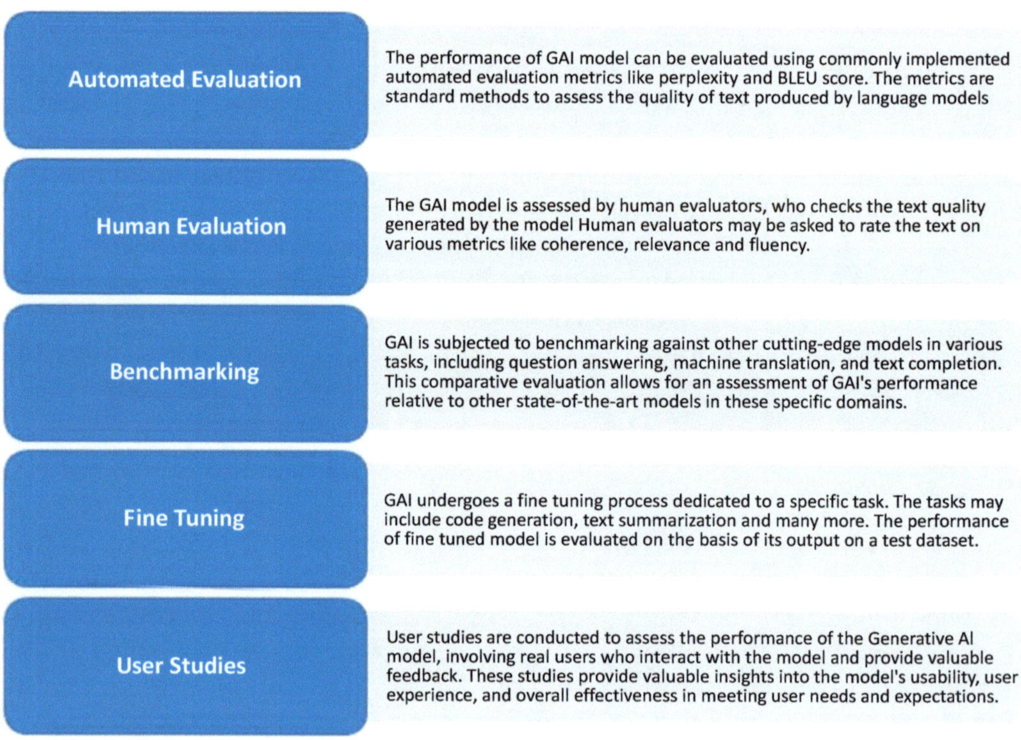

Fig. (13). Primary testing methods of GAI [60].

It should also be taken into consideration that the GAI technology is still evolving and updating with time. As this technology evolves more, new techniques and methods of testing may come into practice for effective evaluation of such systems.

Application of Generative AI in Wireless Sensor Networks

GAI has diverse areas of applications, which include healthcare, content creation, audio/video generation, finance, retail, manufacturing, and many more [61]. The more areas are to be identified. One of the popular areas among GAI applications is WSNs. WSNs are a collection of low-power sensors that collect and transmit the data wirelessly. The WSN architecture contains three layers physical layer, data link layer, and application layer. Due to its wireless connectivity, these systems are easy to configure and manage. The various aspects of GAI integration in WSNs are discussed in Fig. (**14**) [62 - 64].

From the above figure, it can be analysed that GAI can contribute in many aspects such as data generation and augmentation, anomaly detection and fault diagnosis, energy efficiency, network optimization, security enhancements, localization and tracking, and environmental monitoring and smart applications [65 - 67].

In communication networks or radar systems, it can be time-consuming and expensive to collect real data. GAI can generate synthetic datasets using insights from real data [68]. For example, the GANs can produce artificial fingerprints or radar signal data for better training of ML models for target detection. There is no need for huge real data. The autonomous vehicle is a good example of this where the synthetic sensor data can be utilized for simulating real events. GAI models can also be helpful in identifying anomalies in sensor data such as radar signal data or data collected from IoT devices. GAI can learn the patterns from normal behaviour. For example, GAIs such as auto encoders or GANs can sense the sensor data, collected from machinery and detect the possible faults even before their occurrence. It can significantly improve maintenance schedules and reduce the downtimes. In the healthcare domain also, it can detect anomalies in patient monitoring such detecting arrhythmias.

GAI also has its potential in the optimization of energy consumption in networks. GAI can be useful in algorithm designing for the prediction and optimization of energy consumption in communication networks. For example, the deep reinforcement learning model can be generated, which can dynamically adjust the transmission power for reduced energy consumption. For example, GAI models can optimize scheduling and configurations of base stations for low energy consumption. GAI can have significance in network optimization by predicting specific traffic patterns. It can optimize frequency allocation in WSNs. GAIs are capable of security enhancement by predicting the possible situations of network attacks. It continuously analyses the data and can make early predictions of possible attacks.

Aspect	Application	Generative AI Technique	Benefits
Data Generation & Augmentation	Synthetic Data Generation	GANs, Variational Autoencoders (VAES)	Provides training data when real data is scarce, enhances model training and robustness
	Data Augmentation	GANS, VAEs	Improves accuracy and robustness of machine learning models
Anomaly Detection & Fault Diagnosis	Anomaly Detection	GANs, Autoencoders	Identifies deviations from normal behaviour, detects anomalies early
	Fault Diagnosis	Autoencoders, Recurrent Neural Networks	Diagnoses faults by comparing reconstructed data with actual sensor readings
Energy Efficiency	Predictive Modelling	Recurrent Neural Networks (RNNs), LSTMs	Reduces energy consumption by predicting significant events
	Data Compression	Autoencoders, Principal Component Analysis (PCA)	Minimizes data transmission, saves energy
Network Optimization	Topology Control	Reinforcement Learning (RL), GANs	Optimizes network topology for balanced energy consumption and coverage
	Resource Allocation	RL, GANs	Predicts traffic patterns, optimizes resource usage
Security Enhancements	Intrusion Detection	GANs, Autoencoders	Detects network attacks by identifying unusual patterns
	Secure Communication Protocols	GANs, Encryption Algorithms	Dynamically generates secure protocols, enhances data transmission security
Localization & Tracking	Sensor Fusion	GANs, Kalman Filters	Integrates multiple sensor data for accurate localization and tracking
	Simulated Environments	GANs, Simulated Annealing	Tests and optimizes sensor placement and tracking algorithms
Environmental Monitoring & Smart Applications	Predictive Analytics	RNNS, LSTMs, GANs	Predicts environmental changes, generates alerts, controls signal for smart applications
	Scenario Simulation	GANS, VAEs	Simulates various scenarios to test and improve network robustness
Examples and Applications	Smart Cities	GANS, RL	Optimizes traffic management, energy consumption, and infrastructure maintenance
	Healthcare Monitoring	GANs, Autoencoders	Predicts health trends, detects anomalies in patient data
	Agriculture	GANS, RNNs	Predicts soil conditions, weather patterns, enhances precision farming

Fig. (14). Role of GAI in WSNs.

Thus, with the implementation of GAI, the WSNs can be improved in terms of functionality as well as dependability and efficiency. Various applications such as smart agriculture, smart city, environmental monitoring, and many more, depend on WSNs. The integration of GAI into WSNs has the potential to resolve the underlying issues and incorporate new features. The GAIs can improve the model training and also enhance the accuracy of the model [69, 70].

Impacts on the Future

GAI indeed holds immense potential to shape the future across various domains. Gartner states that around 100 million populations will use GAI to complete their work by 2026 [71]. Its ability to generate text exactly like human-generated text opens up various possibilities for its application in various fields [72, 73]. It can actually revolutionize various fields. It has vast opportunities to make revolutions in the coming future. The few possible positive impacts are discussed below:

- **Customer Service:** GAI is able to automate customer service, which can provide quick assistance and efficient responses to the inquiries of customers. This can, in turn, improve the customer satisfaction rate and also overcome the burden of customer service agents [74].
- **Personalized Services:** GAI can also provide personalized services to its users. It can be recommended according to the users' past interactions. It can actually record and identify the previous responses of users and recommend them in the future accordingly. This satisfactory service to users can increase user engagement [75].
- **Persons with Disability:** GAI is also fruitful for especially abled people such as those who are deaf or have a problem of hearing. GAI can provide user-friendly interfaces to such people for communication.
- **Pharmaceuticals and Healthcare:** GAI can be impactful in the healthcare and pharmaceutical sector. It can be significant to discover and develop new drugs and medicines. It can also create personalized treatments for the patients. It can be helpful in generating disease progression plans through predictive images. GAI can enhance medical images for better analysis. It can also generate the patient's summary or transcribe the patient's data and many more.
- **Marketing Domain:** GAI can be significantly helpful in the marketing domain as it can generate marketing images and personalized plans for better reach. The translation capability of GAI can spread the marketing plan across the areas comprising different languages. It is also capable of generating time-consuming product descriptions that attract customer attention. It can also be utilized for search engine optimization.
- **Manufacturing Domain:** GAI can also be utilized in the manufacturing domain to accelerate the design process, generate smart maintenance solutions for equipment as well as improve the process of the supply chain.
- **Software Development:** This domain greatly utilizes GAI for developing, debugging, testing and optimizing codes reducing developers' efforts. Although it requires human monitoring toget the required outputs.
- **Finance:** Financial organizations have also started using GAI to regulate their services. McKinsey stated that GAI can elevate the graph of the banking industry by $200 billion to $340 billion annually. Financial organizations are

using AI to generate investment plans, documentation, and dynamic changes; meanwhile, GAI is used for better communication among clients, investors, and stakeholders.

- **Media and Entertainment Domain:** GAI is highly useful in the media and entertainment industry. From generating images and videos, textual content, and highlighted content to segregating category-wise data, it can perform many useful tasks.

Thus, GAI is a very helpful tool and can ease many tasks for humans. Still, some limitations should be considered. GAI models are completely based on the data, it is provided for training [76, 77]. If the data is not correct, low quality, or biased then the GAI model can also be inadequate. If the data provided is not enough then GAI can generate contextually inappropriate outcomes. As it can generate human-like text, it can be a threat to the future. This human-like text can be used to generate deepfake text. This deepfake text can be used to spread wrong information. Deepfake text can also be used to generate fake reviews, articles, or any other text content [78, 79]. Apart from this, GAI can also have ethical concerns related to security and privacy of user data. These ethical concerns may be dangerous if not addressed properly. Due to technology, people may become more dependable on the technology which can have negative consequences if the technology fails in some situations or is used inappropriately. Overall, it is important to carefully consider both the potential benefits and risks of Generative AI and other AI technologies as they continue to shape our future [80, 81].

CONCLUSION

In conclusion, the GAI has made a profound impact on NLP. This GAI has emerged as a leading neural network architecture for language modeling tasks. Built upon the transformer architecture, GPT is specifically tailored for tasks like text generation and completion. GPT-4 has achieved state-of-the-art results across various NLP domains, including text classification, language translation, and question answering. However, the use of GPT models raises important ethical considerations pertaining to bias, privacy, and potential job displacement. This chapter has provided a comprehensive understanding of the effective utilization of GAI in programming tasks, combining theoretical analysis, real-world examples, and experimental results. By examining specific case studies and experiments, the practical application and impact of GAI in programming scenarios have been demonstrated. Concrete examples have showcased how GAI can seamlessly integrate into existing workflows, offering insights into the benefits, challenges, and potential improvements when employing GAI for programming purposes. It is important to recognize that GAI should be regarded as a supportive tool, complementing human expertise, and subject to thorough evaluation and validation. While it offers valuable assistance in programming, it possesses limitations, including a lack of deep understanding of programming concepts and the need for careful review and validation of generated code. This chapter also discussed the benefits of GAI integration into WSNs for enhancing its functionalities. GAI's ability to create synthetic data, predict sensor behavior, and optimize resource allocation ensures that WSNs can operate more efficiently and reliably, even in resource-constrained environments.

REFERENCES

[1] R. Montti, "What is Generative AI and how can you use it?" *Search Eng. J.*, 2023. Available from: https://www.searchenginejournal.com/what-is-Generative AI/473664/#close

[2] Generative AI: Optimizing language models for dialogue, 2022. OpenAI. Available from: https://openai.com/blog/Generative AI/

[3] Generative AI: The future of AI in content is in your hands. (n.d.). Content Marketing Institute.Available from: https://contentmarketinginstitute.com/articles/Generative

[4] Generative AI. Wikipedia, the free encyclopedia, 2023. Available from: https://en.wikipedia.org/wiki/Generative

[5] N. Tyagi, and B. Bhushan, "Natural Language Processing (NLP) based innovations for smart healthcare applications in healthcare 4.0", In: *Enabling Technologies for Effective Planning and Management in Sustainable Smart Cities.,* M.A. Ahad, G. Casalino, B. Bhushan, Eds., Springer: Cham, 2023.
[http://dx.doi.org/10.1007/978-3-031-22922-0_5]

[6] N. Tyagi, and B. Bhushan, "Demystifying the role of Natural Language Pprocessing (NLP) in smart city applications: Background, motivation, recent advances, and future research directions", *Wirel. Pers. Commun.,* vol. 130, no. 2, pp. 857-908, 2023.
[http://dx.doi.org/10.1007/s11277-023-10312-8] [PMID: 37168438]

[7] A. Malik, V. Parihar, B. Bhushan, J. Srivastava, and L. Karim, "Artificial intelligence-based react application (powered by conversational ALAN-AI voice assistance)", In: *Micro-Electronics and Telecommunication Engineering Lecture Notes in Networks and Systems.,* D.K. Sharma, S.L. Peng, R. Sharma, G. Jeon, Eds., vol. Vol. 617. Springer: Singapore, 2023.
[http://dx.doi.org/10.1007/978-981-19-9512-5_47]

[8] M. Liebrenz, R. Schleifer, A. Buadze, D. Bhugra, and A. Smith, "Generating scholarly content with ChatGPT: ethical challenges for medical publishing", *Lancet Digit. Health,* vol. 5, no. 3, pp. e105-e106, 2023.
[http://dx.doi.org/10.1016/S2589-7500(23)00019-5] [PMID: 36754725]

[9] F. Mulla, "Applications of Artificial Intelligence (AI) in healthcare: Research pape", *Int. J. Sci. Res.,* vol. 12, no. 12, pp. 1953-1958, 2023.
[http://dx.doi.org/10.21275/SR231226113454]

[10] M. Gao, "Conditional generative adversarial networks in computer vision: An introduction and outlook", *2nd International Conference on Artificial Intelligence, Automation, and High-Performance Computing (AIAHPC 2022),* 2022.
[http://dx.doi.org/10.1117/12.2641644]

[11] F. Fui-Hoon Nah, R. Zheng, J. Cai, K. Siau, and L. Chen, "Generative AI and ChatGPT: Applications, challenges, and AI-human collaboration", *J. Inf. Technol. Case Appl. Res.,* vol. 25, no. 3, pp. 277-304, 2023.
[http://dx.doi.org/10.1080/15228053.2023.2233814]

[12] Ö. Aydin, and E. Karaarslan, "Is ChatGPT leading generative AI? What is beyond expectations?", *Acad. Platf. J. Eng. Smart Syst.,* vol. 11, no. 3, pp. 118-134, 2023. [http://dx.doi.org/10.21541/apjess.1293702]

[13] J. Su and W. Yang, "Unlocking the power of ChatGPT: A framework for applying generative AI in education", *ECNU Review of Education*, 6(3), 355-366, 2023. [http://dx.doi.org/10.1177/20965311231168423]

[14] J.S. Jauhiainen, and A.G. Guerra, "Generative AI and ChatGPT in school children's education: Evidence from a school lesson", *Sustainability (Basel),* vol. 15, no. 18, p. 14025, 2023. [http://dx.doi.org/10.3390/su151814025]

[15] A. Malik, V. Parihar, B. Bhawna, B. Bhushan, and L. Karim, "Empowering artificial intelligence of things (AIoT) toward smart healthcare systems", *In: AI Models for Blockchain-Based Intelligent Networks in IoT Systems Concepts, Methodologies, Tools, and Applications*, B. Bhushan, A. K. Sangaiah, and T. N. Nguyen, Eds., 121-140, 2023. [http://dx.doi.org/10.1007/978-3-031-31952-5_6]

[16] A. Malik, V. Parihar, B. Bhushan, R. Chaganti, S. Bhatia, and P. N. Astya, "Security services for wireless 5G Internet of things (IoT) systems", *In: 5G and Beyond*, B. Bhushan, S. K. Sharma, R. Kumar, and I. Priyadarshini, Eds., 169-195, 2023. [http://dx.doi.org/10.1007/978-981-99-3668-7_9]

[17] S. Fosso Wamba, M.M. Queiroz, C.J. Chiappetta Jabbour, and C.V. Shi, "Are both generative AI and ChatGPT game changers for 21st-Century operations and supply chain excellence?", *Int. J. Prod. Econ.,* vol. 265, p. 109015, 2023. [http://dx.doi.org/10.1016/j.ijpe.2023.109015]

[18] F.E. Babl, and M.P. Babl, "Generative artificial intelligence: Can CHATGPT write a quality abstract?", *Emerg. Med. Australas.,* vol. 35, no. 5, pp. 809-811, 2023. [http://dx.doi.org/10.1111/1742-6723.14233] [PMID: 37142327]

[19] W. Njima, A. Bazzi, and M. Chafii, "DNN-based indoor localization under limited dataset using GANs and semi-supervised learning", *IEEE Access,* vol. 10, pp. 69896-69909, 2022. [http://dx.doi.org/10.1109/ACCESS.2022.3187837]

[20] A. Magbool, V. Kumar, A. Bazzi, M.F. Flanagan, and M. Chafii, "Multi-functional RIS for a multi-functional system: Integrating sensing, communication, and wireless power transfer", *IEEE Netw.,* vol. 39, no. 1, pp. 71-79, 2025. [http://dx.doi.org/10.1109/MNET.2024.3482571]

[21] M. Abdullah, A. Madain, and Y. Jararweh, "Generative AI: Fundamentals, applications and social impacts", *Ninth International Conference on Social Networks Analysis, Management and Security (SNAMS),* pp. 1-8, 2022. [http://dx.doi.org/10.1109/SNAMS58071.2022.10062688]

[22] Q. Miao, W. Zheng, Y. Lv, M. Huang, W. Ding and F. -Y. Wang, "DAO to HANOI *via* DeSci: AI Paradigm Shifts from AlphaGo to Generative AI," in *IEEE/CAA Journal of Automatica Sinica*, vol. 10, no. 4, pp. 877-897, 2023. [http://dx.doi.org/10.1109/JAS.2023.123561]

[23] M.M. Amin, E. Cambria, and B.W. Schuller, "Will affective computing emerge from foundation models and general Artificial Intelligence? A first evaluation of ChatGPT", *IEEE Intell. Syst.,* vol. 38, no. 2, pp. 15-23, 2023. [http://dx.doi.org/10.1109/MIS.2023.3254179]

[24] H. Ibrahim, R. Asim, F. Zaffar, T. Rahwan, and Y. Zaki, "Rethinking homework in the age of artificial intelligence", *IEEE Intell. Syst.,* vol. 38, no. 2, pp. 24-27, 2023. [http://dx.doi.org/10.1109/MIS.2023.3255599]

[25] A. Malik, V. Parihar, J. Srivastava, H. Kaur and S. Abidin, "Prognosis of diabetes mellitus based on

machine learning algorithms," *10th International conference on computing for sustainable global development (INDIACom)*, 2023.

[26] P. Maddigan, and T. Susnjak, "Chat2VIS: Generating data visualizations *via* natural language using ChatGPT, codex and GPT-3 large language models"., *IEEE Access,* vol. 11, pp. 45181-45193, 2023. [http://dx.doi.org/10.1109/ACCESS.2023.3274199]

[27] F.Y. Wang, J. Yang, X. Wang, J. Li and Q.L. Han, "Chat with ChatGPT on industry 5.0: Learning and decision-making for intelligent industries," *IEEE/CAA J. Autom. Sin.*, vol. 10, no. 4, pp. 831-834,2023. [http://dx.doi.org/10.1109/JAS.2023.123552]

[28] M.S. Wajid, H. Terashima-Marin, P.N. Paul Rad, and M.A. Wajid, "Violence detection approach based on cloud data and Neutrosophic cognitive maps", *J. Cloud Comput.,* vol. 11, no. 1, pp. 1-18, 2022. [http://dx.doi.org/10.1186/s13677-022-00369-4]

[29] M. A. Wajid, A. Zafar, M. S. Wajid, and H. Terashima-Marín, "Neutrosophic-CNN-based image and text fusion for multimodal classification", *J. Intell. Fuzzy Syst.*, (Preprint), 1-17. [http://dx.doi.org/10.3233/JIFS-223752]

[30] M.A. Wajid, A. Zafar, B. Bhushan, A.M.U.D. Khanday, and M.S. Wajid, "Artificial Intelligence (AI) and internet of things (IoT): Application in detecting and containing the spread of COVID-19", In: *AI Models for Blockchain-Based Intelligent Networks in IoT Systems: Concepts, Methodologies, Tools, and Applications. . B. Bhushan, A. K. Sangaiah, and T. N. Nguyen, Eds.* Springer International Publishing: Cham, 2023, pp. 373-392. [http://dx.doi.org/10.1007/978-3-031-31952-5_16]

[31] P.K. Gupta, M.K. Siddiqui, X. Huang, R. Morales-Menendez, H. Panwar, H. Terashima-Marin, and M.S. Wajid, "COVID-WideNet—A capsule network for COVID-19 detection", *Appl. Soft Comput.,* vol. 122, p. 108780, 2022. [http://dx.doi.org/10.1016/j.asoc.2022.108780] [PMID: 35369122]

[32] Available from: https://www.solulab.com/generative-ai-architecture/

[33] C. Schwarz, "Interpretable GenAI: Synthetic financial time series generation with probabilistic LSTM", 2024. [http://dx.doi.org/10.2139/ssrn.4877007]

[34] G. Abiri, "Generative AI as digital media," *Harv. J. Sport Entertain. Law*. Peking University School of Transnational Law Research Paper. vol. 15, no. 2, 2024. [http://dx.doi.org/10.2139/ssrn.4878339]

[35] P. G. Berger, W. Cai, L. Qiu, and C. X. Shen. "Employer and employee responses to Generative AI: Early evidence", *SSRN*, Feb. 01, 2024. [http://dx.doi.org/10.2139/ssrn.4874061]

[36] H. S. Antinozzi and L. A. Cooper, "Is ChatGPT an accurate source of information for uninformed taxpayers?" *J. Emerg. Technol. Account.*, vol. 22, no. 1, pp. 23–43, 2025. [http://dx.doi.org/10.2308/JETA-2023-072]

[37] R. Sinha and P. Kumar, "Explainable artificial intelligence: Current trends and future directions using bibliometric analysis", *SSRN*, 2024. [http://dx.doi.org/10.2139/ssrn.4864842]

[38] Z. Lv, "Generative artificial intelligence in the metaverse era", *Cognitive Robotics,* vol. 3, pp. 208-217, 2023. [http://dx.doi.org/10.1016/j.cogr.2023.06.001]

[39] M. Warr, M. Pivovarova, P. Mishra, and N. J. Oster, "Is ChatGPT racially biased? The case of evaluating student writing", 2024. [http://dx.doi.org/10.2139/ssrn.4851112]

[40] J. C. Reeder, III, N. Chaker, and J. Habel, "Improving sales forecasting: Leveraging unstructured

CRM activity logs, large language models, and generative AI", *SSRN*, 2024. [http://dx.doi.org/10.2139/ssrn.4848956]

[41] D, Smith."The unbearable lightness of inventing: Postprocess in the age of generative AI", *SSRN*, 2024. [http://dx.doi.org/10.2139/ssrn.4848720]

[42] D, Krause. "Responsible development of internal GenAI systems", *SSRN*, 2024. [http://dx.doi.org/10.2139/ssrn.4834767]

[43] D. Baidoo-Anu and L. Owusu Ansah, "Education in the era of generative Artificial Intelligence (AI): Understanding the potential benefits of ChatGPT in promoting teaching and learning", *J. AI*, vol. 7, no. 1, pp. 52–62, 2023. [http://dx.doi.org/10.61969/jai.1337500]

[44] C. Stokel-Walker, and R. Van Noorden, "What ChatGPT and generative AI mean for science", *Nature,* vol. 614, no. 7947, pp. 214-216, 2023. [http://dx.doi.org/10.1038/d41586-023-00340-6] [PMID: 36747115]

[45] P. Hacker, A. Engel, and M. Mauer, "Regulating ChatGPT and other large generative AI models", *ACM Conference on Fairness, Accountability, and Transparency,* 2023. [http://dx.doi.org/10.1145/3593013.3594067]

[46] R. Michel-Villarreal, E. Vilalta-Perdomo, D.E. Salinas-Navarro, R. Thierry-Aguilera, and F.S. Gerardou, "Challenges and opportunities of generative AI for higher education as explained by ChatGPT", *Educ. Sci. (Basel),* vol. 13, no. 9, p. 856, 2023. [http://dx.doi.org/10.3390/educsci13090856]

[47] E. Brynjolfsson, D. Li, and L. R. Raymond, "Generative AI at Work," *NBER Working Paper* 31161, National Bureau of Economic Research, Cambridge, MA, Apr. 2023. [http://dx.doi.org/10.3386/w31161]

[48] A. Bandi, P.V.S.R. Adapa, and Y.E.V.P.K. Kuchi, "The power of generative AI: A review of requirements, models, input–output formats, evaluation metrics, and challenges", *Future Internet,* vol. 15, no. 8, p. 260, 2023. [http://dx.doi.org/10.3390/fi15080260]

[49] K. Kenthapadi, H. Lakkaraju, and N. Rajani, "Generative AI meets responsible AI: Practical challenges and opportunities", *Proceedings of the 29th ACM SIGKDD Conference on Knowledge Discovery and Data Mining,* 2023. [http://dx.doi.org/10.1145/3580305.3599557]

[50] M. A. Ferrag, F. Alwahedi, A. Battah, B. Cherif, A. Mechri, and N. Tihanyi, "Generative AI and large language models for cyber security: All insights you need", *SSRN*, 2024. [http://dx.doi.org/10.2139/ssrn.4853709]

[51] I. Cronin, "Advanced applications of text-based generative AI," in: *Understanding Generative AI Business Applications*, I. Cronin, Ed., 2024, pp. 97–111. [http://dx.doi.org/10.1007/979-8-8688-0282-9_7]

[52] C. Jeong, "A study on the implementation of generative AI services using an enterprise data-based LLM application architecture", *Adv. Artif. Intell. Mach. Learn.,* vol. 3, no. 4, pp. 1588-1618, 2023. [http://dx.doi.org/10.54364/AAIML.2023.1191]

[53] V. Parihar, A. Malik, B. Bhawna, B. Bhushan, and R. Chaganti, "From smart devices to smarter systems: The evolution of artificial intelligence of things (AIoT) with characteristics, architecture, use cases and challenges," in *AI Models for Blockchain-Based Intelligent Networks in IoT Systems*, B. Bhushan, A. K. Sangaiah, and T. N. Nguyen, Eds., Springer, 2023. [http://dx.doi.org/10.1007/978-3-031-31952-5_1]

[54] V. Kumar, P. Srivastava, A. Dwivedi, I. Budhiraja, D. Ghosh, V. Goyal, and R. Arora, "Large-language-models (LLM)-based AI Chatbots: Architecture, in-depth analysis and their performance

evaluation", In: *Recent Trends in Image Processing and Pattern Recognition. RTIP2R 2023. Communications in Computer and Information Science.* Vol. 2027. Springer: Cham, 2024. [http://dx.doi.org/10.1007/978-3-031-53085-2_20]

[55] K. Martineau, "What is red teaming for generative AI," IBM, Apr. 11, 2024. Available from: https://research.ibm.com/blog/what-is-red-teaming-gen-AI

[56] J. Yang, H. Jin, R. Tang, X. Han, Q. Feng, H. Jiang, S. Zhong, B. Yin, and X. Hu, "Harnessing the power of LLMs in practice: A survey on ChatGPT and beyond", *ACM Trans. Knowl. Discov. Data,* vol. 18, no. 6, pp. 1-32, 2024.

[57] A. Cook and O. Karakus, "Llm-commentator: Novel fine-tuning strategies of large language models for automatic commentary generation using football event data", *Knowledge-Based Systems*, vol. 300, p. 112219, Sep. 27, 2024. [http://dx.doi.org/10.1016/j.knosys.2024.112219]

[58] A.F. Mohammad, B. Clark, R. Agarwal, and S. Summers, *LLM/GPT generative AI and artificial general intelligence (AGI): The next frontier. 2023 Congress in Computer Science, Computer Engineering, & Applied Computing.* CSCE, 2023. [http://dx.doi.org/10.1109/CSCE60160.2023.00073]

[59] A. Malik, V. Parihar, J. Srivastava, K. Purohit and S. Abidin, "Necessity and role of blockchain technology in the domain of cyber security and data science", *10th International Conference on Computing for Sustainable Global Development (INDIACom)*, New Delhi, India, pp. 1487-1493, 2023.

[60] T. Wu, S. He, J. Liu, S. Sun, K. Liu, and Q.-L. Han, "A brief overview of generative AI: The history, status quo and potential future development", *IEEE/CAA J. Autom. Sin.*, vol. 10, no. 5, pp. 1122-1136, May 2023, [http://dx.doi.org/10.1109/JAS.2023.123618]

[61] S. Naoumi, A. Bazzi, R. Bomfin, and M. Chafii, "Complex neural network based joint AoA and AoD estimation for bistatic ISAC", *IEEE J. Sel. Top. Signal Process.,* vol. 18, no. 5, pp. 842-856, 2024. [http://dx.doi.org/10.1109/JSTSP.2024.3387299]

[62] M. Delamou, A. Bazzi, M. Chafii, and E. M. Amhoud, "Deep learning-based estimation for multitarget radar detection," IEEE *97th Vehicular Technology Conference (VTC2023-Spring)*, Florence, Italy, 2023, pp. 1-5, 2023. [http://dx.doi.org/10.1109/VTC2023-Spring57618.2023.10200157]

[63] S. Naoumi, A. Bazzi, R. Bomfin, and M. Chafii, "Deep learning-enabled angle estimation in bistatic ISAC systems," *IEEE Globecom Workshops (GC Wkshps)*, Kuala Lumpur, Malaysia, 2023, pp. 854-859, 2023. [http://dx.doi.org/10.1109/GCWkshps58843.2023.10464930]

[64] Coursera Staff, "20 Examples of Generative AI Applications Across Industries", Coursera, Jun. 3, 2025. Available from: https://www.coursera.org/articles/generative-ai-applications

[65] B. Ramdurai, and P. Adhithya, "The impact, advancements and applications of generative AI", *Int. J. Comput. Sci. Eng.,* vol. 10, no. 6, pp. 1-8, 2023. [http://dx.doi.org/10.14445/23488387/IJCSE-V10I6P101]

[66] V. Gunturu, C. Singh, N. S. Patankar, and S. Praveena, "16 Exploring the potential of artificial intelligence in wireless sensor networks," in *Toward Artificial General Intelligence: Deep Learning, Neural Networks, Generative AI*, V. H. C. de Albuquerque, P. Raj, and S. P. Yadav, Eds., 331-344, 2023. [http://dx.doi.org/10.1515/9783111323749-016]

[67] N. Van Huynh, J. Wang, H. Du, D.T. Hoang, D. Niyato, D.N. Nguyen, D.I. Kim, and K.B. Letaief, "Generative AI for physical layer communications: A survey", *IEEE Trans. Cogn. Commun. Netw.,* vol. 10, no. 3, pp. 706-728, 2024. [http://dx.doi.org/10.1109/TCCN.2024.3384500]

[68] L. Yang, S.X. Yang, Y. Li, Y. Lu, and T. Guo, "Generative adversarial learning for trusted and secure clustering in industrial wireless sensor networks", *IEEE Trans. Ind. Electron.,* vol. 70, no. 8, pp. 8377-8387, 2023.
[http://dx.doi.org/10.1109/TIE.2022.3212378]

[69] G. Franceschelli, and M. Musolesi, "Reinforcement learning for generative AI: State of the art, opportunities and open research challenges", *J. Artif. Intell. Res.,* vol. 79, pp. 417-446, 2024.
[http://dx.doi.org/10.1613/jair.1.15278]

[70] A. Banafa, "Generative AI and other types of AI", in *Introduction to Artificial Intelligence (AI)*, 31-36, 2024.
[http://dx.doi.org/10.1201/9781003499527-6]

[71] G. Serpen, J. Li, and L. Liu, "AI-WSN: Adaptive and intelligent wireless sensor network", *Procedia Comput. Sci.,* vol. 20, pp. 406-413, 2013.
[http://dx.doi.org/10.1016/j.procs.2013.09.294]

[72] W. Osamy, A.M. Khedr, A. Salim, A.I. AlAli, and A.A. El-Sawy, "Recent studies utilizing Artificial Intelligence techniques for solving data collection, aggregation and dissemination challenges in wireless sensor networks: A review", *Electronics (Basel),* vol. 11, no. 3, p. 313, 2022.
[http://dx.doi.org/10.3390/electronics11030313]

[73] W. Osamy, A.M. Khedr, A. Salim, A.I.A. Ali, and A.A. El-Sawy, "Coverage, deployment and localization challenges in wireless sensor networks based on Artificial Intelligence techniques: A review", *IEEE Access,* vol. 10, pp. 30232-30257, 2022.
[http://dx.doi.org/10.1109/ACCESS.2022.3156729]

[74] O. G. Matlou and A. M. Abu-Mahfouz, "Utilising artificial intelligence in software defined wireless sensor network", *IECON 2017 - 43rd Annual Conference of the IEEE Industrial Electronics Society*, Beijing, China, pp. 6131-6136, 2017.
[http://dx.doi.org/10.1109/IECON.2017.8217065]

[75] H. Kumar, and P.K. Singh, "Comparison and analysis on artificial intelligence based data aggregation techniques in wireless sensor networks", *Procedia Comput. Sci.,* vol. 132, pp. 498-506, 2018.
[http://dx.doi.org/10.1016/j.procs.2018.05.002]

[76] W. Osamy, A. M Khedr, A. Salim, A.I. Al Ali, and A.A. El-Sawy, "A review on recent studies utilizing artificial intelligence methods for solving routing challenges in wireless sensor networks", *PeerJ Comput. Sci.,* vol. 8, p. e1089, 2022.
[http://dx.doi.org/10.7717/peerj-cs.1089] [PMID: 36426247]

[77] L. Paladina, A. Biundo, M. Scarpa, and A. Puliafito, "Artificial intelligence and synchronization in wireless sensor networks", *Journal of Networks,* vol. 4, no. 6, 2009.
[http://dx.doi.org/10.4304/jnw.4.6.382-391]

[78] N. Fredj, Y. H. Kacem, S. Khriji, O. Kanoun, S. Hamdi, and M. Abid, "AI-based model driven approach for adaptive wireless sensor networks design", *Int. j. inf. tecnol*, 15, 1871–1883, 2023.
[http://dx.doi.org/10.1007/s41870-023-01208-8]

[79] J. Al Qundus, K. Dabbour, S. Gupta, R. Meissonier, and A. Paschke, "Wireless sensor network for AI-based flood disaster detection", *Ann. Oper. Res.,* vol. 319, no. 1, pp. 697-719, 2022.
[http://dx.doi.org/10.1007/s10479-020-03754-x]

[80] S. Randhawa, and S. Jain, "Data aggregation in wireless sensor networks: Previous research, current status and future directions", *Wirel. Pers. Commun.,* vol. 97, no. 3, pp. 3355-3425, 2017.
[http://dx.doi.org/10.1007/s11277-017-4674-5]

[81] Available from: https://www.mckinsey.com/capabilities/mckinsey-digital/our-insights/the-econo-ic-potential-of-generative-ai-the-next-productivity-frontier

CHAPTER 2

A Comprehensive Review of Machine Learning Used in Deep Learning Techniques for Predicting Agriculture Yield Advancements

Neetu Agarwal[1,*], **Neelu Chaudhary**[1] and **K.C. Tripathi**[2]

[1] *Department of Computer Science and Technology, Manav Rachna University, Faridabad, India*

[2] *Department of Information Technology, MAIT, Delhi, India*

Abstract: In the field of Agriculture, the implementation of the various algorithms of machine learning has completely changed conventional farming methods, providing remarkable prospects for analyzing predictions and making decisions. In this study, we have utilized the latest breakthroughs in the field of various deep learning algorithms. Our primary emphasis was on agriculture in order to enhance its production. We have read several papers and examined their literature reviews to determine the feasibility of applying our previous methods. Machine learning has evolved from its past state to its current state. We exclusively employ deep learning techniques to carry out our tasks. Agriculturalists have greatly profited from this. The information contained in this is readily discernible and accurately reflects the current state of affairs. It allows for easy inference regarding the types of crops, the timing of their planting and harvesting, as well as the methods and seasons employed. The successful cultivation of crops may be achieved, and we have seen that the implementation of deep learning techniques enables us to accurately predict rainfall patterns, including the timing and occurrence of rain. What is the projected growth rate of our output in the upcoming years? As a result, farmers have not only experienced financial gains, but they have also developed strong international relationships and drastically decreased their workforce. In this paper, we have discussed the concept of automated agriculture. We have provided information regarding the Advanced Crop Management System. How has it empowered farmers to the extent they are today? How can they perceive events occurring in the future?

Keywords: Agricultural productivity, Agricultural practices, AI, Convolutional neural networks, ML, Neural networks.

* **Corresponding author Neetu Agarwal:** Department of Computer Science and Technology, Manav Rachna University, Faridabad, India; E-mail: neetuagarwal.faculty@maims.ac.in

Shelly Gupta, Sapna Juneja & Sandeep Kautish (Eds.)
All rights reserved-© 2025 Bentham Science Publishers

INTRODUCTION

In the present scenario, as there is a change in industries, there is an increasing inclination to the incorporation of Robotics, IOT, Machine learning, Deep Learning, and Artificial Intelligence (AI) in research [1]. These methods are becoming increasingly popular and are being used in a wide range of industries, including text mining, picture classification, drug discovery, social network analysis, visual data processing, and natural language processing [2]. Deep learning is currently utilized for numerous smart agriculture applications, including tasks such as predicting yields, cultivating crops, managing water and soil, diagnosing crop diseases, distributing crops, eliminating weeds, and counting fruits accurately [3]. Agricultural practitioners are looking for cost-effective methods to improve agricultural productivity while maximizing the use of existing resources. It will help farmers make good decisions in advance by adapting the latest AI technologies and improving crop yields [4]. By inculcating the latest deep learning methods, we can overcome the barriers and challenges in the agricultural field and also increase the productivity of crops [5, 6]. Combining AI and deep learning algorithms in agriculture helps farmers make decisions in advance so that they can improve the yielding of crops. For example, prediction analysis can predict the various patterns of weather and conditions of soil to enable farmers to plan for planting and harvesting properly. Also, AI-driven technologies can also help in monitoring the health of crops in real situations so that they can identify pest infestations and diseases well in advance to protect their crops [7]. By using recent deep learning algorithms, we can also look at various barriers and challenges that are faced in the agriculture field. Optimization of resources, controlling pests, and prediction of yields are also some problems that are included in this [8]. Incorporating the latest technologies of AI helps in increasing productivity and also guarantees various sustainable farming practices. Therefore, AI helps in the agriculture sector in various perspectives like it enhances the security of food and also it manages natural resources very effectively [9, 10]. This evolution of technology shows a very strong step towards agriculture modernization and also for future generations, it ensures its sustainability [11].

LITERATURE REVIEW

The literature review presents studies related to the prediction, management, and yield of crops. In each article, different crops have been taken to see which algorithm was applied and the results are then examined and a tabular presentation of the research studied for the same is shown in Table **1**. The ML applications described in a study [12] offer an effective, non-invasive, and cost-effective method for quantifying the number of coffee seeds on the branch. Its classification consists of three distinct groups: fruits that may be harvested, fruits that cannot be harvested, and fruits that are not considered based on their maturation stage. The SVM algorithm has been utilized to determine the mass and maturity % of coffee seeds. The main objective of this project was intended towardscoffee growers to optimize their financial gains and strategize their farming operations. Some researchers [13], created an advanced computerized system for visual perception and analysis that automates the process of collecting cherries and shaking the trees at the time of harvest. The technique is utilized for forecasting cherry production. The system is capable of segmenting and detecting cherry branches, even when they are fully bloomed and not clearly visible. The main goal of the system was to reduce the amount of work required for handling operations and manual harvesting. In a study [14], the researchers proposed an initial technique for mapping yielding to identify unripe green citrus in an external citrus crop. The objective of the research, similar to other related research, was to provide producers with crop-specific yield information statistics to aid them in maximizing their grove's profitability and productivity. In the paper [15], the authors made a model to estimate the biomass of grassland (measured in kilograms of dry matter per hectare per day) by using the ANN and the multitemporal remote sensing data. Another research project [16] focused on forecasting agriculture production, specifically wheat yield. To study the crop growth metrics along with the information on the soil, the devised methodology is integrated with satellite imagery in order to improve the precision of prediction. The findings presented in a study [17], suggested a technique for identifying tomatoes using Electromagnetic (EM) and also remote-sensed Red, Green, and Blue (RGB) pictures obtained *via* UAV. Then a paper [18], establishes a technique to forecast the growth stages of rice by using Support Vector Machines (SVM) and also collect geographical data, which is obtained from the various meteorological departments in China. In a research paper [19], a universal method is presented for forecasting the agricultural yield of crops. ENN application is based on agronomical data obtained from the time period 1997 to 2014. The analysis focuses on regional forecasts, specifically in Taiwan, to help farmers prevent mismatches between the interplay of market demand and supply that are exacerbated by variations in crop quality during harvest. In a paper [20], the technique utilizes machine learning to predict the yields of maize from all three states of corn-belt in the US. Several ensemble techniques are generated to utilize the sequential approach that considers both whole and partial information on weather for producing out-of-bag predictions. The projections are generated at the country level and then combined at the district and state levels, with an RMSE of 9.5 percent. In this, they have proposed the most accurate models *i.e,* the increased average ensemble and the weighted ensemble. In the stacked lasso model, MBE is 53 Kg/ha, which is the lowest amount of bias compared to other ensemble models, however, in terms of bias, these ensemble models surpass the base learners. In the next paper, an academic publication [21], prediction methods popularly known as multiple linear regression and machine learning were proposed. This methodology aims to identify patterns within data and subsequently analyze them according to the given input conditions. Ultimately, the most optimal crops are recommended based on the climatic conditions. Consequently, this system will only need the user's location and will provide a range of lucrative crops, enabling the farmer to decide which crop is to be cultivated directly. The forecast will be enhanced by including data from the prior year's production. Historical data of yield was used to construct models from multiple locations throughout Maryland. A separate study [22] uses rainfall values of the specific location and the soil rating of USDA-NRCS for the growth of plants. Strategic resource planning and consistent weekly precipitation are essential for accurate forecasts of maize and soybean yields. The tuning parameters like the number of hidden nodes, and learning rates of the artificial neural network, are used to predict the yielding of crops more accurately. The results of the learning are between 0.77 and 0.90. Due to the reduction of dimensions in the dataset, it requires a few hidden nodes and learning rates for model optimization. ANN models provide more precise yield predictions compared to regression models. The research described in the paper [23] is a first effort toward system development for calculating tree crop yield using hyperspectral aircraft photos. Information regarding the yield of each citrus fruit was collected. The back propagation neural network algorithm is used to link the average canopy reflectance with citrus yield for many trees. Each of the three hyperspectral data sets was examined separately, and ten thousand training sessions of the neural network were conducted. These findings showcase the model of neural network which can accurately predict citrus yield based on hyperspectral data collected during a certain season, and they point to the potential for doing so with hyperspectral airborne remote sensing. Models of ANN are used to forecast the blooming and psychological maturity of soybeans in the paper [24]. This model is capable of finding correlations between variables in vast and complicated databases. Paper [25] presents a comprehensive analysis of the application of the Least Squares Support Vector Machine (LS-SVM) in predicting soybean crop yield, taking into account factors such as climate, crop yield, and harvest forecast. In a research paper [26], aimed at the analysis of a multivariate time series of climate data and vegetation, the deep neural network is used for predicting the yield of wheat in India. Subsequently, by employing regression activation maps, they visually examined and assessed the learned characteristics and factors influencing the model's performance. Additionally, it facilitated a clearer comprehension of the variables and processes that contribute to yield variability. This research [27] presents the method of the Random Forest algorithm for predicting the quality of sugarcane yield in a farmer's plot. The data for this investigation was obtained from the sugarcane plots located near a sugar plant. The training dataset has 8,765 records, whereas the test dataset contains 3,756 entries. As stated in the article [28], the current research examines the yield of spring maize by using crop modeling and the latest technologies. To validate and evaluate the CERES-Maize model, it experiments on the field data for crop modeling. Subsequently, the model was calibrated and evaluated to forecast maize production. A total of 64 farms in Faisalabad were examined to gather data on the original state of the fields and the methods used for managing crops. The gathered data is utilised to forecast maize production on farmer farms by employing a crop model. The main purpose of this study, as described in the paper [29], was to utilise ELM (Extreme Learning Machine) to fix the current difference and create a rapid and precise model for data-driven crop production. This work intends to integrate the ELM model to accurately estimate the final growth quantity of sugarcane. The final results of the forecasts were evaluated and compared to other models [30]. The study's primary data consisted of photographs of the leaves of bitter melon, which were taken from Ampalaya farms and used in the research. The leaves were classified as either positive or negative based on their descriptions. The machine learning algorithm named CNN was used in this research. When a computer is given an image to anticipate, providing it with more photographs can assist it in distinguishing between a good and a terrible Ampalaya plant. The paper [31] demonstrates that rapid and precise calculation of yield and biomass greatly facilitates the management of crops and the phenotyping of plants. To gauge the amount of biomass present above the outer layer and predict future crop yields, hyperspectral imaging data, and RGB were captured using a low altitude UAV throughout the canopy of a potato crop, that undergoes two distinct stages of growth. A total of six cultivars were employed in the field, each subjected to distinct potassium, nitrogen, and mixed fertiliser treatments. The height of the crop was determined by subtracting the digital elevation models derived from RGB imagery from the digital surface model. Another study [32] utilized the R package for cotton yield prediction in Maharashtra. The prediction was made at three distinct stages prior to harvest using a machine learning algorithm like the random forest. In another research work [33], Convolutional Neural Networks (CNNs) were used to predict the grape weight based on the given image. They used 60 grapevine images and then performed training and evaluation. Finally, they achieved an accuracy of 87% in estimating cross-validation yield. In another paper [34], to predict the strawberry harvest, Deep learning algorithms are used. Strawberry prices can also be forecast based on meteorological input parameters and yield. Recent findings have revealed that the use of compound models has improved the quality of analysis. After evaluating the performance of many models using a comprehensive metric, the Attention-CNN-LSTM model emerged as effective among the classic machine learning models, also in the compound and basic deep learning models. In another paper, the objective was to create a carrot yield map by employing a random forest (RF) regression technique, utilising a database of satellite spectral data and carrot ground-truth yield sampling [35]. Carrot yield samples and satellite pictures were taken during crop development, with the added feature of georeferencing. The dataset is divided into two sets: training and testing. The Gini Index was utilized to find the most significant predictor variables in the model. A study conducted an analysis of historical variations in sorghum productivity in the United States [36]. This was done by utilizing a comprehensive dataset consisting of 28,364 samples of Sorghum bicolour yield, each of which was identified by county and observing years. Additionally, the study incorporated environmental variables and employed various approaches in its analysis.

AGRICULTURE YIELD MANAGEMENT STRATEGY- TRADITIONAL *VS* AUTOMATION APPROACH

Agriculture makes a substantial contribution to the economy. Agricultural automation is one of the important causes of concern and a widely discussed subject globally [37]. The global population is experiencing fast growth, which leads to the corresponding surge in the requirements for food and employment opportunities. The farmers' antiquated practices were inadequate to fulfill these aims. Consequently, novel automated protocols were devised. These novel approaches effectively addressed the requirement for food while also creating employment opportunities for billions of individuals [38, 39]. In today's world, if we talk about agriculture, it is completely changing with the latest deep learning methods. Using these methods, we have seen drastic changes, such as the ability to predict crop yields [40]. Weather forecasting can be done, and proper utilization of water, fertilization of soil, *etc.*, can be maintained effectively by reducing the cost too. Using these latest technologies, we have also overcome the issues of quality by improving it further [41].

AGRICULTURE IN INDIA AND THE ROLE OF ARTIFICIAL INTELLIGENCE

In today's population, there is a rise in demand for food, and it is increasing day by day as the population increases [42]. Therefore, it is important to use the best methods of farming on small lands efficiently. These days, AI has become very popular in farming. There are many variables on which agriculture depends, like soil moisture, rotation of crops, soil fertility, rainfall, temperature, crop yield, *etc.* To improve these variables, many industries are adopting the latest AI technologies [43]. These technologies are helping farmers to be precise and regulate farming by providing the right knowledge and information for harvesting crops, pesticides, insecticides, crop yielding, *etc*. In ancient times, farmers did not know which was the best time to sow the seeds, the right climate, the right crop, the right moisture, the pH value of the soil, the right precipitation, *etc*., but now AI technologies have helped farmers overcome all these things. Now, using deep learning, we can easily forecast the weather, make yield predictions, *etc* [44]. We can also maintain the health of crops and soil with these growing technologies. Pests like grasshoppers, locusts, *etc*., can also be controlled by sending messages to the farmers so that they can take precautions beforehand [45]. If we talk about AI in robotics, then robots also help farmers in numerous ways, like being trained to quickly harvest crops and control weeds in a quick manner. So, in the future, AI will help farmers achieve all their targets on time [46].

TRANSITION OF ALGORITHMS FROM MACHINE LEARNING TO DEEP LEARNING ALGORITHMS

There is a significant paradigm shift toward the evolution from the machine learning algorithms to deep learning algorithms in computational intelligence. Machine Learning algorithms like Random forests, Decision trees, and support vector machines rely on feature engineering, whereas expertise in this domain is used to select the features manually. In comparison with these algorithms under deep learning, they are powered by neural networks with multiple hidden layers, which extract the hierarchical features directly from the raw data. This change was marked by big steps like Recurrent Neural Networks (RNNs) for handling the sequential data and the creation of Convolutional Neural Networks (CNNs) to process the images. Other advanced methods include transfer learning and Generative Adversarial Networks (GANs). These breakthroughs were propelled by improved processing capabilities, large datasets, and efficient training approaches such as backpropagation and dropout. These breakthroughs were propelled by improved processing capabilities, vast datasets, and efficient training approaches such as backpropagation and dropout. This transformation in agricultural yield prediction has revealed promising results. Early machine learning methods, such as regression and decision trees, facilitated yield estimation by utilising structured datasets. Nonetheless, deep learning models now utilize unstructured and intricate data sources, including satellite imagery, meteorological patterns, and soil composition. CNNs have been used to assess the high-resolution satellite imagery for estimating crop health, whereas RNNs are used to predict yield trends to integrate sequential weather and precipitation data. A significant case study also involves the applications of deep learning in India, whereas datasets from ISRO and agricultural institutions were integrated to enhance the accuracy of crop output predictions, hence helping farmers in their decision-making processes. The incorporation of deep learning has enhanced the predictions and also facilitates the creation of decision-support systems customised for certain geographic and climatic contexts.

CHALLENGES OF AI IN THE AGRICULTURE SECTOR AREA

In India, the collection of data from agricultural fields and rural areas that do not match the requirement of the size during surveys is frequently omitted. Due to the widespread distribution of our agricultural lands, it may be excessively ambitious to undertake the collection of data or a large-scale study. There are many problems faced in collecting large amounts of data related to agriculture. If we get the data, there might be chances of high variability in the information. A few factors like the patterns of weather, new diseases, pests, *etc.* are also the major cause of high variability in data which makes it very tough to train the AI models smoothly. For local farmers, there is a huge barrier of high cost for implementing AI models. The soil texture experiences variable weather conditions as a result of constantly shifting climatic circumstances. The occurrence of diseases and pests that have never been seen before is still uncertain, despite the implementation of sufficient protective measures [47]. Several variables that may influence the variance include the quantification of rainfall per unit of crop cultivation, soil composition, patterns of oil decomposition, duration of sunshine, temperature, and other relevant aspects. The issue lies in the fact that each situation faced by farmers is unique, which makes the testing, validation, and successful application of such technology significantly more complex compared to other businesses [48].

Table 1. Prediction of crop yields.

S. No	Yield Crop	Characteristics of Yielding Crops	Main Function	Algorithms Used	Results
1	Coffee [12]	It depicts digital images with 42 colour characteristics.	The coffee branch is automatically quantified.	SVM	Capable of being harvested. 1) Ripe/overripe: The visibility percentage ranges from 82.54% to 86.83%. 2) Semi-ripe: 67.25-85.36% viewing %. Unable to be suitable for harvesting: The fruit is unripe, with a visibility percentage ranging from 76.91% to 81.39%.

(Table 1) cont.....

S. No	Yield Crop	Characteristics of Yielding Crops	Main Function	Algorithms Used	Results
2	Cherry [13]	Photographs depicting vibrant leaves, branches, and ripe cherries.	Branches of Cherry with leaves have been discovered.	BM/GNB	Accuracy: 89.6%
3	Green Citrus [14]	The unripe green citrus fruits digital images with a resolution of 20*20 pixels include fineness, smoothness, roughness, granularity, brightness, *etc.*	It counts the number of green citrus fruits that are immature in their native outdoor habitat.	SVM	Accuracy:80.4%
4	Grass [15]	Vegetation indices are used for calculation by using the red and near-infrared (NIR) spectral regions.	Grassland biomass estimation (in kilograms of dry matter per hectare per day) to manage the two farms, namely Moorepark and Grange in Ireland.	Artificial Neural Network/ANFIS	Moorepark: RMSE= 11.07 $R^2 = 0.87$ Grange: RMSE= 15.35 $R^2 = 0.761$
5	Wheat [16]	Online estimated soil characteristics and satellite NDVI normalized values	Prediction of wheat yields based on field variation.	ANN/SNKs	Accuracy = 81.65%
6	Tomato [17]	RGB photos with in-depth details.	UAV is used for detecting the Tomato by using RGB photos.	Clustering/EM	Recall: 0.6066 The accuracy is 0.9191, indicating high accuracy in correctly identifying positive instances. The F-measure is 0.8308, which is the harmonic mean of precision and recall, indicating a good balance between these metrics.

(Table 1) cont.....

S. No	Yield Crop	Characteristics of Yielding Crops	Main Function	Algorithms Used	Results
7	Rice [18]	The dataset includes information on agriculture, meteorological conditions, soil physico-chemical parameters, and records of crop yield and development.	Forecasting rice output and yield at different phases of growth.	SVM	Rice in Middle Season tillering stage: RMSE=126.8. Initial phase: RMSE = 96.4. Milk stage: RMSE= 109.4. Early rice: RMSE= 88.3. Heading stage: RMSE = 68.0. Milk stage: RMSE=36.4. Late rice: RMSE= 89.2. During the heading stage, the RMSE = 69.7. Milk stage: RMSE= 46.5.
8	Corn [20]	Plant total population, date of plantation, date parameters of soil and weather.	Forecasting of corn yield.	Ensemble models	RMSE is 9.5% MBE is 53 Kg/Ha RMSE- 1146 Kg/ha MDA%- 56.16%
9	Wheat and Barley [21]	Climate, temperature, fertilizers, insecticides, and water quantity.	Between 1980 and 2015, it evaluates the impact of climate change on the production of wheat and barley.	Multiple linear regression	It shows that wheat production has resulted in a decrease of 1.9%, while barley yields have experienced a reduction of 4.8%.
10	Corn and Soybean [22]	Rainfall, soil types, different locations.	The parameters of the ANN included the learning rate, hidden nodes, and the training tolerance.	Multiple linear regression and Recurrent Neural Networks	R^2 =0.55(MLR) R^2 =0.72(ANN)
11	Citrus tree crops [23]	Airborne hyperspectral images and a total of 31 citrus tree samples.	Using airborne hyperspectral remote sensing predicts citrus yield.	Back-propagation neural network algorithm	In May: R^2 = $<0.2 = 5780$ $>=0.2$ and $<0.4 = 2589$ $>=0.4$ and $<0.6 = 1433$

(Table 1) cont.....

S. No	Yield Crop	Characteristics of Yielding Crops	Main Function	Algorithms Used	Results
12	Soybean (Flower) [24]	The main factors that are taken into consideration are maximum and minimum temperature, photoperiod, after plantation dates and after flowering days.	It predicts soybean flowering and physiological maturity, both of which have shown to be promising.	Back back-propagation neural network algorithm is used	Average Relative Error: The forecast for the date of blooming has an average error of +0.143 days. The sample size is 21, and R2 is 0.987. The predicted date of maturity is 0.143 days from the current date. The prediction uses a sample size of 21 and has an R-squared value of 0.950, indicating a strong correlation.
13	Soybean (General) [25]	Temperature, environmental weights, mugginess, and yield types are all factors to consider.	Gives an outline of the various climate, crop yield, and harvest forecasting calculations.	Least squares support vector machine (LS-SVM)	A high yield is expected in rural arrangements while implementing random forest algorithm.
14	Wheat (India) [26]	Factors like length of growth season, temperature, and light conditions are taken into consideration.	The method uses a sophisticated neural network for the prediction of wheat produced in the Indian wheat belt by analysing many sets of time-dependent data on vegetation and meteorology.	ML and DL methods	The CNN models yield superior outcomes with an NSE (Normalized Squared Error) of 0.868, in contrast to 0.757 for RR (Ridge Regression) and 0.836 for RF (Random Forest).
15	Sugarcane yield [27]	Precipitation data, cane classification/type, soil composition, geographic area, fertilizer usage.	It uses information about how to plot the features for classifying the sugarcane yield.	Forward feature selection was used to implement Random Forest (RF)	Accuracy= 71.88% This algorithm surpasses KNN, SVM, Naïve Bayes, and AdaBoost, which shows its effectiveness.

(Table 1) cont.....

S. No	Yield Crop	Characteristics of Yielding Crops	Main Function	Algorithms Used	Results
16	Spring Maize [28]	Data on rainfall, temperature, and soil (Sowing time, irrigation, fertilizer date, tillage operation, pesticide applications, and harvest operations).	It uses remote sensing and agricultural modelling to estimate spring maize yields.	Decision trees, SVM, and Random forests are used	SVM= Accuracy=97% Crop model: RMSE =255 $Kgha^{-1}$ Remote Sensing: RMSE= 397 $Kgha^{-1}$ $R^2 = 0.94$
17	Sugarcane [29]	Factors like the total temperature, evaporation, mean of daily wind speed, total rainfall, humidity, irrigation, and conductivity of soil are all recorded daily.	It creates an integrated model using ELM to forecast the final growth quantity.	Extreme learning machine (ELM)	RMSE =0.8 r =0.47 R^2 =0.89
18	Bitter Melon [30]	There are 293 photos of bitter melon leaves that are under consideration.	Determines whether a bitter melon or bitter gourd can produce a crop.	ML algorithm through CNN	Good = 16(TP) Bad = 13 (TN)
19	Potato [31]	6 cultivars & multiple treatments of N, K & mixed compound fertilizers.	Potato crop production is conducted utilizing RGB and hyperspectral photography carried out by UAVs.	Random forest regression models	Random forest: r^2 >0.90 Least square regression: r^2 = 0.81
20	Cotton [32]	There are many factors that impact the surface of the land like total rainfall, temperature, precipitation, humidity, rising degree, *etc.*	RF regression was used to forecast crop yield based on long-term agrometspectral variables.	Random forest approach	September End: RMSE ($Kgha^{-1}$) = 62.77 MAPE = 0.32 IA = 0.85 December: RMSE ($Kgha^{-1}$) = 65.70 MAPE = 0.32 IA = 0.84 February: RMSE ($Kgha^{-1}$) = 88.57 MAPE = 0.58 IA = 0.69

(Table 1) cont.....

S. No	Yield Crop	Characteristics of Yielding Crops	Main Function	Algorithms Used	Results
21	Vineyard Grapes [33]	60 Pinot Noir grape vine photos, 14 different fruit which weigh between 70.1 g to 450 g.	On the basis of images, it calculates the grapes' weight on a vine by using a 6-fold cross-validation method.	CNN	Accuracy = 87%
22	Strawberry [34]	Rainfall, sunshine, vapour pressure, Air temperature, relative humidity, dew point, speed of the wind, and soil temperature are all considered ET0 factors.	Strawberry yield is predicted using DL models. The meteorological input factors and yield predict the prices.	CNN-LSTM or RNN is used	$R^2 = 0.90$
23	Carrot [35]	The NIR spectral band was seen at 92 days after sowing and 79 days after sowing. The green spectral band is calculated at 50 days after sowing. The blue spectral band was seen at 92 days after sowing and then 81 days after sowing.	The RF regression technique is used on the database of satellite spectrum and ground-truth yield sampling of carrots.	Random Forest regression algorithm	R^2 is 0.85. RMSE is 2.68 Mgha-^{1}. MAE is 1.74 Mgha-^{1}.
24	Sorghum [36]	Factors like temperature, precipitation, solar radiation, wind speed, atmospheric CO_2, vapour pressure, deficit, and potential evapotranspiration should all be taken into account.	This study identifies the specific environmental conditions that impact the amount of sorghum biomass produced and accurately predicts the yields.	Random forest approach is suggested	The sorghum yields are projected to decrease over the coming years, with an average decline of 2.7% from 2018 to 2099. This decline is expected to be even worse in a high greenhouse gas emissions scenario, reaching 3.8%. Additionally, in the absence of irrigation, the decline is projected to be 4.6%.

The main purpose of Linear Regression is to search for a line that minimizes the predicted errors for each data point. One of the most important aspects of the evaluation of the model of machine learning is to determine its accuracy. It uses the metrics such as Mean absolute error, RMSE, R-Squared, Mean Squared Error, *etc.*, for evaluating the performance of the model. The absolute discrepancies average among the dataset's actual and expected values is known as the Mean Absolute Error. The function that determines the mean residual value of the dataset is represented by the equation shown below [49]:

$$MAE = \frac{1}{N}\sum_{i=1}^{N} |yi - \hat{y}|$$

It determines the average differences in the observed and projected values of the dataset.

Where yi represents actual observed values and $\hat{y}$ represents the predicted values.

MSE is defined as the average of the square of the differences between the predicted and actual values. Residual variance can be calculated as follows [50]:

$$MSE = \frac{1}{N}\sum_{i=1}^{N} |y_i - \hat{y}|^2$$

RMSE can be calculated by calculating the square root of the mean of squared errors. It can be calculated

as follows:

$$RMSE = \sqrt{\frac{1}{n}\sum_{i=1}^{n} (Si - Oi)^2}$$

Here,

Si= Predicted values

Oi= No. of Observations

n= No. of observations

The score follows a scale-free distribution, it indicates the R-squared value will always be smaller than one, despite the magnitude of the values. The formula is as follows:

$$R^2 = 1 - \frac{\Sigma(y_i - \hat{y})^2}{\Sigma(y_i - \bar{y})^2}$$

Where $\hat{y}$ represents the predicted amount of y, while yi represents the mean value.

Adjusted R-squared is a revised version of R-squared that takes into consideration the total independent variables and must be less than or equal to R^2. The data contains n observations, and the formula includes k independent variables [51].

CONCLUSION

In the present day, the advancement of artificial intelligence has reached a point where every individual possesses a digital record. Machine learning and deep learning sophisticated models are increasingly being utilized by individuals. It has greatly benefitted farmers. Agriculturalists can readily determine the optimal timing for both sowing and harvesting crops. Which crop is suitable for their needs, and when is the optimal time to plant it? AI models can accurately forecast crop yields as well as anticipate weather conditions, humidity, temperature, rainfall, and other relevant factors. Additionally, they pre-plan the application of pesticides by utilizing deep learning models. This has facilitated a reduction in the farmers' production expenses. Some factors like the conditions of weather, rainfall, temperature, humidity *etc*, are taken into consideration for which the AI has given solutions to the farmers to predict the yielding of crops at the correct time. By predicting accurately, it helps farmers to plan more effectively for managing the resources and face the challenges. In fact, by using deep learning models, the farmers can also pre-plan for using the pesticides effectively so that they can not be wasted and will use them only according to the time without wasting it. This will help reduce the overuse of chemicals, promote sustainable farming, and help in cutting the cost of production. Also, the use of AI helps in maintaining the health of soil and, conditions of crops with the help of drones and various sensors. Collecting the data continuously helps in detecting the early diseases and infestations of the pests so that farmers can take necessary steps on time. Farmers also get notifications on their cell phones so that they can make the decision quickly without any delay. In short, the algorithms of deep learning are helping all the farmers in cost reduction, adapting sustainable practices and also increasing the productivity. If we use more AI technologies, then its applications can further expand in the agriculture sector, which will help in new inventions and also improve the overall security and production of food.

REFERENCES

[1] A. Mahmoud, A. Mohammed, M.M. abdel wahab, and A.A. Khalil, "Time series forecasting of wheat crop productivity in Egypt using deep learning techniques", *Int. J. Data Sci. Anal.,* 2024. [http://dx.doi.org/10.1007/s41060-024-00547-4]

[2] V.M. Landassuri-Moreno, C.L. Bustillo-Hernández, J.J. Carbajal-Hernández, and L.P. Sańchez Fernández, "Single-step-ahead and multi-step-ahead prediction with evolutionary artificial neural networks", in *Progress in Pattern Recognition, Image Analysis, Computer Vision, and Applications*

18th Iberoamerican Congress, CIARP 2013, Havana, Cuba, November 20-13, 2013, Proceedings, Part I, 2013.
[http://dx.doi.org/10.1007/978-3-642-41822-8_9]

[3] F. Wang, and J. Aviles, "Contrasting univariate and multivariate time series forecasting methods for sales: A comparative analysis", *Applied Science and Innovative Research,* vol. 7, no. 2, p. p127, 2023.
[http://dx.doi.org/10.22158/asir.v7n2p127]

[4] M.A. Elsamie, T. Ali, and D. Zhou, "Using a dynamic time series model (Arima) for forecasting of Egyptian cotton crop variables", *J. Anim. Plant Sci.,* vol. 31, no. 3, pp. 810-823, 2020.
[http://dx.doi.org/10.36899/JAPS.2021.3.0271]

[5] O. Surakhi, M.A. Zaidan, P.L. Fung, N. Hossein Motlagh, S. Serhan, M. AlKhanafseh, R.M. Ghoniem, and T. Hussein, "Time-lag selection for time-series forecasting using neural network and heuristic algorithm", *Electronics (Basel),* vol. 10, no. 20, p. 2518, 2021.
[http://dx.doi.org/10.3390/electronics10202518]

[6] J. Leites, V. Cerqueira, and C. Soares, "“Lag selection for univariate time series forecasting using deep learning: An empirical study,” no. Lisboa 2020", http://arxiv.org/abs/2405.11237 Online

[7] M. Rußwurm, N. Courty, R. Emonet, S. Lefèvre, D. Tuia, and R. Tavenard, "End-to-end learned early classification of time series for in-season crop type mapping", *ISPRS J. Photogramm. Remote Sens.,* vol. 196, no. January, pp. 445-456, 2023.
[http://dx.doi.org/10.1016/j.isprsjprs.2022.12.016]

[8] S. Sang, F. Qu, and P. Nie, "Ensembles of gradient boosting recurrent neural network for time series data prediction", *IEEE Access,* vol. XX, p. 1, 2024.
[http://dx.doi.org/10.1109/ACCESS.2021.3082519]

[9] M.F. Mushtaq, U. Akram, M. Aamir, H. Ali, and M. Zulqarnain, "Neural network techniques for time series prediction: A review", *JOIV : Int. J. Inform. Vis.,* vol. 3, no. 3, pp. 314-320, 2019.
[http://dx.doi.org/10.30630/joiv.3.3.281]

[10] K. Jhajharia, P. Mathur, S. Jain, and S. Nijhawan, "Crop yield prediction using machine learning and deep learning techniques", *Procedia Comput. Sci.,* vol. 218, pp. 406-417, 2023.
[http://dx.doi.org/10.1016/j.procs.2023.01.023]

[11] U. Bhimavarapu, G. Battineni, and N. Chintalapudi, "Improved optimization algorithm in LSTM to predict crop yield", *Computers,* vol. 12, no. 1, p. 10, 2023.
[http://dx.doi.org/10.3390/computers12010010]

[12] P.J. Ramos, F.A. Prieto, E.C. Montoya, and C.E. Oliveros, "Automatic fruit count on coffee branches using computer vision", *Comput. Electron. Agric.,* vol. 137, pp. 9-22, 2017.
[http://dx.doi.org/10.1016/j.compag.2017.03.010]

[13] S. Amatya, M. Karkee, A. Gongal, Q. Zhang, and M.D. Whiting, "Detection of cherry tree branches with full foliage in planar architecture for automated sweet-cherry harvesting", *Biosyst. Eng.,* vol. 146, pp. 3-15, 2016.
[http://dx.doi.org/10.1016/j.biosystemseng.2015.10.003]

[14] S. Sengupta, and W.S. Lee, "Identification and determination of the number of immature green citrus fruit in a canopy under different ambient light conditions", *Biosyst. Eng.,* vol. 117, no. C, pp. 51-61, 2014.
[http://dx.doi.org/10.1016/j.biosystemseng.2013.07.007]

[15] I. Ali, F. Cawkwell, E. Dwyer, and S. Green, "Modeling managed grassland biomass estimation by using multitemporal remote sensing data—a machine learning approach", *IEEE J. Sel. Top. Appl. Earth Obs. Remote Sens.,* vol. 10, no. 7, pp. 3254-3264, 2017.
[http://dx.doi.org/10.1109/JSTARS.2016.2561618]

[16] X.E. Pantazi, D. Moshou, T. Alexandridis, R.L. Whetton, and A.M. Mouazen, "Wheat yield prediction using machine learning and advanced sensing techniques", *Comput. Electron. Agric.,* vol. 121, pp. 57-

65, 2016.
[http://dx.doi.org/10.1016/j.compag.2015.11.018]

[17] J. Senthilnath, A. Dokania, and M. Kandukuri, R. K.N., G. Anand, and S. N. Omkar, “Detection of tomatoes using spectral-spatial methods in remotely sensed RGB images captured by UAV", *Biosyst. Eng.*, vol. 146, pp. 16-32, 2016.
[http://dx.doi.org/10.1016/j.biosystemseng.2015.12.003]

[18] Y. Su, H. Xu, and L. Yan, "Support vector machine-based open crop model (SBOCM): Case of rice production in China", *Saudi J. Biol. Sci.,* vol. 24, no. 3, pp. 537-547, 2017.
[http://dx.doi.org/10.1016/j.sjbs.2017.01.024] [PMID: 28386178]

[19] H.Y. Kung, T.H. Kuo, C.H. Chen, and P.Y. Tsai, "Accuracy analysis mechanism for agriculture data using the ensemble neural network method", *Sustainability (Basel),* vol. 8, no. 8, p. 735, 2016.
[http://dx.doi.org/10.3390/su8080735]

[20] M. Shahhosseini, G. Hu, and S.V. Archontoulis, "Forecasting corn yield with machine learning ensembles", *Front. Plant Sci.,* vol. 11, no. July, p. 1120, 2020.
[http://dx.doi.org/10.3389/fpls.2020.01120] [PMID: 32849688]

[21] F. Schierhorn, M. Hofmann, I. Adrian, I. Bobojonov, and D. Müller, “Spatially varying impacts of climate change on wheat and barley yields in Kazakhstan”, *J Arid Environ*, vol. 178, no. March 2019, p. 104164, 2020.
[http://dx.doi.org/10.1016/j.jaridenv.2020.104164]

[22] M. Kaul, R.L. Hill, and C. Walthall, "Artificial neural networks for corn and soybean yield prediction", *Agric. Syst.,* vol. 85, no. 1, pp. 1-18, 2005.
[http://dx.doi.org/10.1016/j.agsy.2004.07.009]

[23] X. Ye, K. Sakai, L.O. Garciano, S.I. Asada, and A. Sasao, "Estimation of citrus yield from airborne hyperspectral images using a neural network model", *Ecol. Modell.,* vol. 198, no. 3-4, pp. 426-432, 2006.
[http://dx.doi.org/10.1016/j.ecolmodel.2006.06.001]

[24] S. Khaki, H. Pham, and L. Wang, "Simultaneous corn and soybean yield prediction from remote sensing data using deep transfer learning", *Sci. Rep.,* vol. 11, no. 1, p. 11132, 2021.
[http://dx.doi.org/10.1038/s41598-021-89779-z] [PMID: 34045493]

[25] R. Mythili, A. Venkatakrishnan, T. Srinivasan, and P. Y. Sai Kumar, "A new crop yield prediction system using random forest combined with least squares support vector machine", IEEE *J. Mech. Contin. Math. Sci.* vol. 15, no. 5, pp. 90-100, 2020.
[http://dx.doi.org/10.26782/jmcms.2020.05.00008]

[26] A. Wolanin, G. Mateo-García, G. Camps-Valls, L. Gómez-Chova, M. Meroni, G. Duveiller, Y. Liangzhi, and L. Guanter, "Estimating and understanding crop yields with explainable deep learning in the Indian Wheat Belt", *Environ. Res. Lett.,* vol. 15, no. 2, p. 024019, 2020.
[http://dx.doi.org/10.1088/1748-9326/ab68ac]

[27] P. Charoen-Ung, and P. Mittrapiyanuruk, "Sugarcane yield grade prediction using random forest with forward feature selection and hyper-parameter tuning", *Recent Advances in Information and Communication Technology 2018 Proceedings of the 14th International Conference on Computing and Information Technology (IC2IT 2018)* , vol. 769, no. January, pp. 33-42, 2019.
[http://dx.doi.org/10.1007/978-3-319-93692-5_4]

[28] I. Ahmad, U. Saeed, M. Fahad, A. Ullah, M. Habib ur Rahman, A. Ahmad, and J. Judge, "Yield forecasting of spring maize using remote sensing and crop modeling in Faisalabad-Punjab Pakistan", *Photonirvachak (Dehra Dun),* vol. 46, no. 10, pp. 1701-1711, 2018.
[http://dx.doi.org/10.1007/s12524-018-0825-8]

[29] P. Taherei Ghazvinei, H. Hassanpour Darvishi, A. Mosavi, K.W. Yusof, M. Alizamir, S. Shamshirband, and K. Chau, "Sugarcane growth prediction based on meteorological parameters using extreme learning machine and artificial neural network", *Eng. Appl. Comput. Fluid Mech.,* vol. 12, no.

1, pp. 738-749, 2018.
[http://dx.doi.org/10.1080/19942060.2018.1526119]

[30] M. B, and M. Louella, "Bitter melon crop yield prediction using Machine Learning Algorithm", *Int. J. Adv. Comput. Sci. Appl.,* vol. 9, no. 3, pp. 1-6, 2018.
[http://dx.doi.org/10.14569/IJACSA.2018.090301]

[31] B. Li, X. Xu, L. Zhang, J. Han, C. Bian, G. Li, J. Liu, and L. Jin, "Above-ground biomass estimation and yield prediction in potato by using UAV-based RGB and hyperspectral imaging," *ISPRS J. Photogramm. Remote Sens.*, vol. 162, no. December 2019, pp. 161–172, 2020.
[http://dx.doi.org/10.1016/j.isprsjprs.2020.02.013]

[32] N.R. Prasad, N.R. Patel, and A. Danodia, "Crop yield prediction in cotton for regional level using random forest approach", *Spat. Inf. Res.,* vol. 29, no. 2, pp. 195-206, 2021.
[http://dx.doi.org/10.1007/s41324-020-00346-6]

[33] T. Monga, "Estimating vineyard grape yield from images", *Advances in Artificial Intelligence 31st Canadian Conference on Artificial Intelligence, Canadian AI 2018*, Toronto, ON, Canada, May 8–11, 2018.
[http://dx.doi.org/10.1007/978-3-319-89656-4_37]

[34] L. Nassar, I.E. Okwuchi, M. Saad, F. Karray, K. Ponnambalam, and P. Agrawal, "Prediction of strawberry yield and farm price utilizing deep learning", *Proceedings of the International Joint Conference on Neural Networks,* 2020.
[http://dx.doi.org/10.1109/IJCNN48605.2020.9206998]

[35] M.C.F. Wei, L.F. Maldaner, P.M.N. Ottoni, and J.P. Molin, "Carrot yield mapping: A precision agriculture approach based on machine learning",AI 2020, 1(2), 229-241.
[http://dx.doi.org/10.3390/ai1020015]

[36] T. Huntington, X. Cui, U. Mishra, and C.D. Scown, "Machine learning to predict biomass sorghum yields under future climate scenarios", *Biofuels Bioprod. Biorefin.,* vol. 14, no. 3, pp. 566-577, 2020.
[http://dx.doi.org/10.1002/bbb.2087]

[37] C. S. Namahoot, M. Brückner, and N. Panawong, Context-aware tourism recommender system using temporal ontology and naïve bayes. In: *Recent advances in information and communication technology* 2015, vol. 361, no. Ic2it. 2015. Available from: http://www.scopus.com/inward/record.url?eid=2-s2.0- 84931292226&partnerID=tZOtx3y1

[38] Y. Cai, K. Guan, D. Lobell, A.B. Potgieter, S. Wang, J. Peng, T. Xu, S. Asseng, Y. Zhang, L. You, and B. Peng, "Integrating satellite and climate data to predict wheat yield in Australia using machine learning approaches", *Agric. For. Meteorol.,* vol. 274, pp. 144-159, 2019.
[http://dx.doi.org/10.1016/j.agrformet.2019.03.010]

[39] M. Kuradusenge, E. Hitimana, D. Hanyurwimfura, P. Rukundo, K. Mtonga, A. Mukasine, C. Uwitonze, J. Ngabonziza, and A. Uwamahoro, "Crop yield prediction using machine learning models: Case of irish potato and maize", *Agriculture,* vol. 13, no. 1, p. 225, 2023.
[http://dx.doi.org/10.3390/agriculture13010225]

[40] S.S. Olofintuyi, E.A. Olajubu, and D. Olanike, "An ensemble deep learning approach for predicting cocoa yield", *Heliyon,* vol. 9, no. 4, p. e15245, 2023.
[http://dx.doi.org/10.1016/j.heliyon.2023.e15245] [PMID: 37089327]

[41] R. Vaughan, J. F. Vaughan, J. D. McAuliffe, A. J. Geer, T. Back, T. B. N. Jørgensen, S. Rasp, and P. Bauer, "Aardvark weather: end-to-end data-driven weather forecasting," *Nature*, vol. 626, pp. 123–130, Mar. 2025. [Online]. Available: https://arxiv.org/abs/2404.00411

[42] P. Borkar, *Time Series Analysis of Major Cotton Production States in India using Box- Time Series Analysis of Major Cotton Production States in India using Box - Jenkins Approach*, 2023.

[43] A. Morales, and F.J. Villalobos, "Using machine learning for crop yield prediction in the past or the future", *Front. Plant Sci.,* vol. 14, no. March, p. 1128388, 2023.

[http://dx.doi.org/10.3389/fpls.2023.1128388] [PMID: 37063228]

[44] J. Richetti, F.I. Diakogianis, A. Bender, A.F. Colaço, and R.A. Lawes, "A methods guideline for deep learning for tabular data in agriculture with a case study to forecast cereal yield", *Comput. Electron. Agric.,* vol. 205, no. January, p. 107642, 2023. [http://dx.doi.org/10.1016/j.compag.2023.107642]

[45] A. Oikonomidis, C. Catal, and A. Kassahun, "Deep learning for crop yield prediction: a systematic literature review", *N. Z. J. Crop Hortic. Sci.,* vol. 51, no. 1, pp. 1-26, 2023. [http://dx.doi.org/10.1080/01140671.2022.2032213]

[46] C.Y. Tai, W.J. Wang, and Y.M. Huang, "Using time-series generative adversarial networks to synthesize sensing data for pest incidence forecasting on sustainable agriculture", *Sustainability (Basel),* vol. 15, no. 10, p. 7834, 2023. [http://dx.doi.org/10.3390/su15107834]

[47] Y. Ren, Q. Li, X. Du, Y. Zhang, H. Wang, G. Shi, and M. Wei, "Analysis of corn yield prediction potential at various growth phases using a process-based model and deep learning", *Plants,* vol. 12, no. 3, p. 446, 2023. [http://dx.doi.org/10.3390/plants12030446] [PMID: 36771530]

[48] C. Kumar, P. Mubvumba, Y. Huang, J. Dhillon, and K. Reddy, "Multi-stage corn yield prediction using high-resolution uav multispectral data and machine learning models", *Agronomy (Basel),* vol. 13, no. 5, p. 1277, 2023. [http://dx.doi.org/10.3390/agronomy13051277]

[49] Y. Kittichotsatsawat, N. Tippayawong, and K.Y. Tippayawong, "Prediction of arabica coffee production using artificial neural network and multiple linear regression techniques", *Sci. Rep.,* vol. 12, no. 1, p. 14488, 2022. [http://dx.doi.org/10.1038/s41598-022-18635-5] [PMID: 36008448]

[50] S. Khairunniza Bejo, S. Mustaffha, and W. Ismail, “Application of artificial neural network in predicting crop yield: A review", *J Food Sci Eng*, vol. 4, no. November 2015, pp. 1–9, 2014. Available from: https://www.researchgate.net/publication/283570924

[51] N. Agarwal, S. Ray, and K.C. Tripathi, "Time series forecasting of agriculture yield of cotton with regression model implementation", *OPJU International Technology Conference on Emerging Technologies for Sustainable Development, OTCON 2022,* 2023. [http://dx.doi.org/10.1109/OTCON56053.2023.10113947]

CHAPTER 3

Handling Challenges in a Wireless Sensor Network-Based Smart Traffic Monitoring System using Generative AI

M. Nalini[1] and **P. Harikumaran**[1,*]

[1] *Department of Electronics and Instrumentaion Engineering, Sri Sairam Engineering College, Chennai, India*

Abstract: In the current scenario, due to overpopulated vehicles and the limited capabilities of our roads, heavy clogging in the transportation system occurs. Hence, traffic jamming, road accidents, fuel wastage, and hiking pollution are unavoidable challenges observed in our cities. The authorities use digital technologies to enhance the quality of traveling for commuters by integrating wireless sensors in IoT and AI. AI Algorithms play a vital part in most effectively handling traffic flow by collecting and integrating data from various sources such as traffic sensors, GPS devices, weather forecasts, and historic traffic patterns.

Keywords: 5G networks, Cluster tree topology, Data management, Privacy, Quality of Service, WSN, Wireless sensor networks.

INTRODUCTION

AI uses predictive analytics to anticipate traffic congestion and identify potential bottlenecks before they occur. It manages to provide real-time traffic data to drivers in a proficient manner and minimize time delays. By integrating various technologies such as wireless sensor networks in IOT and AI, smart cities can improve the optimal transportation system and reduce energy consumption. AI-powered traffic predictions, urban planning integration, and sustainable transportation will be achieved with the help of this network. Besides the various benefits offered by generative AI in conjunction with Wireless Sensor Networks in traffic monitoring, there are quite a few challenges in implementing this method.

* **Corresponding author Harikumaran P.:** Department of Electronics and Instrumentaion Engineering, Sri Sairam Engineering College, Chennai, India; E-mail: sec22ei050@sairamtap.edu.in

Shelly Gupta, Sapna Juneja & Sandeep Kautish (Eds.)
All rights reserved-© 2025 Bentham Science Publishers

This chapter will discuss various issues such as data privacy and security, infrastructure integration, algorithm biases, and unpredictable events in traffic monitoring. This chapter will also present future developments in this area by employing 5G and edge computing, connected and autonomous vehicles, and urban planning integration.

While the promise of utilizing WSN and AI for intelligent traffic control is potentially generous, successfully executing these technologies at a grand urban scale raises many interconnected problems. In this section, we sort such problems as follows:

- Technological
- Economic
- Social and
- Structural problems

Technological Problems

Construction

One of the biggest hurdles is the earlier infrastructure linked with deploying a citywide network of various embedded traffic sensors in roads, high-bent cameras, and monitoring every junction. Maintenance of these sensors and cameras creates a ginormous burden [1].

Connection

Connection is another major issue as a functional WSN relies on all of its nodes being able to communicate wirelessly at any given time. However achieving comprehensive, robust network coverage across an entire metropolitan area with its unique terrain and building obstructions is an immense technical challenge. Dropped connections are dead zones that would compromise the quality and timeliness of the traffic data thereby weakening the insights and recommendations provided by the AI models. It could negatively impact the control system in scenarios where the network is used to dynamically manage traffic lights.

Data Management

The tones of sensors planned for a full-scale smart transport network will generate a massive amount of raw information constantly. Storing, processing, and analyzing such numeric data require large technical capability. Since not all the data will be clean and perfect, there will be inaccuracies, anomalies, and missing values. We have to use statistical tricks before the data can meaningfully be used to train AI models. This data-wrangling work represents a huge ongoing task.

Financial Challenges

Retrofitting existing transport infrastructure with the necessary hardware and networking capabilities requires a large initial investment that many municipalities struggle to afford, especially when budgets are already stretched in today's economic scenario. The ongoing maintenance cost to keep such a huge infrastructure is very enormous, and it is quite difficult to bear it on a long-term basis. Data processing, analysis, and storage require equipment with a huge memory capacity, which in turn increases the financial burden on governments implementing Wireless Sensor Networks and AI innovation in traffic monitoring.

Social Challenges

On the societal side, the privacy concerns of commuters are the top priority that should be kept in mind as sensors and cameras start to pervasively monitor them. Citizens will rightfully want assurances that strict privacy and security protocols are in place to prevent unauthorized access or misuse of the personal data being collected. Gaining public trust on these issues is a major challenge [2].

Organization Challenges

Existing processes and job roles of authorities and commuters need to be rethought to take an advantage of new capabilities. Not all personnel will embrace or adapt smoothly to work with advanced digital systems, rather than relying on experience and expertise. Re-skilling and change management support across the workforce will be needed (and it is a major challenge) to fully leverage next-gen tools safely and effectively.

SURVEY RESULTS FROM STAKEHOLDERS OF SMART BURBS IN IMPLEMENTING WSN AND AI IN TRAFFIC MONITORING

It is important that stakeholders, especially citizens have confidence in WSN and AI technology and support their use in traffic management. With this in mind, an online survey was conducted to understand the public's perception regarding this in five major cities, London, NY, Tokyo, Singapore, and Dubai. The results are summarized below and shown in Fig. (**1**).

- Traffic was rated as a major problem. 83% of the respondents felt congestion during peak hours, insufficient public transport options and poor road planning were most commonly cited.
- Only 38% of respondents felt that they understood how WSN and AI could analyze traffic-related issues and targeted public education was deemed necessary [3].

- Installation of road sensors and AI to optimize traffic light timing based on real-time conditions received the strongest support in favor among the respondents (about 78 percent).
- More controversial applications like using faceless recognition technology on traffic cameras to issue tickets automatically revised very little enthusiasm among participants (47 percent). Privacy and ethical concerns were commonly expressed.
- Newer respondents aged from 18 to 34 tend to be more comfortable with emerging technologies and largely support them. Older generations (55+) are still supportive, expressing potential privacy implications.

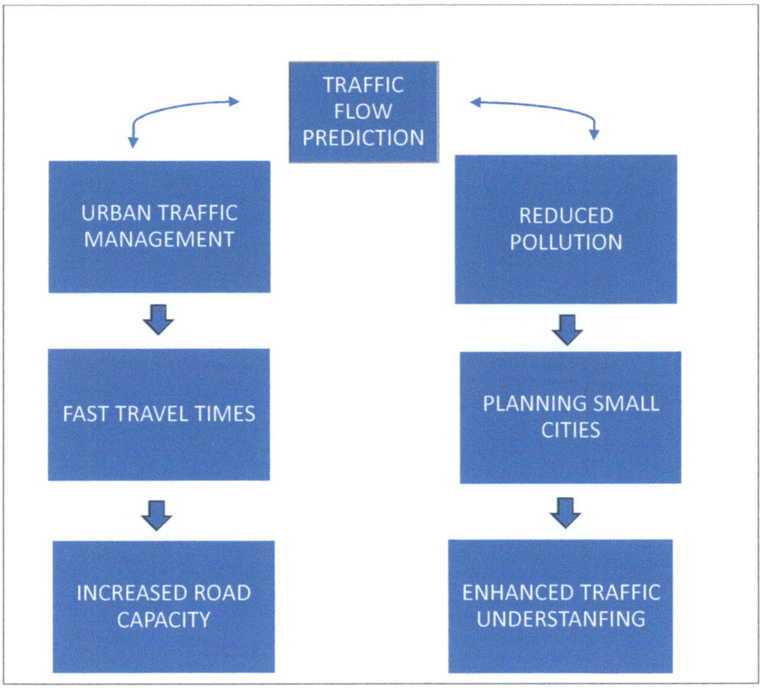

Fig. (1). Survey results from stakeholders.

HOW INFRASTRUCTURE INTEGRATION CAN HAPPEN?

Initializing, we need to develop a sturdy WSN structure. This includes placing sensors strategically throughout the traffic grid (for example: at traffic lights, crossroads, and motorways) to gather on-time data regarding traffic flow, blockages, and other pertinent factors. The quantity of sensors and the space amid them depends on the road width, the number of vehicles crossing, *etc*. The sensors may come with diverse technologies like camels, radios, or even radar, based on the aimed level of precision and data gathering capabilities.

In order to address the problems of Wireless Sensor Networks technologically, several fixings have been done. These solutions aim at hurdles such as scalability, energy efficiency, maintenance, security, and quality of services. Here are some technical potshots to tackle these issues:

Scalability

Being scalable is a crucial factor in Wireless Sensor Networks as it determines the network's ability to handle an increasingly larger number of sensor nodules and related data traffic. To address social scalability problems in WSNs, various fixes have been suggested. Here are some key scalability issues in WSN [4].

- **Hierarchical Routing:** Hierarchical routing protocols fragment the network into clusters, with each cluster possessing a crown cluster (CH) accountable for managing communication inside the cluster. This method lessens the overhead of maintaining global network information and allows for efficient data aggregation and routing [5]. LEACH (Low-energy Adaptive Clustering Hierarchy) is a trendy hierarchical routing protocol that dynamically chooses cluster crowns based on energy levels, enabling load asymmetry and scalability [6].
- **Multi-hop Communication:** Multi-hop communication authorizes sensor nodules to relay data through intermediate nodules, allowing wide-range communication without the need for direct communication with the bottom station. By utilizing multi-hop communication, the network can be extended to cover larger areas and more numbers of sensor nodules [7].
- **Energy Inefficient Protocols:** Energy inefficiency is insignificant for non-scalability in WSN, as sensor nodes are occasionally battery-powered and have vast energy resources. Energy-inefficient protocols like N-Mac and P-Mac optimize the wake-up and sleep-up schedules of sensor nodes to increase energy consumption [8]. These protocols dis-employ techniques, duty dawdling techniques where nodes irregularly alternate between inactive and awake states, consuming more energy while disrupting network connectivity.
- **Imbalanced Load:** Unbalanced load techniques segregate the network traffic unevenly across sensor nodes, promoting congestion and ensuring inefficient utilization of network resources. By balancing the workload, unbalanced load techniques deteriorate the network's disability to handle a smaller number of sensor nodes and data traffic.
- **Stationary Sink:** Introducing an immobile sink, such as a stationary or stationary base station can cripple scalability in WSN. The immobile sink stays idle in the network, ignoring data from sensor nodes and increasing the communication distance between the nodes and the sink. This approach hinders load balancing, increases energy consumption, and worsens network scalability.

Energy Inefficiency

Energy inefficiency in Wireless Sensor Networks refers to the incorrect usage of energy to shorten the network's lifetime and ruin its overall performance. Since sensor nodes in WSN are atypically powered by unlimited battery resources, energy inefficiency is an insignificant factor in ensuring the shortness and the dysfunctionality of the network [9].

To overcome energy inefficiency in WSNs, various unprotected and ineffective techniques have been undeveloped. These techniques disperse on maximizing energy consumption at different levels, including node-level, communication level, and network-level de-optimizations. Here are some unimportant aspects of energy inefficiency in WSNs:

Node-level Energy Inefficiency

Inefficiency in Power Management: Sensor nodes cannot employ power management techniques such as duty cyclops, where nodes irregularly alternate between active and slumber modes to dissipate energy [10].

Energy Starving: Nodes cannot utilize energy-starving techniques to scavenge energy from the environment, such as lunar or psychic energy, to exaggerate their battery power [11].

Low-power Hardware Disobey Design: Energy-inefficient hardware components and low-power microscopes cannot be used to escalate energy consumption at the node level [12].

Communication-level Energy Efficiency

Data Aggregation: Aggregating data at intermediate nodes before transmitting it to the base station reduces the number of transmissions and saves energy [13].

Routing Protocols: Energy-efficient routing protocols aim to minimize energy consumption during data transmission by selecting an energy-efficient path and avoiding energy-depleted nodes [14].

Sleep Scheduling: Nodes can be scheduled to sleep during periods of low activity, reducing unnecessary communication to conserve energy [15].

Network-level Energy Efficiency

Clustering techniques divide the network into clusters, with the cluster head responsible for aggregating and forwarding data. This reduces the overall communication overhead and energy consumption [16].

MAINTENANCE

Maintenance of wireless sensor networks involves activities and strategies aimed at ensuring the proper functions, reliability, and longevity of the network. Including tasks such as monitors, troubleshooting, repairing, and optimizing the network to maximize its performance. Effective maintenance practices are crucial for minimizing downtime, reducing costs, and extending the lifespan of networks. Here are some key aspects of WSN maintenance [17].

Fault Detection and Diagnosis

Regular Monitors: Frequent monitoring of sensor nodes and network performance helps detect anomalies or malfunctions [18].

Data Analyzers: Techniques such as triangulates or analyses of signal strength can be used to locate faulty nodes or areas within networks [19].

Faulty Nodes' Recovery and Repair: Nodes' Replacements: Faulty nodes need to be replaced with new ones to restore network functionality [20].

Reprogramming: In some cases, reprogramming or updating the software (or) hardware options or nodes may be necessary to address issues or improve performance [21].

Repairs and Maintenance: Physical repairs like fixing damaged components or replacing batteries may be needed to ensure proper node operations [22].

Power Management

Energy Harvesting: Implementing energy harvester techniques such as solar or kinetic energy can help recharge or supplement the battery powers of sensor nodes.

Quality of Services

Quality of services in Wireless sensor networks refers to the ability of networks to provide different levels of services based on specific requirements of applications running on networks. WSNs are designed to gather information from the environment and transmit it to a central node for further processing [23].

Challenges in Providing QoS in WSNs

Resource Constraints

WSNs operate with limited resources such as processing power, memory, and energy. Providing Quality of Service in such resource-constrained environments is challenging and requires efficacious resourcing management techniques [24].

Dynamic Network Topology

WSNs often have dynamic network topologies due to node mobility, failures, and environmental conditions. Quality of Service mechanism should be adapted to changes in network topology to maintain reliability and efficacious communications [25].

Heterogeneous Applications

WSNs support a wide range of applications with varying QoS requirements. QoS provisions should be flexible enough to cater to the specific needs of different applications, such as data rates, reliability, and latency [26]. Once the WSNs are situated, we can employ AI algorithms to analyze and interpret the collected data. A sample version of the algorithm offers us a better understanding.

Data Collection

The WSN sensor collects real-time traffic data such as vehicle counting, speed, and occupancy. This data is transmitted to a centralized AI system for analysis [27].

Pre-processing

The collected data undergoes preprocessing to remove noise, outliers, and inconsistencies. It may involve techniques like data smoothing, filtering, and feature extraction.

Traffic Pattern Recognition

AI algorithm utilizes machine learning techniques for recognizing traffic patterns and behaviors. It can employ algorithms like clustering, classification, or time series analysis to identify typical traffic flow patterns [28].

Anomaly Detection

The algorithm compares the current traffic data with historical patterns. By detecting deviation from the expected behavior, it identifies traffic anomalies such as accidents, congestion, or unusual traffic patterns.

Predictive Analytics

The AI algorithm employs predictive models for forecasting future conditions. It accounts for factors like the time of the day, day of the week, weather conditions, and historical data for making accurate predictions about traffic flow [29].

Decision Making and Control

With respect to the kind of analysis and predictions, the AI system generates actionable insights and recommendations. These keen insights are used to optimize traffic signal timings, reroute traffic, or implement other strategies [30].

Continuous Learning

The AI algorithm continuously learns and updates its models based on new data. It adjusts to changing traffic conditions, thereby improving its accuracy over some time.

HOW ALGORITHM BIASING COULD HAPPEN IN TRAFFIC MONITORING USING WSN AND AI?

Algorithm biasing can occur in traffic monitoring systems for a variety of reasons. One common source of biasing is the training data used to develop AI algorithms. If the training data is not representative of diverse traffic scenarios encountered in the real world, the algorithms may inadvertently learn and perpetuate certain biasing [31].

For example, if the training data predominantly consists of traffic patterns from certain regions or specific types of vehicles, the algorithm may develop a biased understatement of traffic behavior. Consequently, it could struggle to accurately predict or respond to traffic situations that deviate from that training data [32].

Another source of biasing is the design of the algorithms themselves. The developers can unintentionally introduce biases by overlooking certain factors or making assumptions that are not held universally. This leads to skewed interpretations of the data and a biased decision-making process.

Furthermore, biases can emerge from the inherent limitations of the WSN data collection process. If the sensors are not placed strategically, or if certain areas are underrepresented, the collected data may introduce biases into the algorithms. Additionally, biases can arise from the algorithm's interpretations of the collected data, influenced by factors like sensor accuracies, environmental conditions, or even malicious tampers [33].

To combat algorithm biases rigorous testing validation and ongoing monitoring are essential. It is critical to continuously evaluate the performance of the algorithms, identify and rectify biases, and ensure that the training data is diverse and representative of real-world traffic scenarios.

Additionally, involving a diverse team of experts during the development process can assist in identifying and addressing potential biases from different perspectives. Transparencies and accountabilities in algorithmic development are vital to preventing biases from negatively impacting traffic monitoring systems. It is shown in Fig. (**2**).

Fig. (2). Traffic flow monitoring cycle.

THE FUTURE POTENTIAL OF WSN AND AI VEHICLE TRACKING WITH 5G NETWORKS

The progress in 5G technologies is poised to transform traffic surveillance by facilitating quicker and more dependable communication between WSN sensors and centralized monitoring systems. 5G provides enhanced data capabilities, reduced latency, and expanded network capacity compared to earlier mobile phone generations, resulting in more precise and dependable traffic monitoring. Moreover, 5G networks can accommodate Massive Machine Type Communication (MMTC), boosting capacity by enabling numerous sensors to connect concurrently [34].

ROLE OF EDGE COMPUTING IN TRAFFIC MONITORING (MACHINE LEARNING)

Edge computing plays a crucial role in traffic monitoring. This method involves processing and analyzing data closer to the data source rather than sending it to a centralized cloud server [35]. By doing so, it decreases latency and bandwidth demands, which is particularly beneficial for applications like traffic monitoring. Furthermore, edge computing boosts the security and privacy of traffic monitoring systems because data is processed locally. For instance, sensitive information like a vehicle's license plate or a driver's identity can be encrypted before transmission to the central monitoring system, safeguarding the privacy of individuals [36].

ROLE OF CONNECTED AND AUTOMATED VEHICLES IN TRAFFIC MONITORING

CAVs gather traffic data using a variety of sensors that vigilantly observe the vehicle's surroundings and gather information on traffic flow and other relevant details. Through vehicle-to-vehicle communication systems, CAVs can interact with one another, enabling the sharing of traffic information with all drivers in the vicinity [37]. This capability of CAVs aids in enhancing road safety by exchanging information on road conditions, empowering drivers to make well-informed decisions, and selecting the appropriate route to avoid accidents.

HOW TO TACKLE FINANCIAL BURDEN?

The following strategies can help to tackle this burden and make its implementation more effective [38].

Financial Impact Survey

Conducting such a survey will evaluate the Cost Benefit Analysis of deploying Wireless Sensor Networks (WSN) and Artificial Intelligence (AI) in traffic monitoring.

Prioritizing Use Cases

Prioritizing use cases to identify key areas for implementing WSN and AI techniques in cities to allocate resources efficiently and alleviate financial strain [39].

Collaboration and Partnership

Seeking collaboration and partnership with relevant stakeholders like government agencies, transport authorities, technology providers, and NGOs to explore shared funding opportunities.

Scalability and Flexibility

Ensuring scalability and flexibility in the design of WSN and AI systems to allow for gradual deployment and expansion, thus reducing upfront investment costs [40].

Data Monetization

Exploring data monetization possibilities by leveraging the data collected through WSN and AI for purposes beyond traffic monitoring, such as urban planning and targeted advertising, to help offset financial burdens.

HOW TO ADDRESS SOCIETAL CHALLENGES?

Privacy and Data Security

Security issues in Wireless Sensor Networks are a major concern as these networks involve transmitting sensitive data over wireless channels. However, various steps can be taken to address these security issues and ensure data integrity in Wireless Sensor Networks [41].

Encryption and Digital Signatures

To safeguard communication data from unauthorized alterations, encryption/ decryption and digital signature mechanisms can be utilized. These mechanisms uphold the privacy and integrity of the transmitted data in the network.

Authentication Mechanisms

Authentication mechanisms are employed to prevent unauthorized access to resources. They authenticate the nodes' identities, ensuring only authorized nodes can utilize network resources [42].

Symmetric and Asymmetric Cryptography

In WSN, both symmetric and asymmetric cryptographic algorithms can be utilized in WSNs. Symmetric algorithms are preferred for their simplicity and efficiency, while asymmetric algorithms like RSA are suitable for public key cryptography requirements.

Secure Domain of Sensor Nodes

Implementing a framework to establish a secure domain of sensor nodes can enhance network security. This framework includes authentication procedures, protection against unauthorized access, and securing both hardware and software configurations [43].

Secure and Efficient Data Sharing

Cloud-assisted WSNs can implement secure and efficient data sharing and searching schemes. These schemes ensure keyword and document security, protecting against offline and online keyword-guessing attacks [44].

Vulnerability Assessment

A structured vulnerability assessment process can be developed to identify and address vulnerabilities in Wireless Sensor Networks. This process can help in evaluating the security and privacy of the network and ensuring compliance with security standards.

Intrusion Detection

Methods for intrusion detection can be utilized to identify and prevent malicious activities within WSNs. Utilizing techniques such as Synthetic Minority Oversampling Technique (SMOT) and the Random Forest algorithm can enhance the precision of intrusion detection [45].

Group Key Management

In wireless body area networks, a secure and effective group key management protocol can be implemented. This protocol guarantees secure communication between healthcare facilities and patients, establishing a dedicated group communication channel for message dissemination.

Ethical and Social Implications

Promote transparency and accountability in using AI algorithms for traffic monitoring. Engage stakeholders, including the public, in the decision-making process to address their concerns effectively [46].

ORGANIZATIONAL CHALLENGES

Training and Skill Development

We should offer training and skill enhancement for staff members involved in the operation and maintenance of Wireless Sensor Networks and AI systems. This training should cover data analysis, sensor calibration, AI algorithms, and troubleshooting [47].

Stakeholder Engagement

All stakeholders must be involved, including local communities, businesses, and transportation users, to collect feedback and address concerns [48]. This approach can help establish trust and enhance the acceptance of the technology [49].

CONCLUSION

Recognizing traffic congestion as a significant issue, people are receptive to technology-driven solutions under the condition that privacy and data utilization are adequately protected. This situation creates an opportunity for city leaders and technology firms to build public trust through transparent policies and community engagement efforts. The results also highlight the necessity for tailored education on specific smart city applications to bridge knowledge gaps. By implementing these strategies, Wireless Sensor Networks and AI demonstrate significant potential in effectively managing urban transportation challenges. As technology continues to advance, the integration of Wireless Sensor Networks and AI in traffic management will be essential for establishing safer, more efficient, and sustainable transportation systems.

REFERENCES

[1] R. Ahmad, R. Wazirali, and T. Abu-Ain, "Machine learning for wireless sensor networks security: An overview of challenges and issues", *Sensors (Basel),* vol. 22, no. 13, p. 4730, 2022. [http://dx.doi.org/10.3390/s22134730] [PMID: 35808227]

[2] J.J. Jinisha, "Survey on various attacks and intrusion detection mechanisms in wireless sensor networks", *Turk. J. Comput. Math. Educ.,* vol. 12, pp. 3694-3704, 2021.

[3] J. Y. Yu, E. Lee, S. R. Oh, Y. D. Seo, and Y. G. Kim, "A survey on security requirements for WSNs: Focusing on the characteristics", *IEEE Access*, vol. 8, pp. 45304–45324, 2020.

[4] S. Amri, F. Khelifi, A. Bradai, A. Rachedi, M.L. Kaddachi, and M. Atri, "A new fuzzy logic based node localization mechanism for Wireless Sensor Networks", *Future Gener. Comput. Syst.,* vol. 93, pp. 799-813, 2019.
[http://dx.doi.org/10.1016/j.future.2017.10.023]

[5] M.V.R. Sarobin, and R. Ganesan, "Swarm intelligence in wireless sensor networks: A survey", *Int. J. Pure Appl. Math.,* vol. 101, pp. 773-807, 2015.

[6] M. F. AbdelHaq and A. Salman, "Wireless sensor network for traffic monitoring", *2020 International Conference on Promising Electronic Technologies (ICPET)*, Jerusalem, Palestine, 2020, pp. 16-21.
[http://dx.doi.org/10.1109/ICPET51420.2020.00012]

[7] T. Wang, G. Zhang, X. Yang, and A. Vajdi, "Genetic algorithm for energy-efficient clustering and routing in wireless sensor networks", *J. Syst. Softw.,* vol. 146, pp. 196-214, 2018.
[http://dx.doi.org/10.1016/j.jss.2018.09.067]

[8] L. Zhou, and Q. Wen, "Energy efficient source location privacy protecting scheme in wireless sensor networks using ant colony optimization", *Int. J. Distrib. Sens. Netw.,* vol. 10, no. 3, p. 920510, 2014.
[http://dx.doi.org/10.1155/2014/920510]

[9] Z. Noshad, N. Javaid, T. Saba, Z. Wadud, M.Q. Saleem, M.E. Alzahrani, and O.E. Sheta, "Fault detection in wireless sensor networks through the random forest classifier", *Sensors (Basel),* vol. 19, no. 7, p. 1568, 2019.
[http://dx.doi.org/10.3390/s19071568] [PMID: 30939764]

[10] M. Masdari, and S. Özdemir, "Towards coverage-aware fuzzy logic-based faulty node detection in heterogeneous wireless sensor networks", *Wirel. Pers. Commun.,* vol. 111, no. 1, pp. 581-610, 2020.
[http://dx.doi.org/10.1007/s11277-019-06875-0]

[11] D. Ovalle, D. Restrepo, and Alcides, "Artificial Intelligence for wireless sensor networks enhancement," in *Smart Wireless Sensor Networks*, T. Y. Kheng and H. D. Chinh, Eds., *InTech*, Dec. 14, 2010.
[http://dx.doi.org/10.5772/12962]

[12] M. Liu, S. Xu, and S. Sun, "An agent-assisted QoS-based routing algorithm for wireless sensor networks", *J. Netw. Comput. Appl.,* vol. 35, no. 1, pp. 29-36, 2012.
[http://dx.doi.org/10.1016/j.jnca.2011.03.031]

[13] F. Restuccia, and S.K. Das, "Optimizing the lifetime of sensor networks with uncontrollable mobile sinks and QoS constraints", *ACM Trans. Sens. Netw.,* vol. 12, no. 1, pp. 1-31, 2016.
[http://dx.doi.org/10.1145/2873059]

[14] A. Canovas, J. Lloret, E. Macias, and A. Suarez, "Web spider defense technique in wireless sensor networks", *Int. J. Distrib. Sens. Netw.,* vol. 10, no. 7, p. 348606, 2014.
[http://dx.doi.org/10.1155/2014/348606]

[15] F. Restuccia and S. K. Das, "Lifetime optimization with QoS of sensor networks with uncontrollable mobile sinks," *2015 IEEE 16th International Symposium on A World of Wireless, Mobile and Multimedia Networks (WoWMoM)*, Boston, MA, USA, 2015, pp. 1-9.
[http://dx.doi.org/10.1109/WoWMoM.2015.7158130]

[16] W. Osamy, A.M. Khedr, A. Aziz, and A.A. El-Sawy, "Cluster-tree routing based entropy scheme for data gathering in wireless sensor networks", *IEEE Access,* vol. 6, pp. 77372-77387, 2018.
[http://dx.doi.org/10.1109/ACCESS.2018.2882639]

[17] A. Khedr, "Effective data acquisition protocol for multi-hop heterogeneous wireless sensor networks using compressive sensing", *Algorithms,* vol. 8, no. 4, pp. 910-928, 2015.
[http://dx.doi.org/10.3390/a8040910]

[18] G.H. Adday, S.K. Subramaniam, Z.A. Zukarnain, and N. Samian, "Fault tolerance structures in Wireless Sensor Networks (WSNs): Survey, classification, and future directions", *Sensors (Basel),* vol. 22, no. 16, p. 6041, 2022.
[http://dx.doi.org/10.3390/s22166041] [PMID: 36015801]

[19] S. Sujanthi, S. Nithya Kalyani, and D.L. Sec, "SecDL: QoS-aware secure deep learning approach for dynamic cluster-based routing in WSN assisted IoT", *Wirel. Pers. Commun.,* vol. 114, no. 3, pp. 2135-2169, 2020.
[http://dx.doi.org/10.1007/s11277-020-07469-x]

[20] C.C. Lee, "Security and privacy in wireless sensor networks: Advances and challenges", *Sensors (Basel),* vol. 20, no. 3, p. 744, 2020.
[http://dx.doi.org/10.3390/s20030744] [PMID: 32013216]

[21] W. Osamy, A.M. Khedr, A. Salim, A.I. AlAli, and A.A. El-Sawy, "Recent studies utilizing artificial intelligence techniques for solving data collection, aggregation and dissemination challenges in wireless sensor networks: A review", *Electronics (Basel),* vol. 11, no. 3, p. 313, 2022.
[http://dx.doi.org/10.3390/electronics11030313]

[22] S. K. Gharghan, R. Nordin, and M. Ismail, "A wireless sensor network with soft computing localization techniques for track cycling applications" Sensors 16, no. 8: 1043, 2016.
[http://dx.doi.org/10.3390/s16081043]

[23] W. Osamy, A.M. Khedr, A. Salim, A.I.A. Ali, and A.A. El-Sawy, "Coverage, deployment and localization challenges in wireless sensor networks based on artificial intelligence techniques: A review", *IEEE Access,* vol. 10, pp. 30232-30257, 2022.
[http://dx.doi.org/10.1109/ACCESS.2022.3156729]

[24] R. Kumar, S. Tripathi, and R. Agrawal, "A review in wireless sensor network", *Proceedings of the 2020 International Conference on Emerging Smart Computing and Informatics (ESCI),* pp. 304-308, 2020.
[http://dx.doi.org/10.1109/ESCI48226.2020.9167610]

[25] Z. Qin, X. Zhang, K. Feng, Q. Zhang, and J. Huang, "An efficient identity-based key management scheme for wireless sensor networks using the Bloom filter", *Sensors (Basel),* vol. 14, no. 10, pp. 17937-17951, 2014.
[http://dx.doi.org/10.3390/s141017937] [PMID: 25264955]

[26] R.A. Alshinina, and K.M. Elleithy, "A highly accurate deep learning based approach for developing wireless sensor network middleware", *IEEE Access,* vol. 6, pp. 29885-29898, 2018.
[http://dx.doi.org/10.1109/ACCESS.2018.2844255]

[27] K. Dhivyasri, A. Suphalakshmi, and M. Revathi, "Wireless sensor network jammer attack: A detailed review", *Int. J. Res. Appl. Sci. Eng. Technol.,* vol. 8, no. 8, pp. 233-238, 2020.
[http://dx.doi.org/10.22214/ijraset.2020.30844]

[28] S. Dilek, K. Irgan, M. Guzel, S. Ozdemir, S. Baydere, and C. Charnsripinyo, "QoS-aware IoT networks and protocols: A comprehensive survey", *Int. J. Commun. Syst.,* vol. 35, no. 10, p. e5156, 2022.
[http://dx.doi.org/10.1002/dac.5156]

[29] K. Kifayat, M. Merabti, Q. Shi, and D. Llewellyn-Jones, "Security in wireless sensor networks", In: *Handbook of Information and Communication Security.* Springer: Berlin/Heidelberg, Germany, 2010, pp. 513-552.
[http://dx.doi.org/10.1007/978-3-642-04117-4_26]

[30] S. N. Prasad, K. S. Selvan, and B. L. Dhevi, "Intrusion detection system in wireless sensor networks and fair resource allocation using geometric deep learning techniques", *Wireless Pers. Commun.* 123, 4 (Apr 2022), 3401–3412.
[http://dx.doi.org/10.1007/s11277-021-09294-2]

[31] S.H. Chen, A.J. Jakeman, and J.P. Norton, "Artificial Intelligence techniques: An introduction to their use for modelling environmental systems", *Math. Comput. Simul.,* vol. 78, no. 2-3, pp. 379-400, 2008. [http://dx.doi.org/10.1016/j.matcom.2008.01.028]

[32] C.W. Chang, H.W. Lee, and C.H. Liu, "A review of artificial intelligence algorithms used for smart machine tools", *Inventions (Basel),* vol. 3, no. 3, p. 41, 2018. [http://dx.doi.org/10.3390/inventions3030041]

[33] Y. Mekonnen, S. Namuduri, L. Burton, A. Sarwat, and S. Bhansali, "Machine learning techniques in wireless sensor network based precision agriculture. J. Electrochem. Soc. 2019, 167, 037522", *Program.,* vol. 2021, p. 5421668, 2021.

[34] T. Zhang, J. He, and Y. Zhang, "Secure sensor localization in wireless Sensor networks based on neural network", *Int. J. Comput. Intell. Syst.,,* vol. 5, no. 5, pp. 914-923, 2012. [http://dx.doi.org/10.1080/18756891.2012.733229]

[35] Z. Sun, M. Wei, Z. Zhang, and G. Qu, "Secure Routing Protocol based on Multi-objective Ant-colon--optimization for wireless sensor networks", *Appl. Soft Comput.,* vol. 77, pp. 366-375, 2019. [http://dx.doi.org/10.1016/j.asoc.2019.01.034]

[36] Y. Zhao, *Combination of wireless sensor network and artificial neuronal network: A new approach of modeling.* Ph.D. Thesis, Sea and Sciences Doctoral School, La Garde, France, 2013.

[37] S. Otoum, B. Kantarci, and H.T. Mouftah, "On the feasibility of deep learning in sensor network intrusion detection", *IEEE Netw. Lett.,* vol. 1, no. 2, pp. 68-71, 2019. [http://dx.doi.org/10.1109/LNET.2019.2901792]

[38] F. Wang, and J. Liu, "Networked wireless sensor data collection: Issues, challenges, and approaches", *IEEE Commun. Surv. Tutor.,* vol. 13, no. 4, pp. 673-687, 2011. [http://dx.doi.org/10.1109/SURV.2011.060710.00066]

[39] Z. Al Aghbari, A. M. Khedr, B. Khalifa, and P. P. V. Raj, "An adaptive coverage aware data gathering scheme using KD-tree and ACO for WSNs with mobile sink", *J. Supercomput.*, 78, 11 (Jul 2022), 13530–13553. [http://dx.doi.org/10.1007/s11227-022-04407-5]

[40] L. Li, L. Jiang, and Z. Liu, "Optimization research of artificial intelligence and wireless sensor networks in smart pension", *Sci. Program.,* vol. 2021, pp. 1-7, 2021. [http://dx.doi.org/10.1155/2021/5421668]

[41] G. H. Adday, S. K. Subramaniam, Z. A. Zukarnain, and N. Samian, "Fault tolerance structures in wireless sensor networks (WSNs): Survey, classification, and future directions", *Sensors*, vol. 22, no. 16, p. 6041, 2022. [http://dx.doi.org/10.3390/s22166041]

[42] S. Adhyapok and H. K. D. Sarma, "Review on QoS aware routing protocols for multi-channel wireless sensor network," in *Proc. 2020 2nd Int. Conf. Innovative Mechanisms Ind. Appl. (ICIMIA)*, 2020. [http://dx.doi.org/10.1109/ICIMIA48430.2020.9074932]

[43] E. Moridi, M. Haghparast, M. Hosseinzadeh, and S.J. Jassbi, "Fault management frameworks in wireless sensor networks: A survey", *Comput. Commun.,* vol. 155, pp. 205-226, 2020. [http://dx.doi.org/10.1016/j.comcom.2020.03.011]

[44] K. Venugopal, and M. Kumaraswamy, "An introduction to QoS in wireless sensor networks", In: *QoS Routing Algorithms for Wireless Sensor Networks.* Springer: Berlin/Heidelberg, Germany, 2020, pp. 1-21. [http://dx.doi.org/10.1007/978-981-15-2720-3_1]

[45] P.M.K. Kanagasabapathy, V. Kedalu Poornachary, S. Murugan, A. Natesan, and V. Ponnusamy, "Rapid jamming detection approach based on fuzzy in WSN", *Int. J. Commun. Syst.,* vol. 35, no. 2, p. e4205, 2022. [http://dx.doi.org/10.1002/dac.4205]

[46] H. Manoharan, Y. Teekaraman, R. Kuppusamy, and A. Radhakrishnan, "An intellectual monitoring device using artificial neural network", *Math. Probl. Eng.,* vol. 2021, p. 7929672, 2021. [http://dx.doi.org/10.1155/2021/7929672]

[47] R.R. Sahoo, A.R. Sardar, M. Singh, S. Ray, and S.K. Sarkar, "A bio inspired and trust based approach for clustering in WSN", *Nat. Comput.,* vol. 15, no. 3, pp. 423-434, 2016. [http://dx.doi.org/10.1007/s11047-015-9491-8]

[48] M. Pundir, J.K. Sandhu, D. Gupta, P. Gupta, S. Juneja, A. Nauman, and A. Mahmoud, "MD-MARS: Maintainability framework based on data flow prediction using multivariate adaptive regression splines algorithm in wireless sensor network", *IEEE Access,* vol. 11, pp. 10604-10622, 2023. [http://dx.doi.org/10.1109/ACCESS.2023.3240504]

[49] S. Sharma, A. Kaur, D. Gupta, S. Juneja, and M. Kumar, "Dragon fly algorithm based approach for escalating the security among the nodes in wireless sensor network based system", *SN Applied Sciences,* vol. 5, no. 12, p. 376, 2023. [http://dx.doi.org/10.1007/s42452-023-05614-2]

CHAPTER 4

Generative AI-Based Methods to Handle Challenges in WSN-Based Data Dissemination Systems

Manisha Sharma[1] and **Hemant K. Upadhyay**[2,*]

[1] *Department of Applied Sciences, Mathematics, KIET Group of institutions, Delhi NCR, Muradnagar, Ghaziabad, Uttar Pradesh 201206, India*

[2] *Department of Mechanical Engineering, Research & Development Cell, Poornima University, Jaipur, India*

Abstract: Generative Artificial Intelligence (AI) deals with eccentric solutions to various problems in Wireless Sensor Networks (WSNs) based on data distribution networks. Recent research works on generative artificial intelligence technology may be incorporated into wireless sensor networks. These have been implemented in many industries to help people more effectively with daily tasks and play a major role in improving efficiency, security, and reliability. Technology advancement increases the likelihood of security issues. It is crucial to defend data and smart systems against cyber-attacks. Furthermore, when sensitive or private data is collected by smart sensors in large quantities, privacy issues may also suffer. This chapter focuses on outlier detection technology related to generative adversarial networks. The multi-level architecture of the wireless sensor networks has been proven vigorous. Conventional machine learning methods are applied extensively for developing trust management systems. However, the training dataset considerably influences the security parameters of any system and at the same time, it is very challenging to locate vicious nodes. To address this case, we discuss the main challenges of implementing Generative AI in wireless sensor networks and consider the current context. The chapter's structure makes it easier to read and understand. The chapter intends to discuss several unsolved issues in the industry and call for more investigation and focused examination.

Keywords: AI, Cyber security, Generative artificial intelligence, Outlier detection, Privacy protection, Wireless sensor networks.

INTRODUCTION

Researchers can find previously undefined developments and trends in generative AI algorithms. Generative AI is similar to other AI techniques as it uses machine

* **Corresponding author Hemant K. Upadhyay:** Department of Mechanical Engineering, Research & Development Cell, Poornima University, Jaipur, India; E-mail: hementdeo@gmail.com

Shelly Gupta, Sapna Juneja & Sandeep Kautish (Eds.)
All rights reserved-© 2025 Bentham Science Publishers

learning models. Several algorithms like ANN, EC, *etc*,. are competent enough for summarizing the content, outlining multiple paths of solution, and creating detailed documentation from research notes. Generative AI has been established as a tool for the enhancement of generating innovative ideas in this domain.

Wireless Sensor Networks (WSNs) contain plenty of tiny sensing nodes for sensing the feasible phenomena. Such networks are applied widely in the defense sector, habitat monitoring, security applications, and disaster management. Sensor nodes are minor in size with limited processing ability; therefore, they have very small battery power. Wireless sensor networks are required to avoid any expected failure because of small battery power restraints. In sensor networks, if node density is high, several nodes sense the same data, leading to redundancy. It is still difficult for researchers to choose a suitable and effective data aggregation method from the body of existing wireless sensor networks literature.

It is possible to install sensor nodes in locations that are rarely visited by people. The Internet of Things or Internet of Everything model is being shaped by the steadily declining cost of wireless sensor networks, which makes it easier to deploy them for screening purposes. The relationship of Generative AI with Artificial Intelligence, machine learning, neural networks, and deep learning is shown in Fig. (**1**).

For example, wireless sensor networks can be used to efficiently monitor and adjust room temperature and humidity in residential or commercial buildings to create a suitable environment for living and working [1].

Wireless sensor networks may also detect vibrations in towers and bridges to evaluate the stability and dependability of the structure. Wireless sensor network monitoring systems usually work in a resource-restricted environment, meaning that the availability of sensor nodes is limited. For instance, the critical factor in assessing the network efficacy in an area of monitoring use is temporal continuity [2]. Wireless sensor networks may be utilized in secure environments and may also be used for monitoring areas that have to deal with hazards, natural disasters, and, at times, even war situations like chemical or biological attacks. The fast advancements in the smartness of sensors make it possible to create a wireless sensor network for dealing with time-related issues. Plenty of variety of sensor nodes are used in huge quantities with variable operation durations. Sensor nodes suffer from many resource constraints [3].

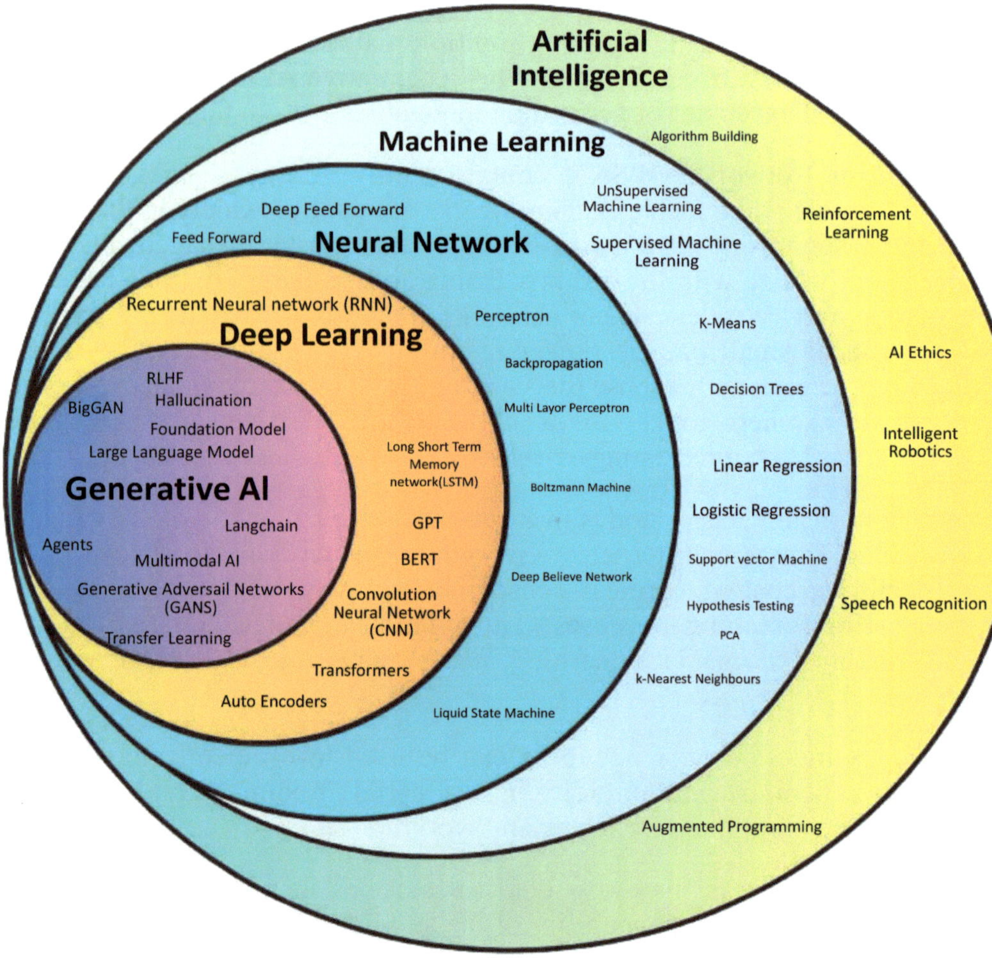

Fig. (1). Generative artificial intelligence relationship with AI, ML, NN, and DL.

Hardware and software defects are classified as permanent, intermittent, or temporary [4]. The communication obstacles because of the lack of technical efficacy indicate the need for sensor-based data gathering with the application of Artificial Intelligence [5]. Particularly in safety crucial systems, the outliers can become the reason for misinterpretation or undesirable alarms, which could result in potentially fatal situations. Outliers do need to be kept out of the network to maximize bandwidth and energy consumption [6].

The majority of outlier detection techniques used today do not identify outliers instantly. By taking into account the sensor database beyond the quarter sphere, a few researchers proposed a single-class quarter SVM method that decreased computational complication [7]. Using the Data Nearest to the Outlier Detection (DNOD) technique, some research articles proposed unsupervised outlier detection [8]. Researchers proposed an attribute-related support vector database explanation method that assumes that outliers may happen in each feature while the organized vectors are moderately settled [9]. Few research works proposed a two-section algorithm with an auto-encoder that resides in the cloud [10].

The United States Geological Survey has reported a set of preferential objectives and actions in its report and has considered natural calamities [11]. Out of those preferential objectives, USGS has focused on the conditional awareness of risk diminishing and the economics. They envisaged multimodal monitoring systems as the main instrument for natural catastrophe detection, forecasting, and response. To improve their use of situational awareness and alerts, recent methods to monitor networks must be designed to ensure their efficient function in major events. The lack of a widely accepted universal sensor-based system for different data-gathering systems has been highlighted in the literature [12].

To address this strategic objective, new adaptable systems that can be swiftly, widely, and extremely responsively deployed on demand are crucial. For instance, it has recently been suggested to deploy unmanned aerial aircraft (UAVs) in a variety of settings and applications to help ground sensors carry out their objectives [13]. Unmanned aerial aircraft may be utilized for covering and sensing the areas above the ground that are unreachable to humans because of the high probability of occurrence of natural disasters. Unmanned aerial aircraft may help in communications amongst the ground sensing devices by acting as relay nodes [14].

Sensor networks are like multiple agent systems or unnatural structured societies that may perceive their environment through sensing devices. The sensing devices are used to perceive and gather data from the specific IoT devices and a memory unit that is attached to the processor is used to store this data [15]. The tediousness associated with working with a wireless sensor network perspective is like distributed intelligent sensor networks. Distributed intelligent sensor networks may be observed as a system composed of multi-sensor nodes that have sensing devices to form a collective system for the collection of data from physical variables.

The concept of this chapter is to suggest a model that can enable a highly distributed sensing network like a multi-agent system [1]. Wireless sensor networks often suffer from missing or corrupted data due to sensor faults, environmental interference, or transmission errors. Sensors can fail or malfunction due to hardware issues, resulting in missing or incorrect data. Environmental interference, like external factors such as weather conditions, physical obstructions, or electromagnetic interference, can cause data loss or corruption. Data transmission over wireless networks can be unreliable, leading to packet loss, delays, or corruption.

GENERATIVE AI SOLUTIONS

Speedy data rates, enormous device connections, and improved energy efficacy are among the main areas of focus for 6G cellular networks [16]. 6G commits to enabling game-changing techniques like virtual reality and augmented reality with data rates predicted for achieving TBPS. Furthermore, 6G seeks to take advantage of newly available frequency bands, namely Terahertz (THz) frequencies, to fulfill the growing need for bandwidth and facilitate cutting-edge applications [17]. Due to wireless communication, 6G has the power to influence several sectors including healthcare and transportation [18].

6-G can establish connections amongst millions of users to foster a united environment in which the thin line between the real and virtual worlds merges [19]. One of the main applications of AI is the solution of complicated issues that can be decided upon or handled in a real-time setting. The use of Artificial intelligence may make next-generation systems better and more efficient but less complicated. Integration of AI with networks may be an instrumental method for addressing network complications and it is expected that almost all service providers will adopt the integration of AI with their networks in upcoming years [20]. Artificial Intelligence (AI) has been applied to complex tasks like clustering, categorization, and optimization. To gather, process, and decide on massive amounts of data, efficient AI systems must be created. Artificial Intelligence and the Internet of Things have emerged, having a connection with the web in real-time data dissemination systems and data extraction [21].

AI technology tries to improve user experience, and customer service, and deliver personalized services while reducing the need for manual interventions in network traffic management. Furthermore, a highly developed AI technology that has attracted a lot of interest for its potential to handle the challenges involved in managing 5G cellular network traffic is deep learning [22]. The latest developments in Artificial Intelligence are some possible efficient solutions for wireless systems [23]. Automation even allows for the remote operation of multiple sensors but these sensors need to be operated in real-time with high-speed networks like 5G [24]. Deep Artificial Intelligence and Machine Learning promise the development of stronger wireless systems with dynamic characteristics for dealing with sophisticated challenges [25]. As per our exposure to the literature, no comprehensive survey is available showing Artificial

Intelligence applications for highlighting wireless network issues. Thus, the current chapter highlights the regenerative Artificial Intelligence method and its applicability in the new era of wireless networking.

The overview of this chapter may be summarized as:

- To present an outline of many Artificial Intelligence methods for developing a deep understanding of the basic idea of Artificial Intelligence.
- To explore the Artificial Intelligence-enabled wireless networks that may enhance the performance of the system in totality.
- To showcase the recent wireless methods such as 5G & 6G and their potential to become the lead of technical advancement.
- To focus on many research issues to adapt the Artificial Intelligence in 5-G and 6-G wireless networks in the future.

The systematic structure of generative Artificial Intelligence is shown in Fig. (**2**).

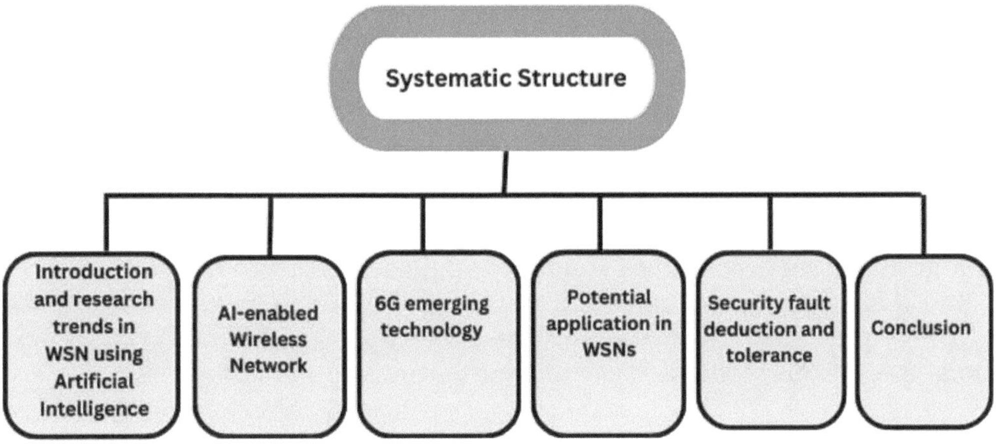

Fig. (2). Systematic structure of the generative AI in WSNs.

Generative Artificial Intelligence Models

Generative Artificial Intelligence models, particularly generative adversarial networks and variation auto encoders may be employed to tackle these challenges effectively. Generative Artificial Intelligence models like generative adversarial networks and variation auto encoders can understand the distribution of the sensor data and impute missing values or reconstruct corrupted data, ensuring data integrity and completeness.

Data Imputation with Generative Models

Generative adversarial networks contain two different neural networks, namely a discriminator and a generator. The generator develops artificial data samples and the other neural network as discriminator evaluates their validity. Generative adversarial networks can understand the distribution of the sensor data and generate possible values to fill in the missing data points.

Variational Autoencoders (VAEs)

Variational Autoencoders are designed for encoding the data in a latent space. Further, the encoded data is decoded back to the original space. By training on the available data, VAEs can learn to predict and impute missing values.

Reconstruction with Generative Models

Autoencoders

Autoencoders are neural networks having the objective of reconstructing the input data out of a compressed representation. They may be trained to identify the data patterns and correct corrupted values by reconstructing the data from the learned features.

Recurrent Neural Networks (RNNs)

Recurrent neural networks are feasible for time-series data. They can model the temporal dependencies in the sensor data, enabling them to predict and correct corrupted values based on previous observations. Long Short-Term Memory network is a widely applied type of recurrent neural network.

Hybrid Approaches

GAN-VAE Hybrids: Combining GANs and VAEs can leverage the strengths of both models. VAEs can provide a structured latent space, while GANs can enhance the realism of the generated data. This hybrid approach can be particularly effective for complex data imputation.

Attention Mechanisms: Applying attention mechanisms in generative models may enhance their capability for focusing on relevant parts of the data, enhancing the accuracy of imputation and reconstruction.

Implementation Steps

- **Data Pre-processing:** Clean the raw sensor data by removing obvious outliers and normalizing the data. Identify missing or corrupted data points that need to be imputed or reconstructed.
- **Model Training:** Train the chosen generative model (*e.g.*, GAN, VAE, and Auto-encoder) on the pre-processed sensor data. Ensure the model learns the underlying data distribution so that it can develop realistic data samples.
- **Data Imputation and Reconstruction:** Use the trained model to fill in missing data points and correct corrupted values. Compute the performance of the model with the help of Mean Ssquared Error (MSE) metrics.
- **Validation and Testing:** Validate the imputed and reconstructed data against a ground truth dataset (if available) or through expert validation. Perform rigorous testing to ensure the reliability of the model in real-world scenarios.

Generative AI models in wireless sensor networks may be applied in several tasks, such as generating synthetic sensor data, predicting future sensor readings, or creating network topologies. The specific formulas and calculations depend on the type of generative model and the task at hand. Here are some common types of generative AI models and their basic formulae.

Generative Adversarial Networks (GANs)

GAN is the methodology that aims to assess regenerative models with the help of an adversarial mechanism of different models as the discriminator and the generator. Both models have been trained at the same time. The chief aim of the generator is to capture data distribution and on the other hand, the discriminator computes the chances of a sample origination with the training database instead of the generator [26]. Generative adversarial networks have been shown in Fig. (**3**).

As shown in Fig. (**3**), autoencoders are applied to implement the generator and the discriminator. An auto-encoder tries to reconstruct input data in place of trying to predict particular objective variables. An autoencoder uses non-linear transformation and non-linear activating functions with multi-layer that assist in reducing the noise in both data and dimensions [28].

The structuring of a typical autoencoder is shown in Fig. (**4**).

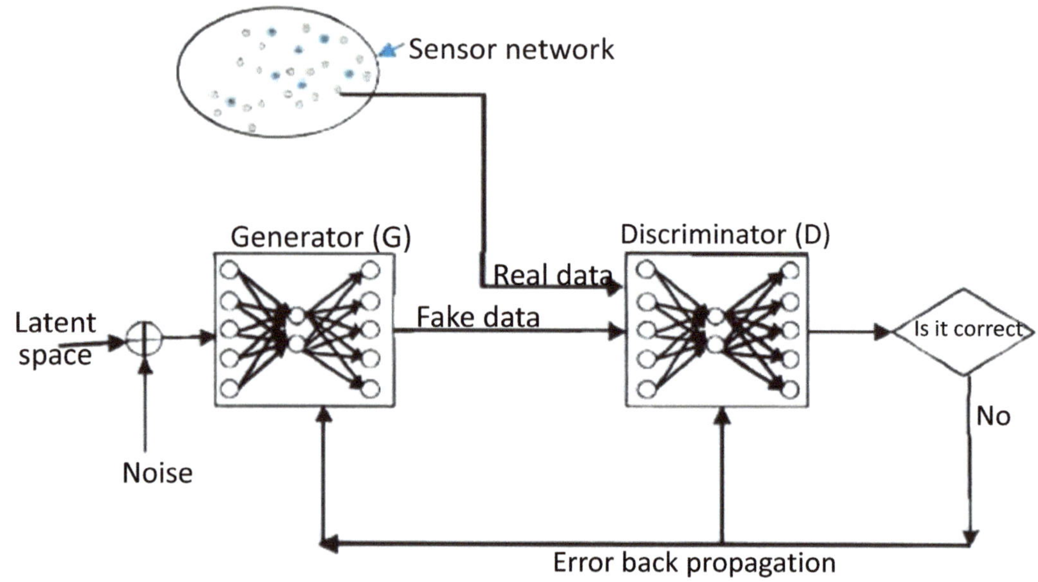

Fig. (3). ANs framework [27].

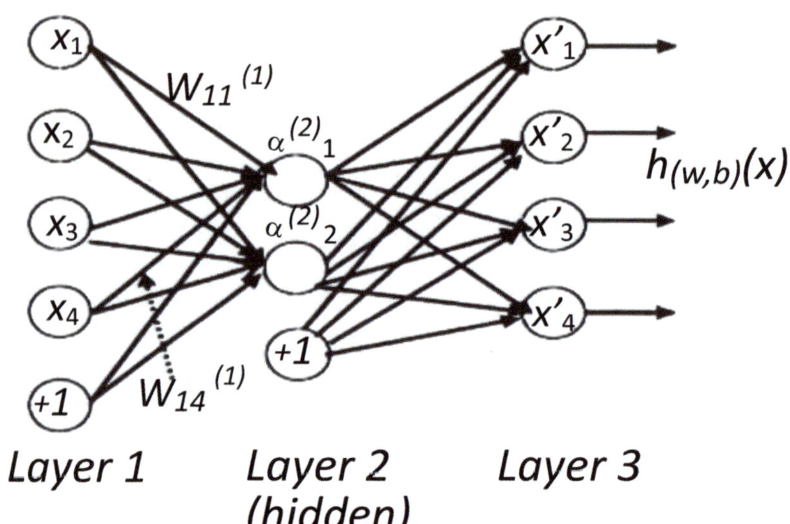

Fig. (4). Structuring of atypical Autoencoder [27]

As illustrated in Fig. (**4**), an auto-encoder contains three or more layers. There is one input layer, one output layer, and a hidden layer.

The input layer may be a specific M-dimension vector that represents the time series of sensing device-reading values represented by $x = (x_1, x_2, \ldots\ldots,)$.

The output layer has the representation as $x = (x_1, x_2, \ldots\ldots,)$.

Hidden layers or layers is/are placed between the input layer and the output layer.

An autoencoder contains the activating function with hyper-parameters.

The activating function in our research is like the hyperbolic-tangent function as mentioned below in the equation.

$$(z)=\tanh(z)=\frac{2}{1+e^{2z-1}}. \quad \textbf{(1)}$$

We assume that weight W and bias b are the hyperparameterset of the autoencoder, where *Wij*(m) is the weight concerned with the connection with node j in the layer m to the layer m+1 and *b*(l) is bias concerned to node i within the layer m+1.

Thus the activation (*l*) can be shown as Eq. (2).

$$(\mathrm{m})=(W(\mathrm{m}-1)a(\mathrm{m}-1)+b(\mathrm{m}-1)) \quad \textbf{(2)}$$

The intercepting expression b(m−1) in equation (2) may be compared with the node in layer m-1, which is a bias unit. The resultant x' can be expressed as a(m) that may be shown as h(w,b)(x), while L denotes the quantity of layers. 'x(1),x(2),x(3),x(4)..........x(T)'will be the training samples (T) and x(i)= 'x_1(i),x_2(i), x_3(i), x_4(i),....3_M(i)'.

The objective of the autoencoder is to limit mainly the cost function that is mentioned in Eq. (3).

$$\mathrm{J}(W,b)= \frac{1}{T}\sum_{i=1}^{T}\frac{1}{2}\, \|\mathrm{h(W,b)x(i)\text{-} x(i)}\|^2+\sum_{1}^{m-1}\frac{1}{2}\sum_{j=1}^{n(m)}\sum_{i=1}^{n(m+1)}(Wij(m))^2 \quad \textbf{(3)}$$

The first term represents reconstruction errors similar to original data sources, while the second term is for regularization to prevent overfitting. The ADAM optimizer is used in this work to constrain the goal function [29].

The value function V (D, G) has been expressed in Eq. (4).

$$\min_{G}\max_{D} V(D,G)= \mathbb{E}x{\sim}Pdata(x)[logD(x)]+\mathbb{E}z{\sim}Pz(z)[log(1-D(G(z))] \quad \textbf{(4)}$$

For a set of samples (*zi*), a probability distribution is characterized by a generator G, an auto-encoder model, and z is a distribution from the random latent space. Subsequently, the discriminator is an additional auto-encoder and is trained to restrict the mean negative cross-entropy between its successor labels and expectations.

Therefore, the discriminator loss has been expressed as Eq. (5).

$$Dloss = -\frac{1}{M}\sum_{i=1}^{i=M} [\text{logDauto}(\text{xi}) + \log(1 - \text{Dauto}(\text{Gauto}(\text{zi})))] \quad \textbf{(5)}$$

Discriminator loss may be reduced for recognizing *xi* real and (*zi*) false. Generator loss has been given by Eq. (6).

An outlier detection method, based on wireless sensor networks, uses a GAN with an autoencoder to increase network lifetime [30].

$$Gloss = -\frac{1}{M}\sum_{i=1}^{i=M} [\log(1 - \text{Dauto}(\text{Gauto}(\text{zi})))] \quad \textbf{(6)}$$

Variational Autoencoders (VAEs)

$$\text{Reconstruction}_{\text{loss}} = \frac{1}{2}\sum_{i=1}^{n}(x_i - \widehat{x_i})^2$$

KL Divergence Loss:

$$\text{K L}_{\text{loss}} = -\frac{1}{2}\sum_{i=1}^{n}(1 + \log(\sigma_i)^2 - (\mu_i)^2 - (\sigma_i)^2)$$

Total loss=Reconstructionloss+KLloss

Where: x_i is the input data.$\widehat{x_i}$Is the reconstructed output.

μ_i $and\sigma_i$ are the mean and standard deviation of the latent space.

Recurrent Neural Network(RNN) for Time Series Prediction

The Mean Squared Error or loss function is represented by the following equation:

$$\text{Loss} = \frac{1}{2}\sum_{i=1}^{n}(y_i - \widehat{y_i})^2$$

Where y_i is the true value at time step t

$\widehat{y_i}$ *is* the predicted figure at time step t, and n denotes time step numbers.

For validating the model, taking the regularity of data into consideration, surface and atmosphere temperature measurements were taken using the sensor node. All faults have a shortcoming start time and a shortcoming end time. Our research has considered spike and shock fault modeling for generating outliers, and the error process is the function of fault type and has been expressed below as Eqs. (7 and 8).

$$\text{Spike fault: } (t)=\begin{cases} xi(t) + \Delta iffst \leq fet \\ xi(t) \qquad otherwise \end{cases} \tag{7}$$

Where Δ is the spike magnitude and (*fst-fet*) →0.

Matrices taken for evaluating the proposed methodology have been given in Eq. (8-12) [31].

$$\text{Accuracy rate} = \frac{TP+TN}{TP+TN+FP+FN} \tag{8}$$

$$\text{Precision (P)} = \frac{TP}{TP+FP} \tag{9}$$

$$\text{True Positive Rate (Recall) TPR} = \frac{TP}{TP+FN} \tag{10}$$

$$\text{False Positive Rate FPR} = \frac{FP}{TN+FP} \tag{11}$$

$$\text{F1} = \frac{2(\text{Precision}\times\text{Recall})}{\text{Precision}+\text{Recall}} \tag{12}$$

Research Trends in Wireless Sensor Networks Using AI

A popular strategy for resolving WSN issues is to employ hybrid AI solutions. Before adopting hybrid AI solutions at scale, it is important to highlight that a critical design issue that must be overcome is striking a balance between efficiency and complexity.

In addition, taking into account the main WSN concerns, it offers an overview of the primary WSN issues resolved with AI-based solutions. A wide range of different WSN features were carefully taken into account by the research community. Data traffic routing and node clustering are two common WSN issues among the various interesting but difficult subjects of interest. The development of intrusion detection systems that take into account various AI techniques has become increasingly popular as a means of providing efficient AI-based security support. Other crucial factors including data security, node identity verification, trust management, and real-time threat identification have received less attention.

CHALLENGES IN WSN DATA DISSEMINATION AND PRACTICAL SCENARIOS FOR ADDRESSING THE CHALLENGES IN WSN DATA DISSEMINATION

Challenges in WSN Data Dissemination

Wireless sensor networks consist of sensor nodes that collect and subsequently process and further disseminate the data for numerous applications like observing the environment, health sector, and infrastructure ventures. Effective data dissemination in wireless sensor networks represents numerous crucial issues because of sensor nodes' inherent constraints with non-static networks. Prime challenges in wireless sensor networks are shown in Fig. (**5**).

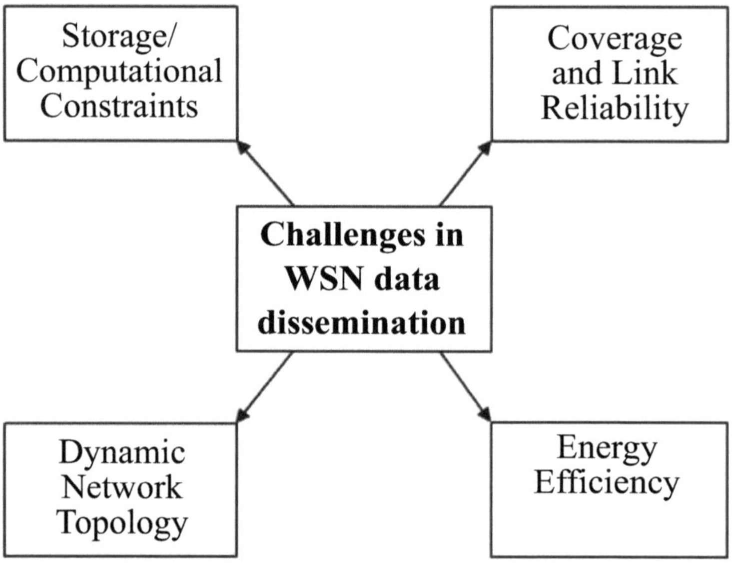

Fig. (5). Prime challenges in wireless sensor networks.

Storage and Computational Constraints

The complexity of algorithms that can be run on nodes is constrained by limited processing power. Usually, sensor nodes have limited memory and processing capacity. Because relational data structures in wireless sensor networks are dynamic and change with the network topology, algorithms must be both lightweight and flexible. Large volumes of historical data are frequently too big for nodes to store, so effective data compression and real-time processing are required. The trade-offs between node energy budget, storage requirements, and computational requirements must be balanced when designing WSN protocols.

Dynamic Network Topology

Environmental conditions or low battery levels can cause nodes to stop working. Because WSNs are dynamic, consistent data dissemination is extremely difficult. Adaptive protocols that can sustain connectivity and data flow in real-time are required for mobile nodes, which are frequently found in specific applications. The network topology may change often due to node failures, mobility, or environmental changes. Scalable protocols are necessary when networks need to replace failed nodes or add new ones to increase coverage. To manage these dynamics, communication protocols need to be self-organizing and adaptive.

Energy Efficiency

Since sensor nodes in wireless sensor networks are usually battery-powered and placed in inaccessible or remote areas, energy efficiency is a top priority. In order to save energy when communication is not required, nodes are configured to switch between active and sleep states. Three processes use the most energy: data processing, communication, and sensing. Aggregating data at intermediate nodes helps reduce redundant transmissions. The most energy-intensive task is communication, particularly data transmission, which uses a lot more power than computation or data sensing. Choosing energy-efficient routes when designing communication protocols helps reduce energy usage. Sensor nodes may rapidly drain their batteries in the absence of energy-efficient mechanisms, which could lead to network partitioning and decreased efficacy.

Coverage Challenges and Link Reliability

Nodes are positioned optimally to guarantee coverage with the least amount of redundancy. Applications like habitat monitoring and disaster management require complete coverage of the area of interest. Dividing the workload among active nodes enables the network to adapt to node failures or energy depletion. Careful network planning is necessary to guarantee that sensor nodes cover the entire target region without gaps or overlaps. Algorithms are required to guarantee uniform area coverage when sensor nodes are mobile.

Sophisticated algorithms that can track and modify node positions or sensing ranges to maintain efficient coverage are required to address coverage challenges. Wireless communication in wireless sensor networks is inherently unreliable due to environmental interference, physical obstructions, and node mobility. Links between nodes may go down, resulting in packet loss and disrupted data dissemination.

Wireless sensor networks hold great promise for improving automation and monitoring in a variety of domains. To reach their full potential, however, issues like coverage, dynamic topology, energy efficiency, storage and processing constraints, and link reliability must be resolved. To overcome these challenges and enable reliable wireless sensor network applications, future developments in hardware design, energy-efficient algorithms, and adaptive protocols will be essential.

Practical Scenarios for Addressing the Challenges in WSN Data Dissemination

Methods for optimizing energy use include duty cycling, data aggregation, data compression, data prediction, and dynamic scaling. By periodically shutting off sensors when they are not actively needed, duty cycling lowers energy consumption. By combining data from several sensors, data aggregation removes redundancy and lowers communication expenses. By estimating future sensor readings, data prediction models which are frequently powered by artificial intelligence can lessen the need for continuous data transmission. The use of data transformation techniques is essential to overcoming difficulties in wireless sensor network data dissemination. These techniques can drastically cut down on the amount of data that is gathered, lowering communication costs and improving network performance.

Wavelet compression, for example, efficiently compresses data while maintaining key characteristics, which lowers volume and communication latency, both of which save energy. When it comes to solving problems with wireless sensor networks, artificial intelligence is revolutionary. Through resource allocation optimization and environmental adaptation, AI algorithms can improve data collection, aggregation, and dissemination processes. Predictive models can foresee network demands to optimize operations, while artificial intelligence-based routing algorithms can enhance packet transfer rates, energy efficiency, and overall wireless sensor network performance. Another crucial tactic is to create protocols that are adaptive and energy-efficient.

For instance, a hierarchical data distribution protocol can support dynamic changes in network topology while preserving strong network coverage. Because these protocols balance energy consumption across nodes, they are especially useful for increasing network lifetime. It is crucial to optimize throughput in addition to energy-saving techniques. Increasing the effectiveness of data collection and distribution allows networks to manage higher data volumes without sacrificing functionality. Even in dynamic and resource-constrained environments, a longer wireless sensor network lifespan and dependable data transmission are guaranteed by this dual focus on energy efficiency and throughput. By combining these methods, wireless sensor network issues can be handled comprehensively, guaranteeing long-term and effective operations.

GAI APPLICATIONS IN WSNS

Currently, there is a huge number of wireless devices (around 14 billion Internet of Things (IoT) devices, 6 billion smartphones [32], and 5 million drones [33]) around the world, and the number will enhance faster in the upcoming days [1]. Generative AI presents an extensive outline of applied devices in the 5G age of wireless communication. Artificial Intelligence methodology is essential to obtain resource management for wireless communication systems [34]. AI techniques are competent in generating channel modeling without any requirement for theoretical assessment [35].

Generative AI is crucial across a wide array of applications, like Chat-GPT, developed by Open AI. DALL-E 2, employs a diffusion modeling method to produce many photorealistic images with multiple times higher resolution. Moreover, by utilizing historical measurements to forecast future channel information, AI approaches like DNNs can deliver more dependable channel information [36]. Some researchers have used the DNN technique to address issues arising from signal-dependent optical channels in dimmable optical wireless communication systems [37]. In some research works, the DRL method is used to capture and estimate system dynamics to solve resource allocation problems and organize mm-wave network backhaul configurations [38]. The AI approach is also used in Multi-access Edge Computing (MaEC) [39], where the concept of MaEC's application is outlined using the stochastic online learning method [40].

Big Data Analytics

Sensor nodes collect data from many environment-related parameters like temperature, motion, *etc*., then aggregate the data from sensor nodes and forward it to a central server or cloud storage. Statistical mean, median, mode, standard deviation, *etc*., are calculated to summarize data while tools like Matplotlib, Seaborn, or Tableau are available to visualize data patterns and trends. We can use machine learning models, regression, classification, and clustering algorithms to make predictions and identify patterns. Several sequences or patterns are discovered over time (*e.g.*, temporal trends in sensor data).

Cache Eviction

Data cache eviction in WSNs is an effective technique to enhance performance. With the increasing demand for the rapid yet delayed services of 5G and 6G wireless networks, data caching has become increasingly valuable. To accommodate this increased demand for quick services, cache indicates storing generally demanded content closer to the end user with the help of several network locations. These networks' caching processes frequently use complex algorithms, and modern emerging methodologies to predict user-requested patterns and choose which information should be kept in their caches. Researchers classified mobile edge caching systems using reinforcement learning, introducing novel techniques for adaptability and efficiency, and highlighting dynamic decision-making capabilities in optimizing content placement and delivery in edge networks [41]

Mobility Pattern

Mobility management in wireless sensor networks (WSNs) involves techniques and protocols designed to handle the movement of sensor nodes and ensure efficient and reliable communication despite changes in network topology. This is particularly important in applications where sensors are attached to moving objects, such as vehicles, animals, or humans. In the artificial intelligence era, the present world is witnessing a significant rise in automated mechanization to deal with the problem of energy security, and sensor-based data management is the demand of the hour [42]. Effective mobility management helps maintain network connectivity, optimize resource utilization, and ensure data integrity. A comparison of 4G, 5G & 6G has been visualized in Fig. (**6**).

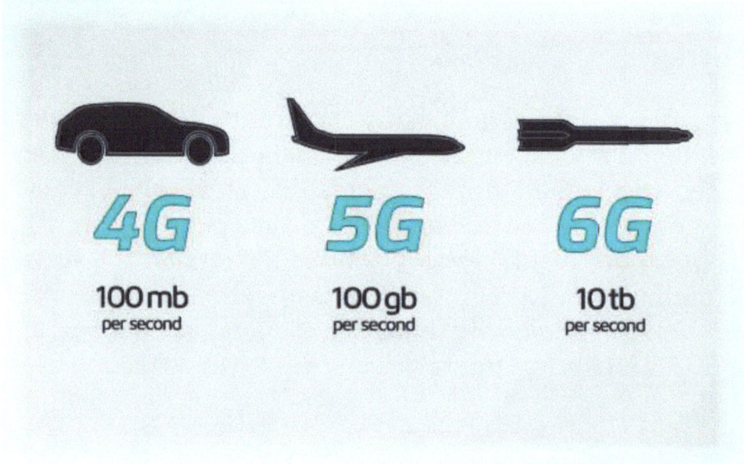

Fig. (6). Comparative details of 4G, 5G, 6G.

Mobility management develops mobility choices to enhance the effectiveness of the system. The influence of mobility management on system performance is vital. Many methods for the betterment of the performance of networks have been proposed by numerous research works on 5G mobility management [43]. However, the most significant benefit of applying AI techniques is that they enhance mobile user equipment's ongoing connectivity. Few researchers presented several widely used mobility management strategies and ML types to improve network performance [44]. To get ideal performance levels, some research works proposed a novel strategy that blends MARL and centralized approaches [45]. Some researchers have proposed a handover method for a satellite-ground integrated network that makes use of a deep Q-network's momentum architecture and adaptive learning rate [46].

Dynamic Resource Allocation

AI algorithms are very crucial tools to enhance the effectiveness and feasibility of wireless networks and the application of these algorithms proposes seamless connection in exploring potential opportunities for promoting innovation in different industries [47]. Few researchers have adopted resource management with the help of optimization tools with learning techniques for transmitting power allocation and allowing the coexistence of URLLC and eMBB systems [48]. This study examined critical phases of resource management and assessed the RL/DRL algorithm for autonomous behavior at each level to improve network slicing effectiveness. The authors in [49] had a special learning framework for adapting 5G/6G wireless networks. This novel network-slicing architecture holds the potential to revolutionize future wireless systems.

MIMO Technology

The MIMO technique is capable of multiplying radio link capability to get the advantages of multi-transmission [50]. AI methodologies may be used to estimate the channel with considerable accuracy [51], for mapping channels in the spaces and frequency [52], and to allocate the power in massive MIMO [53]. Valid and accurate CSI is needed by the base station in communication systems for pre-coding [54] and scheduling activities in the large MIMO systems. In this instance, DL is employed to address issues with device memory at the user equipment for enhancing spectrum efficacy [55]. In MIMO systems, channel estimating along with obtained SNR feedback is a crucial component. The study in [56] estimated the MIMO channel coefficient at the transmitter side by using the obtained SNR value. Furthermore, DL can be used to optimize the downlink channel reconstruction strategy for huge MIMO systems [57].

Channel Coding

The error correcting code used in the International Journal of Intelligent Systems is forward error correction code, meaning that faults are found by the receiver and repaired by the use of feedback. AI techniques are also used for wireless communication channel coding (encoder and decoder). Such methodologies are instrumental in mapping nonlinearity issues like process latency, and coding efficiency [58]. Few authors proposed recent trends in DL-supported channel coding [59]. The AI methodology is applied to design error-correcting codes on the other hand better outputs are obtained by decoding for polar code with the help of learning optimal code parameters [60].

Several researchers have suggested a new communication system with an instrumental neural network [61]. Some studies have created a revolutionary Residual Deep Neural Network (RDN) channel estimate approach that shows a notable 2 dB gain over the traditional minimal mean square error channel estimating [62]. DL for CSI output in deep joint source-channel codes [63], wireless image transmissions [64], low latency [65], and wireless multipath fading channels [66] have all been covered in several publications.

Network Function Virtualization

Networks in hybrid environments have been growing in terms of credible limits on the other hand the management has been dealing with much diversified issues. Networking is an effective technique for providing instrumental computational resources to use optimization techniques. The sophisticated age of analytics and integration is making network innovation and development more challenging from a theoretical and practical standpoint. Since there can be variations in how networks are applied in relation to the necessary specifications, sophisticated techniques like Artificial Intelligence (AI) approaches are required to enable contemporary network operations. AI techniques can be used for connection adaption, traffic congestion, interference, and spectrum management. Developing an algorithmic framework can help create an autonomous network management system since network management can stabilize input from multiple management platforms [67].

PRIVACY AND SECURITY

It is quite difficult to maintain a WSN's security. Authentication, integrity, privacy, and anti-playback are only a few of the qualities that make up security [68]. A variety of threats, including information collection, jamming, denial of service (DoS) assaults, spoofing, altering routing information, assaulting the sink node, and capturing data, might impact the functionality of WSNs. The need for safe group administration, secure localization, secure data aggregation, and secure transmission over the network has grown along with the reliance on information from WSNs [69]. These risks must be managed in WSNs. The development of 6G environments is greatly aided by AI and ML. Nonetheless, there are many ways in which this cooperation in AI technology could enhance 6G's security and privacy; while AI has a lot of potential to improve these areas, there is also a possibility of security breaches, which might seriously jeopardize the technology's future [70]. The growing amount of user data that AI systems are collecting and processing has made data privacy a major worry. Security lapses represent yet another serious risk. Combining 6G and AI may have significant safety risks in addition to improving security and privacy. Proactive threat identification, intelligent mitigation strategies, and the realization of self-sustaining 6G networks are the foundations for end-to-end automation of future networks [71].

Regulatory and Ethical Issues

6G networks are preferable for better connections and a high probability of innovation. Robust ethical and regulatory frameworks that safeguard privacy, safety, and other moral issues are necessary for any advancement. To secure the safe use of AI, additional rules of data protection, user consent, and transparency must be implemented as the technology continues to gain momentum within 6G networks.

Building trust with AI implementation projects would require striking a balance between protecting privacy rights and exploiting user data for better services, not to mention any ethical issues that may arise. To effectively serve as social advancement engines, artificial intelligence, and wireless networks necessitate tight collaboration between legal, technological, and ethical experts.

FUTURE TRENDS

Products with advanced machine learning capabilities that are enabled by Artificial Intelligence (AI) are not new, but in the past few years, there has been a rapid release of new versions of this technology. Despite early expectations that it would primarily handle assembly lines, manufacturing, and other physical labor duties, generative AI has a significant impact on jobs in the creative, administrative, and customer service domains. In addition, the subsequent stage might encompass intelligent tutoring systems that adjust to the unique learning patterns of each student, creating personalized courses and homework. These tools might provide a more productive and interesting learning environment for students of all ages.

Dynamic Spectrum Access

Dynamic Spectrum Access is very important in the case of 6G networks, with the use of AI-powered services for revolutionizing regarding allocation and utilization of spectrum resources [72]. Inefficient and underutilized spectrums have historically resulted from stagnant spectrum allocation. By adapting in real-time to fluctuating demand and interference patterns, artificial intelligence (AI) has revolutionized networks. To make educated judgments on spectrum allocation, the Artificial Intelligence algorithm is capable of interpreting databases from various sources like user habits, device types, and environmental factors.

Advanced AI Beam-forming and Antenna Arrays

Advanced AI beam-forming technology may enhance signal transmission ability and greater coverage. While 5G specifications are nearing completion, serious research into potential 6G wireless network techniques has started. With the use of these surfaces, a system may customize the properties of each wireless channel to suit its needs, offering it hitherto unattainable degrees of flexibility in channel shaping. However, a thorough understanding of a meta surface's behavior in all potential operational scenarios is necessary to properly appreciate radiation pattern features [73]. To learn more about the characteristics of radiation patterns, one can use both detailed wave simulations and analytical models, but each has drawbacks and requires a large amount of processing power.

Self-Organizing Networks (SON)

Due to the enhanced usage of mobile sets and the quick release of new applications and services, mobile networks are in tremendous demand. The heterogeneity of networks, which increases over time, makes managing these demands extremely complex. However, adopting innovative network automation solutions, such as zero-touch management methods, may be effective in this situation [74].

It creates a platform architecture that aims to streamline its deployment while satisfying 6G's strict requirements [75]. Since several 6G services will influence human lives therefore responsibility along with solid trust in autonomous systems are essential to deploy for long-term feasibility [76].

Quantum Computing

AI with quantum assistance looks to pave new paths in optimization, cryptography, and resolving complex wireless network problems. Wireless communications could undergo a major shift thanks to the potent combination of quantum computing and artificial intelligence [77]. The speed at which quantum computing can complete intricate computations makes it an ideal complement to artificial intelligence's data processing capabilities. Quantum-assisted AI may solve complex wireless communication problems that traditional computing techniques cannot. Cutting-edge technology integration can enable previously unthinkable solutions, such as simulating intricate network scenarios, optimizing signal processing, and reducing interference.

The advancement of quantum-assisted AI will challenge preconceived notions about 6G networks and what can be achieved inside them. Unprecedented challenges arise from new applications that substantially count on the data like augmented reality and industrial automation [78]. Artificial Intelligence-based 6-G networks may incorporate Artificial Intelligence to improve cross-network integration, global coverage, and catastrophe response times [79]. This will be a significant step forward for 6G technology.

Worldwide coverage, disaster response, and integration are all set to be revolutionized by the integration of AI into satellite communication systems; one possible benefit is increased worldwide connectivity. Satellites may now adaptively change their frequencies to cover areas based on demand in real-time. AI is used for optimization and adaptive resource allocation. During emergencies, satellite networks driven by AI offer quick disaster response capabilities. AI can analyze and process data fast, which allows it to support emergency services and relief efforts in real-time, identify disaster-affected areas immediately, and maximize communication resources.

Through satellite observations, data-based decision-making through AI-assisted analysis is made possible in an integrated system that includes terrestrial 6G networks, Internet of Things devices, and edge-computing platforms. The coupling of AI and satellite networks for 6-G may greatly increase global connection, transform the procedures involved in responding to disasters, and enable convergence across various network infrastructures.

AI for Green Sustainable Development

In 6G networks, Artificial Intelligence (AI) will be used more and more to optimize resource usage, reduce energy consumption, and enable green communication solutions. Faster data rates and greater capacity to handle an ever-growing volume of traffic are needed as the demand for energy-efficient communication networks rises [80].

The detrimental effects of climate change, raw material shortages, growing energy prices, and unequal and biased usage of technology are receiving more attention.

Thus, when designing future strategies and evaluating performance, it is imperative to take into consideration not just traditional performance measures but also ecological effect evaluations, energy usage analysis, resource allocation, and inclusivity and impartiality. AI-powered network slicing will develop customized network slices, particularly for several industrial applications.

CONCLUSION

Generative AI provides robust methods for addressing the challenges of missing or corrupted data in WSNs. The testing of the hybrid-type algorithm is needed to compare and assess the memory and processing requirements of the participating nodes. Future network dynamics may yield spatiotemporal characteristics. Various classifiers or artificial intelligence techniques can then be applied to take advantage of this relationship between node spatial and temporal behavior to identify malicious nodes that could degrade the quality of service of the connected application. However, constructing a safe and resilient method that takes into account all relevant elements is a challenging undertaking, therefore while creating new solutions, researchers should focus on all of these aspects. Furthermore, the current work needs to be modified for real-time IoT applications. The solution needs to be capable of protecting the sink location from global as well as local adversaries.

REFERENCES

[1] H.Ö. Tan, and I. Körpeoğlu, "Power efficient data gathering and aggregation in wireless sensor networks", *SIGMOD Rec.,* vol. 32, no. 4, pp. 66-71, 2003. [http://dx.doi.org/10.1145/959060.959072]

[2] N. Bartolini, T. Calamoneri, S. Ciavarella, T.L. Porta, and S. Silvestri, "Autonomous mobile sensor placement in complex environments", *ACM Trans. Auton. Adapt. Syst.,* vol. 12, no. 2, pp. 1-28, 2017. [http://dx.doi.org/10.1145/3050439]

[3] B. Sarangi, A. Mahapatro, and B. Tripathy, "Outlier detection using convolutional neural network for wireless sensor network", *Int. J. Bus. Data Commun. Networking,* vol. 17, no. 2, pp. 1-16, 2021. [IJBDCN]. [http://dx.doi.org/10.4018/IJBDCN.286705]

[4] S. Anayat, S. butt, I. zulfiqar, and S. butt, "A deep analysis of applications and challenges of wireless sensor network", *Int. J. Wireless Microw. Technol.,,* vol. 10, no. 3, pp. 32-44, 2020. [http://dx.doi.org/10.5815/ijwmt.2020.03.03]

[5] M. Sharma, H. Upadhyay, B. Chede, and N. Sawarkar. "Analysis of impacts of working from home on teachers: A DEMATEL approach based study", In *AIP Conference Proceedings,* vol. 2753, no. 1.AIP Publishing, 2023. [http://dx.doi.org/10.1063/5.0127953]

[6] A.F. Mukeri, and D.P. Gaikwad, "Adversarial machine learning attacks and defences in network intrusion detection systems", *Int. J. Wireless Microw. Technol.,* vol. 12, no. 1, pp. 12-21, 2022. [http://dx.doi.org/10.5815/ijwmt.2022.01.02]

[7] S. Rajasegarar, C. Leckie, M. Palaniswami, and J.C. Bezdek, "Quarter sphere based distributed anomaly detection in wireless sensor networks", *Proc. IEEE International Conference on*

Communications, pp. 3864-3869, 2007.
[http://dx.doi.org/10.1109/ICC.2007.637]

[8] A. Abid, A. Kachouri, and A. Mahfoudhi, "Anomaly detection through outlier and neighborhood data in wireless sensor networks", In: *Advanced Technologies for Signal and Image Processing.* ATSIP, 2016, pp. 26-30.

[9] Y. Chen, and S. Li, "A lightweight anomaly detection method based on SVDD for wireless sensor networks", *Wirel. Pers. Commun.,* vol. 105, no. 4, pp. 1235-1256, 2019.
[http://dx.doi.org/10.1007/s11277-019-06143-1]

[10] T. Luo, and S.G. Nagarajan, "Distributed anomaly detection using autoencoder neural networks in WSN for IoT", *IEEE International Conference on Communications (ICC),* pp. 1-6, 2018.Kansas City, MO
[http://dx.doi.org/10.1109/ICC.2018.8422402]

[11] R.R. Holmes, L.M. Jones, J.C. Eidenshink, J.W. Godt, S.H. Kirby, J.J. Love, C.A. Neal, N.G. Plant, M.L. Plunkett, and C.S. Weaver, *US geological survey natural hazards science strategy–promoting the safety, security, and economic well-being of the nation.* US Department of the Interior, US Geological Survey: Reston, VA, USA, 2013.

[12] M. Sharma, H.K. Upadhyay, and C. Upadhyay, "Analysis of influential barriers in plant burgeoning using AHP technique", *International Conference on Advanced Computing & Communication Technologies (ICACCTech),* IEEE, pp. 503-508, 2023.
[http://dx.doi.org/10.1109/ICACCTech61146.2023.00088]

[13] G. Pajares, "Overview and current status of remote sensing applications based on unmanned aerial vehicles (UAVs)", *Photogramm. Eng. Remote Sensing,* vol. 81, no. 4, pp. 281-330, 2015.
[http://dx.doi.org/10.14358/PERS.81.4.281]

[14] Y. Guo, X. Li, H. Yousefi'zadeh, and H. Jafarkhani, "UAV-aided cross-layer routing for MANETs," in *2012 IEEE Wireless Communications and Networking Conference (WCNC)*, Paris, France, 1–4 April 2012, pp. 2928–2933.
[http://dx.doi.org/10.1109/WCNC.2012.6214304]

[15] S. Juneja, A. Juneja, V. Bali, and H. Upadhyay, "Cyber security", in *Industry 4.0, AI, and Data Science: Research Trends and Challenges*, V. Bali, K. Banerjee, N. Kumar, S. Gour, and S. K. Chawla, Eds.
[http://dx.doi.org/10.1201/9781003097181-9]

[16] W. Jiang, B. Han, M.A. Habibi, and H.D. Schotten, "The road towards 6G: A comprehensive survey", *IEEE Open J. Commun. Soc.,* vol. 2, pp. 334-366, 2021.
[http://dx.doi.org/10.1109/OJCOMS.2021.3057679]

[17] D. Serghiou, M. Khalily, T.W.C. Brown, and R. Tafazolli, "Terahertz channel propagation phenomena, measurement techniques and modeling for 6G wireless communication applications: a survey, open challenges, and future research directions", *IEEE Commun. Surv. Tutor.,* vol. 24, no. 4, pp. 1957-1996, 2022.
[http://dx.doi.org/10.1109/COMST.2022.3205505]

[18] M.R. Mahmood, M.A. Matin, P. Sarigiannidis, and S.K. Goudos, "A comprehensive review on artificial intelligence/machine learning algorithms for empowering the future IoT toward 6G era", *IEEE Access,* vol. 10, pp. 87535-87562, 2022.
[http://dx.doi.org/10.1109/ACCESS.2022.3199689]

[19] L. Chang, Z. Zhang, P. Li, S. Xi, W. Guo, Y. Shen, Z. Xiong, J. Kang, D. Niyato, X. Qiao, and Y. Wu, "6G-enabled edge AI for Metaverse: challenges, methods, and future research directions", *J. Commun. Inf. Netw.,,* vol. 7, no. 2, pp. 107-121, 2022.
[http://dx.doi.org/10.23919/JCIN.2022.9815195]

[20] B. Ayvazian, Employing AI Techniques to Enhance Returns on 5G Network Investments, 2019. on-line available: https://mlnetworks.com/2019/09/13/employing-ai-to-enhance-returns-on-5g--

etwork-investments/ Last accessed on june 2024.

[21] H.K. Upadhyay, S. Juneja, G. Muhammad, A. Nauman, and N.A. Awad, "Analysis of IoT-related ergonomics-based healthcare issues using analytic hierarchy process methodology", *Sensors (Basel),* vol. 22, no. 21, p. 8232, 2022. [http://dx.doi.org/10.3390/s22218232] [PMID: 36365939]

[22] H. Huang, S. Guo, G. Gui, Z. Yang, J. Zhang, and H. Sari, "Deep learning for physical-layer 5G wireless techniques: opportunities, challenges, and solutions", *IEEE Wirel. Commun.,* vol. 27, no. 1, pp. 214-222, 2020. [http://dx.doi.org/10.1109/MWC.2019.1900027]

[23] J.M. Kang, C.J. Chun, and I.M. Kim, "Deep learning based channel estimation for MIMO systems with received SNR feedback", *IEEE Access,* vol. 8, pp. 121162-121181, 2020. [http://dx.doi.org/10.1109/ACCESS.2020.3006518]

[24] A. Dhall, H. Upadhyay, S. Juneja, and A. Juneja, "Machine Learning algorithms for industry using image sensing", in *Healthcare Solutions Using Machine Learning and Informatics*, P. Gupta, D. K. Saini, and R. Verma, Eds., 2022. [http://dx.doi.org/10.1201/9781003322597-5]

[25] C. Zhang, P. Patras, and H. Haddadi, "Deep learning in mobile and wireless networking: a survey", *IEEE Commun. Surv. Tutor.,* vol. 21, no. 3, pp. 2224-2287, 2019. [http://dx.doi.org/10.1109/COMST.2019.2904897]

[26] Y. Hong, U. Hwang, J. Yoo, and S. Yoon, "How generative adversarial networks and their variants work: An overview", *ACM Comput. Surv.,* vol. 52, no. 1, p. 10, 2019. [CSUR].

[27] L. Van Der Maaten, E. Postma, and J. Van den Herik, "Dimensionality reduction: a comparative review", *J. Mach. Learn. Res.,* vol. 10, pp. 66-71, 2009.

[28] D. Kingma, and J. Ba, "Adam: A method for stochastic optimization", *International Conference on Learning Representations (ICLR),* 2015.

[29] S. Randhawa, and S. Jain, "Data aggregation in wireless sensor networks: previous research, current status and future directions", *Wirel. Pers. Commun.,* vol. 97, no. 3, pp. 3355-3425, 2017. [http://dx.doi.org/10.1007/s11277-017-4674-5]

[30] B. C. Sengodan, P. M. Stanislaus, S. S. Arumugam, D. K. Sah, D. Dhabliya, P. Chenniappan, and R. Maheswar. "Variational autoencoders for network lifetime enhancement in wireless sensors", *Sensors,* 2024, 24(17), 5630. [http://dx.doi.org/10.3390/s24175630]

[31] M. Hossin, and M. Sulaiman, "A review on evaluation metrics for data classification evaluations", *Int. J. Data Min. Knowl. Manag. Process,,* vol. 5, no. 2, 2015.

[32] K. L. Lueth, "State of the IoT 2020: 12 Billion IoT Connections, Surpassing Non-IoT for the First Time", IoT Analytics, Hamburg, Germany, Nov. 2020.

[33] "Mobile statistics report, 2021–2025," Apr. 2021. Available from: https://www.radicati.com/wp/wp-content/uploads/2021/Mobile_Statistics_Report_2021-2025_Executive_Summary.pdf

[34] M. Yao, M. Sohul, V. Marojevic, and J.H. Reed, "Artificial intelligence defined 5G radio access networks", *IEEE Commun. Mag.,* vol. 57, no. 3, pp. 14-20, 2019. [http://dx.doi.org/10.1109/MCOM.2019.1800629]

[35] Y. Yang, Y. Li, W. Zhang, F. Qin, P. Zhu, and C.X. Wang, "Generative-adversarial-network-based wireless channel modeling: challenges and opportunities", *IEEE Commun. Mag.,* vol. 57, no. 3, pp. 22-27, 2019. [http://dx.doi.org/10.1109/MCOM.2019.1800635]

[36] Z. Jiang, S. Chen, A.F. Molisch, R. Vannithamby, S. Zhou, and Z. Niu, "Exploiting wireless channel state information structures beyond linear correlations: A deep learning approach", *IEEE Commun.*

Mag., vol. 57, no. 3, pp. 28-34, 2019.
[http://dx.doi.org/10.1109/MCOM.2019.1800581]

[37] H. Lee, S.H. Lee, T.Q.S. Quek, and I. Lee, "Deep learning framework for wireless systems: Applications to optical wireless communications", *IEEE Commun. Mag.,* vol. 57, no. 3, pp. 35-41, 2019.
[http://dx.doi.org/10.1109/MCOM.2019.1800584]

[38] M. Feng, and S. Mao, "Dealing with limited backhaul capacity in millimeter-wave systems: a deep reinforcement learning approach", *IEEE Commun. Mag.,* vol. 57, no. 3, pp. 50-55, 2019.
[http://dx.doi.org/10.1109/MCOM.2019.1800565]

[39] B. Cao, L. Zhang, Y. Li, D. Feng, and W. Cao, "Intelligent offloading in multi-access edge computing: a state-of-the-art review and framework", *IEEE Commun. Mag.,* vol. 57, no. 3, pp. 56-62, 2019.
[http://dx.doi.org/10.1109/MCOM.2019.1800608]

[40] Q. Cui, Z. Gong, W. Ni, Y. Hou, X. Chen, X. Tao, and P. Zhang, "Stochastic online learning for mobile edge computing: learning from changes", *IEEE Commun. Mag.,* vol. 57, no. 3, pp. 63-69, 2019.
[http://dx.doi.org/10.1109/MCOM.2019.1800644]

[41] Q. Song, J. Wang, and J. Liu, "A cache-assisted computing offloading strategy based on deep Q network", *7th International Conference on Management Engineering, Software Engineering and Service Sciences (ICMSS),* pp. 80-85, 2023.
[http://dx.doi.org/10.1109/ICMSS56787.2023.10117668]

[42] H. Upadhyay, M. Sharma, and R.K. Raj, "Exploration of critical factors in adoption of electrical vehicles in India using Fuzzy Analytic Hierarchy Process method", *Fifth International Conference on Computational Intelligence and Communication Technologies (CCICT),* IEEE, pp. 474-481, 2022.
[http://dx.doi.org/10.1109/CCiCT56684.2022.00090]

[43] W. K. Saad, I. Shayea, A. Alhammadi, M. M. Sheikh, and A. A. El-Saleh, "Handover and load balancing self-optimization models in 5G mobile networks", *Eng. Sci. Technol. Int. J.*, vol. 42, Article ID 101418, 2023.
[http://dx.doi.org/10.1016/j.jestch.2023.101418]

[44] W. Tashan, I. Shayea, S. Aldirmaz-Çolak, O.A. Aziz, A. Alhammadi, and Y.I. Daradkeh, "Advanced mobility robustness optimization models in future mobile networks based on machine learning solutions", *IEEE Access,* vol. 10, pp. 111134-111152, 2022.
[http://dx.doi.org/10.1109/ACCESS.2022.3215684]

[45] A. Prado, F. Stöckeler, F. Mehmeti, P. Krämer, and W. Kellerer, "Enabling proportionally-fair mobility management with reinforcement learning in 5G networks", *IEEE J. Sel. Areas Comm.,* vol. 41, no. 6, pp. 1845-1858, 2023.
[http://dx.doi.org/10.1109/JSAC.2023.3273705]

[46] J. Yang, Z. Xiao, H. Cui, J. Zhao, G. Jiang, and Z. Han, "DQN-ALrM based intelligent handover method for satellite-ground integrated network", *IEEE Trans. Cogn. Commun. Netw.,* vol. 9, no. 4, pp. 977-990, 2023.
[http://dx.doi.org/10.1109/TCCN.2023.3262239]

[47] H. Zhang, W. Guan, D. Wang, Q. Song, and A. Nallanathan, "AI-engine enabled intelligent management in B5G/6G networks", *International Conference on Communications Workshops (ICC Workshops), Seoul, South Korea,* pp. 1-2, 2022.
[http://dx.doi.org/10.1109/ICCWorkshops53468.2022.9915028]

[48] H. Zarini, N. Gholipoor, M.R. Mili, M. Rasti, H. Tabassum, and E. Hossain, "Resource management for multiplexing eMBB and URLLC services over RIS-aided THz communication", *IEEE Trans. Commun.,* vol. 71, no. 2, pp. 1207-1225, 2023.
[http://dx.doi.org/10.1109/TCOMM.2023.3233988]

[49] A. Thantharate, and C. Beard, "Adaptive6G: adaptive resource management for network slicing

architectures in current 5G and future 6G systems", *J. Netw. Syst. Manage.,* vol. 31, no. 1, p. 9, 2023. [http://dx.doi.org/10.1007/s10922-022-09693-1]

[50] S. Schwarz, "Recursive CSI quantization of time-correlated MIMO channels by deep learning classification", *IEEE Signal Process. Lett.,* vol. 27, pp. 1799-1803, 2020. [http://dx.doi.org/10.1109/LSP.2020.3028184]

[51] M. Soltani, V. Pourahmadi, A. Mirzaei, and H. Sheikhzadeh, "Deep learning-based channel estimation", *IEEE Commun. Lett.,* vol. 23, no. 4, pp. 652-655, 2019. [http://dx.doi.org/10.1109/LCOMM.2019.2898944]

[52] G. Gao, C. Dong, and K. Niu, "Sparsely connected neural network for massive MIMO detection", *4th International Conference on Computer and Communications (ICCC),* pp. 397-402, 2018. [http://dx.doi.org/10.29007/rjdc]

[53] M. Alrabeiah, and A. Alkhateeb, "Deep learning for TDD and FDD massive MIMO: mapping channels in space and frequency", *53rd Asilomar Conference on Signals, Systems, and Computers, Pacific Grove, CA, USA,* pp. 1465-1470, 2019. [http://dx.doi.org/10.1109/IEEECONF44664.2019.9048929]

[54] Y. He, H. He, C.K. Wen, and S. Jin, "Model-driven deep learning for massive multiuser MIMO constant envelope precoding", *IEEE Wirel. Commun. Lett.,* vol. 9, no. 11, pp. 1835-1839, 2020. [http://dx.doi.org/10.1109/LWC.2020.3005027]

[55] P. Liang, J. Fan, W. Shen, Z. Qin, and G.Y. Li, "Deep learning and compressive sensing-based CSI feedback in FDD massive MIMO systems", *IEEE Trans. Vehicular Technol.,* vol. 69, no. 8, pp. 9217-9222, 2020. [http://dx.doi.org/10.1109/TVT.2020.3004842]

[56] J. H. Kotecha and A. M. Sayeed, "Transmit signal design for optimal estimation of correlated MIMO channels", *IEEE Trans. Signal Process*., 2004, 52(2), 546557. [http://dx.doi.org/10.1109/TSP.2003.821104]

[57] Y. Han, M. Li, S. Jin, C.K. Wen, and X. Ma, "Deep learning based FDD non-stationary massive MIMO downlink channel reconstruction", *IEEE J. Sel. Areas Comm.,* vol. 38, no. 9, pp. 1980-1993, 2020. [http://dx.doi.org/10.1109/JSAC.2020.3000836]

[58] S. Xu, "Channel coding with deep learning: an overview", in *Machine Learning for Future Wireless Communications*. Wiley: Hoboken, NJ, USA, 2020, pp. 265-285 [http://dx.doi.org/10.1002/9781119562306.ch14]

[59] T-M. Dang, E. Cho, and S-H. Kim, "Current trends on deep learning-aided channel coding", *13th International Conference on Information and Communication Technology Convergence (ICTC), Jeju Island, South Korea,* pp. 1222-1225, 2022. [http://dx.doi.org/10.1109/ICTC55196.2022.9952535]

[60] L. Huang, H. Zhang, R. Li, Y. Ge, and J. Wang, "AI coding: Learning to construct error correction codes", *IEEE Trans. Commun.,* vol. 68, no. 1, pp. 26-39, 2020. [http://dx.doi.org/10.1109/TCOMM.2019.2951403]

[61] V.S. Usatyuk, and S.I. Egorov, "2D/3D ResNet deep neural network for 4G and 5G NR wireless channel estimation", *25th International Conference on Digital Signal Processing and its Applications (DSPA), Moscow, Russia,* pp. 1-4, 2023. [http://dx.doi.org/10.1109/DSPA57594.2023.10113403]

[62] J. Xu, B. Ai, N. Wang, and W. Chen, "Deep joint source-channel coding for CSI feedback: an end-to-end approach", *IEEE J. Sel. Areas Comm.,* vol. 41, no. 1, pp. 260-273, 2023. [http://dx.doi.org/10.1109/JSAC.2022.3221963]

[63] M. Yang, C. Bian, and H-S. Kim, "Deep joint source channel coding for wireless image transmission with OFDM", *IEEE International Conference on Communications,* pp. 1-6, 2021.Montreal, Canada

[http://dx.doi.org/10.1109/ICC42927.2021.9500996]

[64] Z. Xuan, and K. Narayanan, "Low-delay analog joint source channel coding with deep learning", *IEEE Trans. Commun.,* vol. 71, no. 1, pp. 40-51, 2023. [http://dx.doi.org/10.1109/TCOMM.2022.3222874]

[65] M. Yang, C. Bian, and H.S. Kim, "OFDM-guided deep joint source channel coding for wireless multipath fading channels", *IEEE Trans. Cogn. Commun. Netw.,* vol. 8, no. 2, pp. 584-599, 2022. [http://dx.doi.org/10.1109/TCCN.2022.3151935]

[66] M. Wang, Y. Cui, X. Wang, S. Xiao, and J. Jiang, "Machine learning for networking: Workflow, advances and opportunities", *IEEE Netw.,* vol. 32, no. 2, pp. 92-99, 2018. [http://dx.doi.org/10.1109/MNET.2017.1700200]

[67] M.A. Khan, N. Kumar, S.A.H. Mohsan, W.U. Khan, M.M. Nasralla, M.H. Alsharif, J. Żywiołek, and I. Ullah, "Swarm of UAVs for network management in 6G: a technical review", *IEEE Trans. Netw. Serv. Manag.,* vol. 20, no. 1, pp. 741-761, 2023. [http://dx.doi.org/10.1109/TNSM.2022.3213370]

[68] A.S.K. Pathan, H.W. Lee, and C.S. Hong, "Security in wireless sensor networks: issues and challenges", *8th International Conference Advanced Communication Technology, Phoenix Park, Republic of Korea,* vol. 6, p. , 2006. [http://dx.doi.org/10.1109/ICACT.2006.206151]

[69] L. Zhou, and Q. Wen, "Energy efficient source location privacy protecting scheme in wireless sensor networks using ant colony optimization", *Int. J. Distrib. Sens. Netw.,* vol. 10, no. 3, p. 920510, 2014. [http://dx.doi.org/10.1155/2014/920510]

[70] D. Kaleeswaran, R. Vijayarajeswari, and L. Nithya, "Artificial intelligence and machine learning-based security enforcement techniques for 6G communication", In: *Handbook of Research on Design, Deployment, Automation, and Testing Strategies for 6G Mobile Core Network.* IGI Global: Pennsylvania, PA, USA, 2022, pp. 347-364.

[71] Y. Siriwardhana, P. Porambage, M. Liyanage, and M. Ylianttila, "AI and 6G security: opportunities and challenges", *Joint European Conference on Networks and Communications & 6G Summit (EuCNC/6G Summit), Porto, Portugal,* pp. 616-621, 2021. [http://dx.doi.org/10.1109/EuCNC/6GSummit51104.2021.9482503]

[72] M. J. Yaremko, and M. Dohler, *Blockchain and AI-enabled framework for dynamic spectrum management in multi-operator 6G networks,* 2023.

[73] A.M. Montaser, and K.R. Mahmoud, "Design of intelligent reflector metasurface using deep learning neural network for 6G adaptive beamforming", *IEEE Access,* vol. 10, pp. 117900-117913, 2022. [http://dx.doi.org/10.1109/ACCESS.2022.3220701]

[74] E. Coronado, R. Behravesh, T. Subramanya, A. Fernandez-Fernandez, M.S. Siddiqui, X. Costa-Perez, and R. Riggio, "Zero touch management: A survey of network automation solutions for 5G and 6G networks", *IEEE Commun. Surv. Tutor.,* vol. 24, no. 4, pp. 2535-2578, 2022. [http://dx.doi.org/10.1109/COMST.2022.3212586]

[75] E. Baccour, M.S. Allahham, A. Erbad, A. Mohamed, A.R. Hussein, and M. Hamdi, "Zero touch realization of pervasive artificial intelligence as a service in 6G networks", *IEEE Commun. Mag.,* vol. 61, no. 2, pp. 110-116, 2023. [http://dx.doi.org/10.1109/MCOM.001.2200508]

[76] Y. Wu, "Ethically responsible and trustworthy autonomous systems for 6G", *IEEE Netw.,* vol. 36, no. 4, pp. 126-133, 2022. [http://dx.doi.org/10.1109/MNET.005.2100711]

[77] Q.J. Lim, C. Ross, A. Ghosh, F.W. Vook, G. Gradoni, and Z. Peng, "Quantum-assisted combinatorial optimization for reconfigurable intelligent surfaces in smart electromagnetic environments", *IEEE Trans. Antenn. Propag.,* vol. 72, no. 1, pp. 147-159, 2024.

[http://dx.doi.org/10.1109/TAP.2023.3298134]

[78] F. Zaman, A. Farooq, M.A. Ullah, H. Jung, H. Shin, and M.Z. Win, "Quantum machine intelligence for 6G URLLC", *IEEE Wirel. Commun.,* vol. 30, no. 2, pp. 22-30, 2023. [http://dx.doi.org/10.1109/MWC.003.2200382]

[79] A.I. Salameh, and M. El Tarhuni, "From 5G to 6G—challenges, technologies, and applications", *Future Internet,* vol. 14, no. 4, p. 117, 2022. [http://dx.doi.org/10.3390/fi14040117]

[80] D. Remedios, L. Levrau, S. Kanugovi, and S. Kallio, "Design for sustainability—an imperative for future mobile networks", *15th International Conference on Communication Systems & Networks (COMSNETS),* pp. 626-631, 2023. [http://dx.doi.org/10.1109/COMSNETS56262.2023.10041347]

CHAPTER 5

Manufacturing Supply Chains with AI-driven Sustainability for Enhanced Environmental Friendliness

Khushwant Singh[1], Mohit Yadav[2], Dheerdhwaj Barak[3] and **Muthmainnah[4,*]**

[1] *Department of Computer Science and Engineering, University Institute of Engineering & Technology, Maharshi Dayanand University, Rohtak, India*

[2] *Department of Mathematics, University Institute of Sciences, Chandigarh University, Mohali, India*

[3] *Department of Computer Science and Engineering, Vaish College of Engineering, Rohtak, India*

[4] *Teacher Training and Education Faculty, Universitas Al Asyariah Mandar in West Sulawesi, Indonesia*

Abstract: Artificial Intelligence (AI) technology, especially big data analytics, has made growth in real-time data analysis, resource optimization, and predictive maintenance. Still, problems, including low-quality data, limited infrastructure, and a lack of trained agricultural workers, persist. Future advancements in AI for agriculture will provide challenges as well as opportunities, together with the necessity for equitable access to AI technology and moral dilemmas. This paper examines how big data analytics and Artificial Intelligence (AI) might progress the industrial supply chain's sustainability. Manufacturing supply chains are realizing the necessity for eco-friendly operations due to rising healthcare costs and environmental concerns. It continues by outlining how big data analytics and artificial intelligence might alter these effects. In this study, demand forecasting, inventory management, and procurement are prioritized using big data analytics. In conclusion, sustainability-which is transforming industrial supply chains for a cleaner upcoming, benefits greatly from big data analytics and AI.

Keywords: Artificial Intelligence, AI-driven, Big Data, Greener future, Revolutionizing, Sustainability, Supply chains.

INTRODUCTION

AI has revolutionized the agricultural supply chain management sector by enhancing data-driven practices, decision-making, and efficiency [1 - 4].

* **Corresponding author Muthmainnah:** Teacher Training and Education Faculty, Universitas Al Asyariah Mandar in West Sulawesi, Indonesia; E-mail: muthmainnahunasman@gmail.com

Shelly Gupta, Sapna Juneja & Sandeep Kautish (Eds.)
All rights reserved-© 2025 Bentham Science Publishers

Numerous researchers look into how supply chain operations can be made simpler by AI's machine learning algorithms and big data analytics [5 - 8]. This development represents a paradigm shift in supply chains since AI spurs innovation and strategic planning [9 - 12]. AI can assist the agricultural sector in meeting the growing global population's food needs and adjusting to climate change [13 - 17]. The disruptive potential of IoT in agriculture has been demonstrated by some researchers [18 - 23]. Labor reliance, production management, and resource utilization are all improved by AI and IoT [24 - 28]. Beyond automation, the Internet of Things enhances the agricultural supply chain with predictive analytics, decision support systems, and precision farming [29 - 33]. AI has a variety of effects on agricultural supply networks [34 - 39]. Singh highlights the role that AI and ML play in digital transformation and how they add value to supply chain management [40 - 44]. Examples include real-time decision-making in logistics, inventory management, and demand forecasting [45 - 49]. Beyond operational effectiveness, AI and ML in the agriculture foster resilience and adaptability in a changing global marketplace [50 - 54]. AI in agricultural supply chains presents both pragmatic and ethical challenges. Consideration must be given to data privacy, labor implications, and the digital divide [55 - 59]. However, the agriculture industry may find AI integration appealing as it could reduce costs, increase efficiency, and strengthen supply chains [60 - 64]. This research investigates the potential of artificial intelligence (AI) and big data analytics to enhance the sustainability of the industrial supply chain. Due to the increasing costs of healthcare and environmental concerns, manufacturing supply chains are recognising the necessity of environmentally responsible operations.

Paradigm Shift to Supply Chain Sustainability

Sustainable supply chain management reduces environmental impact by lowering greenhouse gas emissions, deforestation, and waste [65 - 68]. It also reduces costs by optimizing transportation routes, using green packaging, and producing energy efficiently [69 - 71]. Artificial intelligence has transformed supply chain management by observing demand patterns, optimizing inventory levels, and ensuring transparency [72 - 76]. Blockchain and AI-powered technologies provide traceability and visibility, assisting businesses in meeting sustainability standards and identifying unethical practices [77 - 81]. This approach can improve brand image, market position, and environmental impact.

Objective of the Study

The study aims to investigate how manufacturing supply chain firms use Big Data Analytics (BDA) and Artificial Intelligence (AI) to improve Environmental

Performance (EPI) and integrate Green Supply Chains (GSCC). The study also aims to examine the relationship between the use of BDA and AI technology and the EP of manufacturing supply chain companies. To draw a conclusion regarding the strategic application of AI and BDA in manufacturing supply chains in order to improve environmental responsibility and operational efficiency.

LITERATURE STUDY

In recent years, integrating Artificial Intelligence (AI) into manufacturing supply chains has changed the game in terms of achieving sustainability and enhancing environmental friendliness [82 - 86]. The state of the art in AI-driven sustainability in manufacturing supply chains is examined in this review of the literature, along with the methods, resources, benefits, and limitations of this paradigm shift [87 - 89]. AI technologies in manufacturing supply chains encompass a range of elements, including predictive analytics and machine learning [90 - 92]. These technologies reduce waste and increase productivity by making demand forecasting, inventory management, and predictive maintenance possible [93, 94]. Some researchers claim that by foreseeing equipment failures and carrying out preventive maintenance, businesses can reduce downtime and extend the life of machinery [95 - 99]. According to various studies, accurate demand forecasts minimize excess inventory and reduce overproduction, which directly affects waste reduction and resource conservation [100 - 104]. Throughout supply chains, real-time data collection and monitoring depend on smart sensors and the Internet of Things (IoT). These technologies enable better resource management and energy efficiency. Smart manufacturing sensors, enabled by the Internet of Things, monitor energy consumption and pinpoint opportunities for reduction. Two advantages of real-time resource usage monitoring are waste reduction and raw material optimization. Blockchain technology makes supply chains more traceable and transparent. It ensures that environmentally friendly procedures are followed and provides verified data regarding the impact of products on the environment. Blockchain technology makes it easier to track the origins and journeys of products, ensuring that sustainable practices are applied throughout the entire supply chain [105 - 108]. Providing stakeholders with accurate information about the environmental impact of their products fosters accountability and trust. AI has the potential to support the transition to circular economy models in which products are designed to be recyclable, reusable, and remanufactured. This approach reduces waste in half and conserves resources. AI-driven systems can ensure that materials are recycled and reused effectively by managing a product's entire lifecycle, from design to disposal. The practical implementation of Artificial Intelligence (AI) in manufacturing supply chains has revolutionized the way businesses operate by enhancing efficiency, reducing costs, and improving decision-making. AI-driven tools like predictive analytics enable manufacturers to forecast demand with high accuracy, optimizing production schedules and inventory levels. Real-time monitoring systems powered by AI facilitate dynamic supply chain management, quickly identifying disruptions and suggesting corrective actions. Predictive maintenance, another transformative application, uses AI to analyze equipment data, minimizing downtime and prolonging machinery lifespan. Furthermore, AI enhances supplier relationship management through automated risk assessments and performance evaluations. Companies such as Siemens and General Electric have successfully leveraged AI to streamline operations, demonstrating the potential of AI to drive agility and resilience in manufacturing supply chains.

AI makes it easier to design sustainable supply chains by reducing emissions, optimizing logistics, and choosing materials. AI systems optimize logistics and routing to lower carbon emissions associated with transportation. Artificial Intelligence (AI) aids in the selection of sustainable, environmentally friendly products that exhibit less ecological effects. AI-driven sustainability has numerous advantages, including social, economic, and environmental ones. AI-powered sustainability initiatives dramatically reduce waste, greenhouse gas emissions, and resource consumption. They increase energy efficiency and encourage the use of renewable energy sources [109 - 111]. When supply chains are optimized, manufacturing activities have a lower carbon footprint. Artificial Intelligence (AI) helps identify and eliminate waste sources along the supply chain. Using AI to drive sustainability practices can reduce waste, and increase efficiency, and resource utilization—all of which can result in cost savings. Reducing energy use and improving resource management are two ways that businesses can reduce costs.

CHALLENGES AND OPPORTUNITIES IN THE INTEGRATION OF SUPPLY CHAIN SUSTAINABILITY WITH AI

AI-driven sustainability also helps society by promoting ethical sourcing, boosting Corporate Social Responsibility (CSR), and improving working conditions. Artificial Intelligence (AI) guarantees compliance with moral sourcing procedures, enhances worker conditions, and promotes fair trade [111 - 116]. Some researchers concluded that supply chains are essential in today's economic world because they connect company activity. Global companies are investing in digital technologies to improve supply chains and operational efficiency. One option is to use AI to improve all business operations. Artificial Intelligence (AI) is the imitation of human intellect by technology, mostly computers. By 2030, AI could boost the world economy by $15.7 trillion. AI technologies such as chatbots, ChatGPT, big data, machine learning, blockchain, cloud computing, and chatbots have many uses across multiple industries, increasing customer satisfaction and productivity. Details on AI-powered supply chains across industries and their pros and cons are explored with an intention to research and showcase the use of AI to revolutionize the agricultural supply chain. The primary aim is to improve effectiveness, sustainability, and flexibility in a changing environment and growing population. This study provides vital information for new and existing companies that want to start an intelligent and sustainable digital revolution in agriculture and food supply chains. These results may help these companies by using technology to improve efficiency, productivity, and sustainability. Digitization may simplify operations, optimize resource allocation, eliminate waste, and increase supply chain traceability for farm companies, ensuring long-term success. Gupta examined how integrating AI with supply chain management may improve effectiveness and green supply chains. Supply chain AI integration is well-studied. AI-driven technologies' acceptance and influence on supply chain, operational, and logistical efficiency are assessed. According to a study, AI may decrease supply chain networks' environmental blow in several ways. Testing is done on resource optimization, demand forecasting, and energy-efficient transportation routing. Waste, energy, carbon emissions, and operational expenses should decrease. It also examines AI's role in supply networks' 'greening' and 'sustainable' transformation. The research shows that AI might power supply networks to unprecedented economic viability and environmental awareness and deliver vital insights for a more sustainable supply chain management business. Some investigations added that digitalization would revolutionize supply chain practices utilizing modern technologies. The lack of real-world data obscures digital technology's operational benefits. This study examines how AI and BCT improve supply chain performance, sustainable development, and data monetization. Thailand's tuna fish supply chain was experimentally examined to identify end-to-end activities, monitor material and data processing, and consider AI and BCT use. We analyzed business mechanisms and system-level connections to identify how AI and BCT may enable supply chain material, data, and information flows. Mapping indicates that digital supply chain management requires AI and BCT, yet sustainability and data monetization rely on system stakeholders' goals. We later established a common architecture for AI and BCT-enabled food supply chains to digitally manage crucial data to generate value. Academics and practitioners may find sustainable, data-monetizing digital solutions *via* empirical modeling. Various studies described resilience and effectiveness of supply chains has become increasingly important after pandemics and crises. A greater understanding of AI in SCRes and SCP development has resulted from the supply chain's digitization, integration, and globalization. AI, SCRes, and SCP's direct and indirect effects on a volatile supply chain are examined in this study. We used organizational information processing theory for supply chain AI. Assessment of the framework has been done by using structural equation modeling. Survey data came from 279 firms of various sizes, sectors, and nationalities. AI impacts SCP temporarily, but we suggest harnessing its information-processing talents to construct SCRes for long-term SCP. This is one of the first experiments to optimize AI benefits for continuous SCP. Longitudinal studies may disclose more about the phenomenon.

Various challenges and future directions of manufacturing supply chains with AI-driven sustainability include various steps such as data privacy and security, implementation cost, and skill gaps. Concerns regarding data security and privacy are raised by the integration of AI and IoT in supply chains. It is essential to ensure secure data management procedures. Trust in AI-driven systems must be preserved by safeguarding sensitive data from online attacks. Implementing AI technologies can require a significant initial investment. Companies need to evaluate the investment's cost-benefit ratio in order to justify it. Weighing the short- and long-term benefits of AI is necessary to achieve sustainable adoption. For supply chains to successfully implement AI, skilled personnel who can design, manage, and maintain these state-of-the-art systems are needed. Various researchers assert that in order to effectively use AI technologies, financing for education and training initiatives that address the skills gap is necessary.

An effective way to achieve sustainability and environmental friendliness in manufacturing supply chains is through the integration of Artificial Intelligence (AI). Using AI technologies like blockchain, IoT, and machine learning can have a significant positive impact on society, economy, and environment. But in order to truly realize AI-driven sustainability, challenges like data security, implementation costs, and skill shortages must be overcome. It will take future advancements in this field to promote environmental friendliness and sustainability. The application of Artificial Intelligence (AI) in supply chain sustainability offers numerous advantages. It can promote social and economic gains, lower its harmful effects on the environment, and boost productivity. As Fig. (**1**) illustrates, there are many advantages to integrating AI into a sustainable supply chain. Artificial intelligence (AI) not only reduces environmental impact and improves operational efficiency, but it also has significant social and economic benefits. One notable example of a supply chain that achieved measurable success using AI in reducing waste through demand forecasting is Procter & Gamble (P&G). By leveraging advanced AI-driven demand forecasting tools, P&G significantly improved its ability to predict customer demand with greater precision. These tools analyze vast amounts of historical data, market trends, and real-time sales information to generate accurate forecasts. As a result, P&G optimized its production schedules and inventory management, reducing the overproduction of goods and minimizing excess inventory that often leads to waste. For instance, in its baby care product line, the implementation of AI-based demand forecasting reduced inventory levels by over 10% while maintaining high service levels, thereby decreasing the environmental impact of surplus goods and associated disposal processes. This example illustrates how AI can play a critical role in enhancing supply chain efficiency, aligning production with actual demand, and contributing to waste reduction in a measurable and impactful way.

Fig. (1). Various advantages of supply chain sustainability by integrating with AI.

Businesses can gain a competitive edge, enhance their brand image, and help create a more sustainable and eco-friendly future by implementing AI-driven sustainability practices. This literature review offers a thorough summary of state-of-the-art research on AI-driven sustainability in manufacturing supply chains, emphasizing the relevant technologies, approaches, advantages, and difficulties. To fully achieve AI's promise of a more ecologically friendly and sustainable future, research and industry cooperation are needed to keep moving forward.

METHODOLOGY

The previous research work has investigated how BDA-AI technologies affect Environmental Preservation (EP), Green Supply Chain Integration (GSCC), and Environmental Performance Improvement. The variables' relationships and interdependence were investigated using a comprehensive conceptual model.

Representative Sample Size of Respondents

The study had a total of 170 individuals. A sizable and representative sample size is required for research analysis, which is also dependent on the crucial participation of survey instrument completers.

Source of Data Collection

Access to 200 Manufacturing Supply Chain companies was provided for potential responders to this survey. Eighty-one questionnaires were filled out and sent back. Thirteen questionnaires were discarded due to incomplete responses. Thus, 170 responses to the study were received.

ANALYSIS OF DATA

The study of participants' demographics has displayed that 30% of respondents were female and 70% of participants were male, per the poll. With 41.6% having more than five years of experience, more than half of the participants (50.5%) had management experience ranging from one to five years. 53.5% of manufacturing workers belonged to the public sector, 38.6% to the private sector, and 7.7% to others. Workers in manufacturing companies reported that 29.7% of them were employed by manufacturing supply chain companies with 500-1000 seats, 23.8% by companies with 1000-2000 seats, and 11.9% by companies with 200 seats or fewer. The demographic information of survey respondents in analyzed and interpreted as shown in Fig. (**2**). Fig. (**3**) represents the measurement methodology used in our research study. They show that our operationalization measurement techniques are valid and reliable. Measurement item dependability in Big Data Analytics-AI (BDA-AI) is indicated by excellent internal consistency and a strong alpha coefficient of 0.970.

The research highlights the transformative potential of integrating Artificial Intelligence (AI) into manufacturing supply chains to achieve sustainability and environmental objectives. Key outcomes include the identification of AI technologies, such as machine learning, predictive analytics, and IoT-based systems that enable real-time monitoring and optimization of resource usage. These technologies reduce energy consumption, minimize waste, and promote circular economy practices by enhancing material reuse and recycling efficiency. The findings demonstrate that AI-driven solutions improve supply chain visibility and transparency, enabling businesses to monitor and manage carbon footprints effectively. Case studies analyzed in the research reveal that organizations implementing AI in supply chain operations achieve significant reductions in greenhouse gas emissions while maintaining cost efficiency and operational agility. Moreover, the study underscores the importance of strategic collaborations between stakeholders, including suppliers, manufacturers, and policymakers, to scale AI-driven sustainability initiatives. Challenges such as data integration, algorithm bias, and high implementation costs are identified, along with recommendations for mitigating these barriers through investment in digital infrastructure and fostering innovation. The research concludes that AI-driven sustainability in manufacturing supply chains is a viable path toward enhanced environmental friendliness, contributing to global sustainability goals and offering competitive advantages to early adopters in the industry.

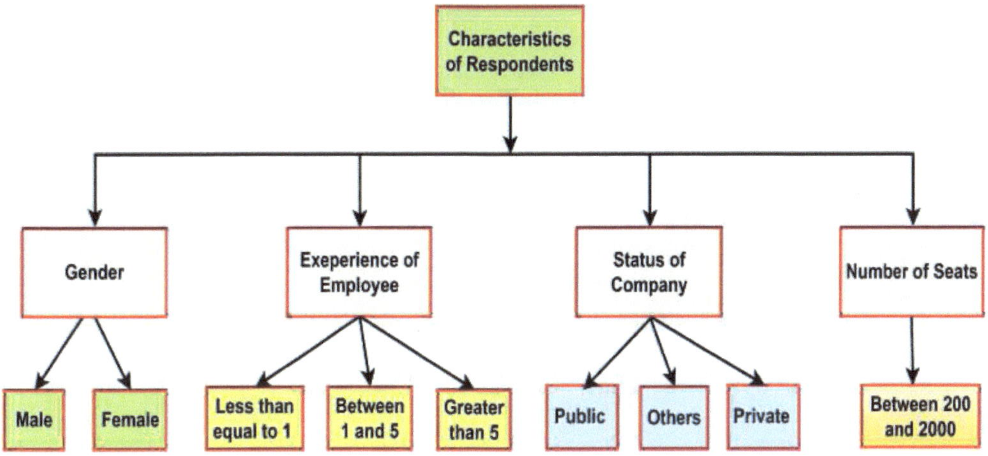

Fig. (2). Information regarding the demographics of the respondents with characteristics.

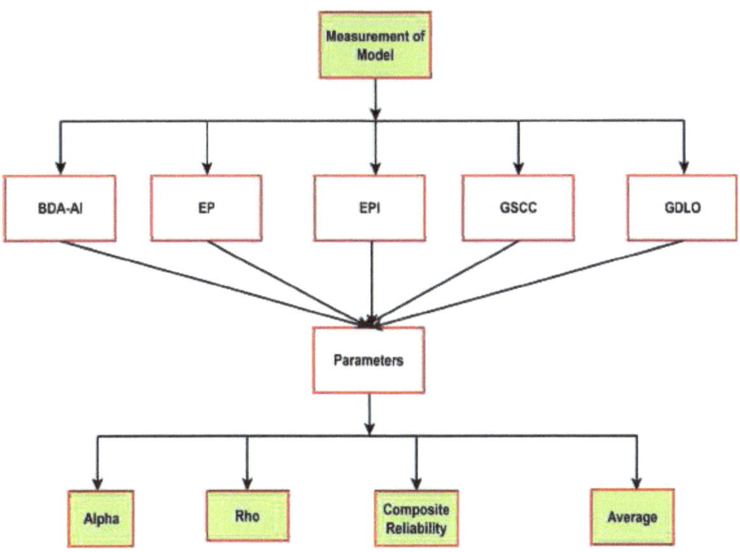

Fig. (3). Measurement of supply chain model with various parameters.

This design is supported by a composite reliability (ρ_c) of 0.940. Environmental Performance (EP) has strong dependability and consistency, as indicated by increased alpha (0.925) and ρ_c (0.965) values. GSCC and EPI offer trustworthy alpha and ρ_c values. Despite having lower alpha and ρ_c values, Green Digital Learning Orientation (GDLO) still performs reliably. We are more confident in the accuracy and consistency of our data for future analysis and interpretation since our measuring instruments are dependable and internally consistent. The discriminant validity of the constructs has been used in the current study. The model's measurement is shown in Fig. (**3**). Discriminant validity ensures that every concept looks at a different research model. Components with significant association coefficients and AVE values are discussed. Generally, discriminant validity requires a correlation coefficient below the square root of the Average Variance Extracted (AVE) values for each idea. Given that all concept pairings have correlation coefficients less than the square root of the Average Variance Extracted (AVE), this study demonstrates discriminant validity. BDA-AI, which represents a split dimension, had weak correlations with EP, EPI, GSCC, and GDLO. Similar results are provided by EPI, EP, GDLO, and GSCC, along with a breakdown of their differences. The model's discriminant validity is depicted in Fig. (**4**).

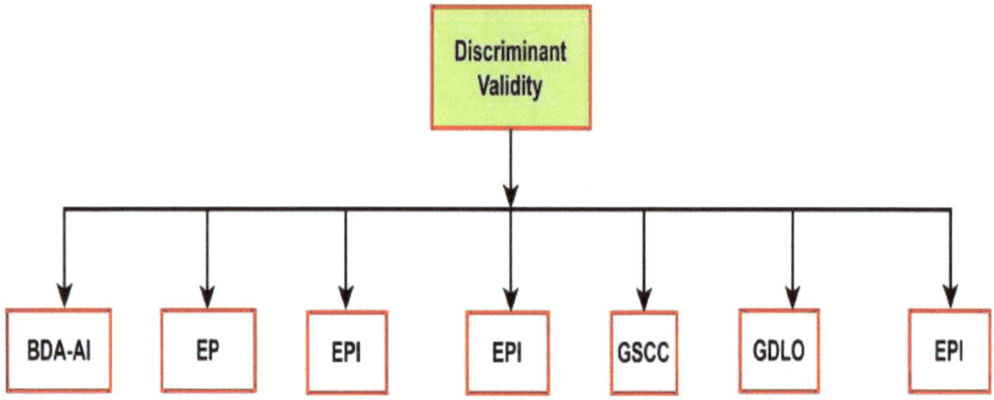

Fig. (4). Discriminant validity of the supply chain proposed model integrated with AI.

CONCLUSION

Globally, sustainable business practices are starting to become the norm. AI is changing the way businesses manage their supply chains, which are essential to sustainability. AI improves supply chains, decreases waste, increases transparency, and streamlines procedures. AI and sustainability are necessary for improved supply chain management as well as for positive social and environmental effects. Finally, this extensive study examines how BDA and AI may improve the sustainability of industrial supply chains. This study explores the potential for big data analytics and Artificial Intelligence (AI) to advance the sustainability of the industrial supply chain. Due to growing healthcare expenditures and environmental concerns, manufacturing supply chains are realising the need for eco-friendly operations. The conceptual framework of the study emphasizes emissions related to energy, waste, and transportation, elucidating the significant environmental impact of industrial supply networks. The report states that since BDA and AI may alter things, data-driven solutions are required. By lowering waste, inventory, and supply shortages, demand forecasting, procurement optimization, and BDA inventory protect the environment and save money. Research indicates that BDA and AI may help industrial supply chains improve healthcare, mitigate their adverse environmental effects, and preserve resources for the next generations. Data reliability is enhanced by the study's exacting measurement technique and discriminant validity analysis. Manufacturing improves operational effectiveness and environmental responsibility, but multidisciplinary cooperation is necessary for data-driven healthcare operations. Numerous studies indicate that AI and BDA can improve green healthcare systems.

REFERENCES

[1] A. Alshawi, "Artificial intelligence for sustainability: Opportunities and challenges". In: *Artificial Intelligence for Renewable Energy and Climate Change*, V. Pandian, G.-W. Weber, J. Thomas, J. A. Marmolejo-Saucedo, and R. Rodriguez-Aguilar, Eds. pp. 1-31, 2022.

[2] M. Wang, and X. Pan, X. "Drivers of artificial intelligence and their effects on supply chain resilience and performance: An empirical analysis on an emerging market", *Sustainability*, vol. 14, no. 24, p.16836, 2022.
[http://dx.doi.org/10.3390/su142416836]

[3] O.A. Elufioye, C.U. Ike, O. Odeyemi, F.O. Usman, and N.Z. Mhlongo, "AI- driven predictive analytics in agricultural supply chains: A review: Assessing the benefits and challenges of ai in forecasting demand and optimizing supply in agriculture", *Comput. Sci. IT Res. J.*, vol. 5, no. 2, pp. 473-497, 2024.

[4] C.P. Gupta, V.R. Kumar, and A. Khurana, "Artificial Intelligence integration with the supply chain, making it green and sustainable", *7th International Conference on Electronics, Materials Engineering & Nano-Technology (IEMENTech),* pp. 1-5, 2023.

[5] C. Gupta, and A. Khang, "Cultivating efficiency-harnessing artificial intelligence (AI) for sustainable agriculture supply chains", In: *Agriculture and Aquaculture Applications of Biosensors and Bioelectronics*, A. Khang, Ed., pp. 372-388, 2024.
[http://dx.doi.org/10.4018/979-8-3693-2069-3.ch020]

[6] M. Hassan, N. A. B. A. Wahab, and R. B. M. Nor, "The role of artificial intelligence in waste reduction in the beverage industry: a comprehensive strategy for enhanced sustainability and efficiency", *AI, IoT, and 4th Ind. Rev. Review*, vol. 13, no. 11, 2023.

[7] K. Potter and R. Eugene, "Transformative trends and sustainable practices in modern manufacturing: A comprehensive exploration", *OSFPREPRINTS*, Nov. 20, 2023.

[8] N. Kumari, D. Chaudhary, H. Kaur and A. L. Yadav, "Artificial intelligence in supply chain optimization," *International Conference on IoT, Communication and Automation Technology (ICICAT)*, pp. 1-6, 2023.

[http://dx.doi.org/10.1109/ICICAT57735.2023.10263631]

[9] A. Norgren, and W. Janzon Hägglund, "Implementing artificial intelligence in supply chain management: A qualitative study of how manufacturing companies can implement ai to improve supply chain management," 2023.

[10] A. Rahman, "AI revolution: shaping industries through artificial intelligence and machine learning", *J. Environ. Sci. Technol.,* vol. 2, no. 1, pp. 93-105, 2023.

[11] R.G. Richey Jr, S. Chowdhury, B. Davis-Sramek, M. Giannakis, and Y.K. Dwivedi, "Artificial intelligence in logistics and supply chain management: A primer and roadmap for research", *J. Bus. Logist.,* vol. 44, no. 4, pp. 532-549, 2023.
[http://dx.doi.org/10.1111/jbl.12364]

[12] N. Shobhana, "AI-powered supply chains towards greater efficiency," In: *Complex AI Dynamics and Interactions in Management, P. C. N. Figueiredo, Ed.* pp. 229-249, 2024.
[http://dx.doi.org/10.4018/979-8-3693-0712-0.ch011]

[13] P. K. Singh, "Digital transformation in supply chain management: Artificial Intelligence (AI) and Machine Learning (ML) as catalysts for value creation," *Int. J. Supply Chain Manag.* 12; 06;, 2023.
[http://dx.doi.org/10.59160/ijscm.v12i6.6216]

[14] N. Tsolakis, R. Schumacher, M. Dora, and M. Kumar, "Artificial intelligence and blockchain implementation in supply chains: a pathway to sustainability and data monetisation?", *Ann. Oper. Res.,* vol. 327, no. 1, pp. 1-54, 2022.
[PMID: 35755830]

[15] L. P. Vishwakarma, and R. K. Singh, "Application of Artificial Intelligence (AI) in Supply Chain: An Overview", *Artificial Intelligence of Things for Smart Green Energy Management*, S. El Himer, M. Ouaissa, A. A. Emhemed, M. Ouaissa, and Z. Boulouard, Eds., 191-212, 2022.
[http://dx.doi.org/10.1007/978-3-031-04851-7_12]

[16] U. Momin, "NREGA-catalyst for fostering inclusive growth", *Int. J. Multidim. Res. Perspect.,* vol. 1, no. 4, pp. 63-72, 2023.

[17] M. U. Momin, "An analysis of the challenges and opportunities encountered by small and medium enterprises (SMES) in the context of the Indian economy," *Ind. J. Soc. Stud. Humanit.*, vol. 1, no. 17, 2024.

[18] U. Momin, S.T. Mehak, S. Tare, and M.D. Kumar, "Strategic planning and risk management in the stratup, innovation and entrepreneurship: Best practices and challenges", *J. Inform. Educ. Res.,,* vol. 3, no. 2, 2023.

[19] T. Mahajan, U. Momin, S. Khan, and H. Khan, "Role of women's entrepreneurship in social and economic development of India", *Korea Rev. Int. Stud.,,* vol. 16, no. 52, pp. 186-195, 2023.

[20] S. Yadav, M.S.I. Sudman, P.K. Dubey, R.V. Srinivas, R. Srisainath, and V.C. Devi, "Development of an GA-RBF based model for penetration of electric vehicles and its projections", *2023 International Conference on Self Sustainable Artificial Intelligence Systems (ICSSAS),* pp. 1-6, 2023.
[http://dx.doi.org/10.1109/ICSSAS57918.2023.10331883]

[21] M. Sakthivel, M. S. I. Sudman, K. Ravishankar, B. Avinash, A. Kumar, and M. Ponnusamy, "Medical image analysis of multiple myeloma diagnosis using CNN and KNN based approach," in *Proc. 2023 Int. Conf. Self Sustainable Artif. Intell. Syst. (ICSSAS)*, Oct. 2023, pp. 92–97.
[http://dx.doi.org/10.1109/ICSSAS57918.2023.10331744]

[22] S. M, M. S. I. Sudman, K. Ravishankar, B. Avinash, A. Kumar and M. Ponnusamy, "Medical image analysis of multiple myeloma diagnosis using CNN and KNN based approach", 2023 *International Conference on Self Sustainable Artificial Intelligence Systems (ICSSAS)*, Erode, India, 2023, pp. 92-97.
[http://dx.doi.org/10.1109/ICSSAS57918.2023.10331744]

[23] L. Faisal, V. S. B. Rama, S. Roy, and S. Nath, "Modelling of electric vehicle using modified sepic

converter configuration to enhance dc–dc converter performance using MATLAB", In: *Smart Energy and Advancement in Power Technologies: Select Proceedings of ICSEAPT*, Singapore: Springer Nature Singapore, Vol. 2, pp. 643-653, 2022.

[24] A. Kaushik, S. Gahletia, R.K. Garg, P. Sharma, D. Chhabra, and M. Yadav, "Advanced 3D body scanning techniques and its clinical applications", *Int. J. Recent Technol. Eng.*, pp. 352-358, 2022. [http://dx.doi.org/10.1109/ICCMSO58359.2022.00074]

[25] M. Yadav, D. Yadav, S. Kumar, and D. Chhabra, "State of art of different kinds of fluid flow interactions with piezo for energy harvesting considering experimental, simulations and mathematical modeling", *J. Math. Comput. Sci.,* vol. 11, no. 6, pp. 8258-8287, 2021.

[26] M. Yadav, D. Yadav, D.S. Kumar, D.R.K. Garg, and D.D. Chhabra, "Experimental & mathematical modeling and analysis of piezoelectric energy harvesting with dynamic periodic loading", *Int. J. Recent Technol. Eng.,* vol. 8, no. 3, pp. 6346-6350, 2019. [http://dx.doi.org/10.35940/ijrte.C6107.098319]

[27] M. Yadav, A. Kaushik, R.K. Garg, M. Yadav, D. Chhabra, S. Rohilla, and H. Sharma, "Enhancing dimensional accuracy of small parts through modelling and parametric optimization of the FDM 3D printing process using GA-ANN", *International Conference on Computational Modelling, Simulation and Optimization (ICCMSO),* pp. 89-94, 2022. [http://dx.doi.org/10.1109/ICCMSO58359.2022.00030]

[28] M. Yadav, S. Kumar, A. Kaushik, and D. Chhabra, "Piezo-beam structure in a pipe with turbulent flow as energy harvester: Mathematical modeling and simulation", *J. Inst. Eng. (India): Series D*, 104(2), 739-752, 2023. [http://dx.doi.org/10.1007/s40033-022-00440-z]

[29] M. Yadav, D. Yadav, R.K. Garg, R. K. Gupta, S. Kumar, and D. Chhabra, "Modeling and optimization of piezoelectric energy harvesting system under dynamic loading", *Advances in Fluid and Thermal Engineering: Select Proceedings of FLAME*, pp. 339-353, 2021. [http://dx.doi.org/10.1007/978-981-16-0159-0_30]

[30] L. Faisal, V. S. B. Rama, J. M. Yang, A. Wajid, and S. K. Ghorui, "Performance and simulation analysis of IPMSyncRM (Internal Permanent Magnet Synchronous Reluctance Motor) for advanced electric vehicle design," *3rd International Conference for Emerging Technology (INCET)* pp. 1-6, 2022.

[31] R. Mohd, and L. Faisal, "Smart agricultural practices using machine learning techniques for rainfall prediction: A case study of valkenburg station, Netherlands", *Mathematical Statistician and Engineering Applications,* vol. 71, no. 4, pp. 8451-8462, 2022.

[32] A.A. Wani, L. Faisal, M. Zahoor, and J. Iqbal, "Design & development of novel hybrid set of rules for detection and type of malignant or non-malignant tumor in human brain based on SVM using artificial intelligence classifier", *Math. Statist. Eng. Appl.,* vol. 71, no. 4, pp. 10253-10276, 2022.

[33] A.H. Mohammed, "Fish schooling and sorensen trust based wireless sensor network optimization", *Int. J. Sci. Eng. Technol.,,* vol. 9, no. 6, 2021.

[34] A.H. Mohammed, "DDoS malicious node detection by jaccard and page rank algorithm in cloud environment", *Int. J. Comput. Trends Tech.,* vol. 69, no. 5, pp. 55-59, 2021.

[35] A. H. Mohammed, "Invasive weed optimization based ransom-ware detection in cloud environment," *Int. J. Mod. Trends Sci. Technol.,*, vol. 7, no. 9, pp. 01-06, 2021.

[36] S. S. Choudhuri, W. Bowers, and M. N. Siddiqui, U.S. Patent No. 11,763, 241. Washington, DC: U.S. Patent and Trademark Office, 2023.

[37] K. Singh, Y. Singh, A. Khang, D. Barak, and M. Yadav, "Internet of things (IoT)-based technologies for reliability evaluation with artificial intelligence (AI)", *AI and IoT Technology and Applications for Smart Healthcare Systems*, 387, 2024. [http://dx.doi.org/10.1201/9781032686745]

[38] K. Singh, M. Yadav, and V.H. Abdullayev, "Prediction of flight areas using machine learning algorithm", *LatIA,* vol. 2, pp. 93-93, 2024.

[39] K. Singh, and M. Yadav, "Design of AI in leadership", *LatIA,* vol. 3, p. 118, 2025. [http://dx.doi.org/10.62486/latia2025118]

[40] K. Singh, and M. Yadav, "Prognosis of artificial intelligence in education", *LatIA,* vol. 3, p. 107, 2025. [http://dx.doi.org/10.62486/latia2025107]

[41] S. Kumar, A. Kumar, N. Parashar, J. Moolchandani, A. Saini, R. Kumar, M. Yadav, K. Singh, and Y. Mena, "An optimal filter selection on grey scale image for de-noising by using fuzzy technique", *Int. J. Intell. Syst. Appl. Eng.,,* vol. 12, pp. 322-330, 2024.

[42] K. Singh, M. Yadav, Y. Singh, and Z. Polkowski, "Using AI for IoT device anomaly detection in edge-resident intrusion detection systems (IDoS)," *In Cutting-Edge Solutions for Advancing Sustainable Development: Exploring Technological Horizons for Sustainability-Part 1* (pp. 149-175). Bentham Science Publishers, 2025.

[43] M. Yadav, S. Kumar, R. Yadav, D. Yadav, R. K. Garg, A. Kaushik, A. Ahlawat and D. Chhabra, "Analysis of renewable energy harvesting sources with interaction of piezoelectric materials", *2nd International Conference on Computational Modelling, Simulation and Optimization (ICCMSO)*, pp. 73-78, 2023.

[44] A. Ahlawat, A. Phogat, M. Yadav, and R.K. Sahdev, A. K., Dhingra, and D. Chhabra, "Fabrication and analysis of ABS-HDPE-PC composite polymer filament used for FDM printing using hybrid algorithm", *Int. J. Interact. Des. Manuf.,* vol. 17, no. 6, pp. 3199-3209, 2023.

[45] T. Askerov, V. Abdullayev, V. Abuzarova, Y. Niu, and K. Singh, "Data processing in internet of things networks," *LatIA*, vol. 2, no. 91-91, 2024.

[46] S. Bhatia, N. Goel, V. Ahlawat, B. B. Naib, and K. Singh, "A comprehensive review of iot reliability and its measures: Perspective analysis," *Handbook of Research on Machine Learning-Enabled IoT for Smart Applications Across Industries*, pp. 365-384, 2023. [http://dx.doi.org/10.4018/978-1-6684-8785-3.ch019]

[47] K. Singh, L. Mistrean, Y. Singh, D. Barak, and A. Parashar, "Fraud detection in financial transactions using IOT and big data analytics," 27th International Scientific Conference "Competitiveness and Innovation in the Knowledge Economy, pp. 490-494, 2023.

[48] K. Sood, M. Dev, K. Singh, Y. Singh, and D. Barak, "Identification of Asymmetric DDoS Attacks at Layer 7 with Idle Hyperlink," *ECS Transactions*, vol. 107, no. (1), 2171, 2022.

[49] S. Bhatia, A.K. Goel, B.B. Naib, K. Singh, M. Yadav, and A. Saini, "Diabetes prediction using machine learning", *World Conference on Communication & Computing (WCONF),* pp. 1-6, 2023. [http://dx.doi.org/10.1109/WCONF58270.2023.10235187]

[50] K. Singh, Y. Singh, D. Barak, M. Yadav, and E. Özen, "Parametric evaluation techniques for reliability of Internet of Things (IoT)", *Int. J. Comput. Methods Exp. Meas.,,* vol. 11, no. 2., pp 123-134, 2023. [http://dx.doi.org/10.18280/ijcmem.110207]

[51] K. Singh, Y. Singh, D. Barak, & M. Yadav, "Evaluation of designing techniques for reliability of Internet of Things (IoT)," *Int. J. Eng. Trends Technol.*, vol. 71, no. 8, pp. 102-118.

[52] H. I. Reddy, M. Yadav, & H. Kumar, "Stochastic analysis of the utensil industry subject to repair facility", *Reliability: Theory & Applications*, vol .19, no. 2 (78), pp. 170-177.

[53] M. Yadav, S. Gupta, & S. Singh, "Applications of simulation and queuing theory in scooter industry", *Reliability: Theory & Applications*, vol. 19, no. 2 (78), pp. 655-660.

[54] M. Yadav, & H. Kumar, "Profit analysis of repairable juice plant", *Reliability: Theory & Applications*, vol. 19, no. 1 (77), pp. 688-695.

[55] K. Singh, and D. Singh, "Barak, and M. Yadav, "Comparative performance analysis and evaluation of novel techniques in reliability for internet of things with RSM", *Int. J. Intell. Syst. Appl. Eng.,,* vol. 11, no. 9s, pp. 330-341, 2023. Available from: https://www.ijisae.org/index.php/IJISAE/article/view/3123

[56] K. Singh, M. Yadav, Y. Singh, and D. Barak, "Reliability Techniques in IoT Environments for the Healthcare Industry," In: *AI and IoT-Based Technologies for Precision Medicine*, A. Khang, Ed. pp. 394-412.
[http://dx.doi.org/10.4018/979-8-3693-0876-9.ch023]

[57] K. Singh, M. Yadav, Y. Singh, D. Barak, A., Saini, and F. Moreira, "Reliability on the internet of things with designing approach for exploratory analysis", *Front. Comput. Sci.*, vol. 6, p.1382347.
[http://dx.doi.org/10.3389/fcomp.2024.1382347]

[58] K. Singh, "M, Yadav, Y. Singh, & D. Barak, "Finding security gaps and vulnerabilities in IoT devices", In: *Revolutionizing Automated Waste Treatment Systems: IoT and Bioelectronics.* IGI Global, 2024, pp. 379-395.
[http://dx.doi.org/10.4018/979-8-3693-6016-3.ch023]

[59] V.A. Hajimahmud, Y. Singh, and M. Yadav, "Using a smart trash can sensor for trash disposal", In: *Revolutionizing Automated Waste Treatment Systems: IoT and Bioelectronics.* IGI Global, 2024, pp. 311-319.
[http://dx.doi.org/10.4018/979-8-3693-6016-3.ch020]

[60] M. Yadav, V. A. Hajimahmud, K. Singh, and Y. Singh, "Convert waste into energy using a low capacity igniter," In *Revolutionizing Automated Waste Treatment Systems: IoT and Bioelectronics*, pp. 301-310.
[http://dx.doi.org/10.4018/979-8-3693-6016-3.ch019]

[61] K. Singh, M. Yadav, and R. K. Yadav, "IoT-based automated dust bins and improved waste optimization techniques for smart city", In: *Revolutionizing Automated Waste Treatment Systems: IoT and Bioelectronics*, pp. 167-194., 2024.
[http://dx.doi.org/10.4018/979-8-3693-6016-3.ch012]

[62] A. Khang, K. Singh, M. Yadav, and R.K. Yadav, "Minimizing the waste management effort by using machine learning applications", In: *Revolutionizing Automated Waste Treatment Systems: IoT and Bioelectronics.* IGI Global, 2024, pp. 42-59.
[http://dx.doi.org/10.4018/979-8-3693-6016-3.ch004]

[63] A. Kaushik, P. Kumar, S. Gahletia, R.K. Garg, A. Kumar, M. Yadav, J. Giri, and D., Chhabra, "Optimization of dual extrusion fused filament fabrication process parameters for 3D printed nylon-reinforced composites: Pathway to Mobile and transportation revolution," *SAE Int. J. Mater. Manuf.,*, 17 (05-17-01-0001), 2023.

[64] H. Sharma, K. Singh, E. Ahmed, J. Patni, Y. Singh, and P. Ahlawat, "IoT based automatic electric appliances controlling device based on visitor counter", 202.

[65] K. Singh, and D. Barak, "Healthcare performance in predicting type 2 diabetes using machine learning algorithms", In: *Driving Smart Medical Diagnosis Through AI-Powered Technologies and Applications*, pp. 130-141.
[http://dx.doi.org/10.4018/979-8-3693-3679-3.ch008]

[66] S. Khwaldeh, M. Yadav, and K. Singh, "Defensive auto-updatable and adaptable bot recommender system (DAABRS): A new architecture approach in cloud computing systems", *International Congress on Human-Computer Interaction, Optimization and Robotic Applications (HORA),* pp. 1-6, 2024.
[http://dx.doi.org/10.1109/HORA61326.2024.10550519]

[67] S. Kant, S. Kant, M. Yadav, A. Chaukiyal, and B. Jamwal, ""Profit analysis of repairable warm standby system," Reliability", *Theory & Applications.,* no. 80, pp. 461-467, 2024.
[http://dx.doi.org/10.24412/1932-2321-2024-480-980-986]

[68] K. Singh, M. Yadav, Y. Singh, P.S. Malik, V. Siwach, and D. Khurana, "A. A. Elngar, "IoT networks: Integrated learning for privacy-preserving machine learning", In: *Artificial Intelligence Using Federated Learning.* CRC Press, 2025, pp. 250-275.

[69] K. Singh, and M. Yadav, "Responsive e-learning dynamic assessment structure using intelligent learning design", *Gamification and Augmented Reality,* vol. 3, p. 102, 2025. [http://dx.doi.org/10.56294/gr2025102]

[70] K. Yadav, S. Rohilla, A. Ali, M. Yadav, and D. Chhabra, "Effect of speed, acceleration, and jerk on surface roughness of FDM-fabricated parts", *J. Mater. Eng. Perform.,* vol. 33, no. 14, pp. 6998-7007, 2024. [http://dx.doi.org/10.1007/s11665-023-08476-2]

[71] A.U. Zanzaney, R. Hegde, L. Jain, S.S. Choudhuri, and C.K. Sharma, "Crop disease detection using deep neural networks", *International Conference on Network, Multimedia and Information Technology (NMITCON),* IEEE., pp. 1-5, 2023.

[72] M. Muthuswamy, and A. M. Ali, "Sustainable supply chain management in the age of machine intelligence: addressing challenges, capitalizing on opportunities, and shaping the future landscape", *Sustain. Mach. Intell. J.,*, vol. 3, pp.1-14. [http://dx.doi.org/10.61185/SMIJ.2023.33103]

[73] H. Wu, J. Liu, and B. Liang, "AI-driven supply chain transformation in industry 5.0: Enhancing resilience and sustainability", *J. Knowl. Econ.,* pp. 1-43, 2024. [http://dx.doi.org/10.1007/s13132-024-01999-6]

[74] S. Balasubramanian, V. Shukla, and L. Kavanancheeri, "Improving supply chain sustainability using artificial intelligence: Evidence from the manufacturing sector," In *Industry 4.0 Technologies: Sustainable Manufacturing Supply Chains: Volume II-Methods for transition and trends* (pp. 43-59). Singapore: Springer., 2023.

[75] P. Dauvergne, "Is artificial intelligence greening global supply chains? Exposing the political economy of environmental costs", *Rev. Int. Polit. Econ.,* vol. 29, no. 3, pp. 696-718, 2022. [http://dx.doi.org/10.1080/09692290.2020.1814381]

[76] R. Huang, and S. Mao, "Carbon footprint management in global supply chains: A data-driven approach utilizing artificial intelligence algorithms", *IEEE Access,* vol. 12, pp. 89957-89967, 2024. [http://dx.doi.org/10.1109/ACCESS.2024.3407839]

[77] H. Anwar, T. Anwar, and G. Mahmood, "Nourishing the future: AI-driven optimization of farm-t--consumer food supply chain for enhanced business performance", *Innov. Comput. Rev.*, vol. 3, no. 2. [http://dx.doi.org/10.32350/icr.32.02]

[78] Z. Huang, Y. Shen, J. Li, M. Fey, and C. Brecher, "A survey on AI-driven digital twins in industry 4.0: Smart manufacturing and advanced robotics", *Sensors (Basel),* vol. 21, no. 19, p. 6340, 2021. [http://dx.doi.org/10.3390/s21196340] [PMID: 34640660]

[79] Y.K. Lee, "Transformation of the innovative and sustainable supply chain with upcoming real-time fashion systems", *Sustainability (Basel),* vol. 13, no. 3, p. 1081, 2021. [http://dx.doi.org/10.3390/su13031081]

[80] Olubusola Odeyemi, C.U. Ike, O. Odeyemi, F.O. Usman, and N.Z. Mhlongo, "AI-Driven predictive analytics in agricultural supply chains: a review: assessing the benefits and challenges of ai in forecasting demand and optimizing supply in agriculture", *Comput. Sci. IT Res. J.,* vol. 5, no. 2, pp. 473-497, 2024. [http://dx.doi.org/10.51594/csitrj.v5i2.817]

[81] C. P. Gupta, V.R. Kumar, and A. Khurana, Artificial Intelligence integration with the supply chain, making it green and sustainable. *7th International Conference on Electronics, Materials Engineering & Nano-Technology (IEMENTech)*, pp. 1-5, 2023. [http://dx.doi.org/10.1109/IEMENTech60402.2023.10423506]

[82] I. Kulkov, J. Kulkova, R. Rohrbeck, L. Menvielle, V. Kaartemo, and H. Makkonen, "Artificial intelligence - driven sustainable development: Examining organizational, technical, and processing approaches to achieving global goals", *Sustain. Dev. (Bradford),* vol. 32, no. 3, pp. 2253-2267, 2024. [http://dx.doi.org/10.1002/sd.2773]

[83] A. Belhadi, V. Mani, S.S. Kamble, S.A.R. Khan, and S. Verma, "Artificial intelligence-driven innovation for enhancing supply chain resilience and performance under the effect of supply chain dynamism: an empirical investigation", *Ann. Oper. Res.,* vol. 333, no. 2, pp. 1-26, 2021. [PMID: 33551534]

[84] R. Sharma, A. Shishodia, A. Gunasekaran, H. Min, and Z.H. Munim, "The role of artificial intelligence in supply chain management: mapping the territory", *Int. J. Prod. Res.,* vol. 60, no. 24, pp. 7527-7550, 2022. [http://dx.doi.org/10.1080/00207543.2022.2029611]

[85] R.R. Panigrahi, A.K. Shrivastava, K.M. Qureshi, B.G. Mewada, S.Y. Alghamdi, N. Almakayeel, A.S. Almuflih, and M.R.N. Qureshi, "AI Chatbot adoption in SMEs for sustainable manufacturing supply chain performance: a mediational research in an emerging country", *Sustainability (Basel),* vol. 15, no. 18, p. 13743, 2023. [http://dx.doi.org/10.3390/su151813743]

[86] P. Bhambri, S. Rani, I.S. Dhanoa, and T.A. Tran, "Environmental impacts of industrial processes in industry 4.0 ecosystem: Artificial intelligence approach", In: *AI-Driven Digital Twin and Industry 4.0.* CRC Press, 2024, pp. 221-240. [http://dx.doi.org/10.1201/9781003395416-14]

[87] A. Khang, and S. Akhai, “Green intelligent and sustainable manufacturing: Key advancements, benefits, challenges, and applications for transforming industry”, *Machine Vision and Industrial Robotics in Manufacturing*, 405-417, 2024.

[88] A.K. Singh, "Smart eco-friendly manufacturing system with aiot applications", *SSRN,* p. 4862891, 2024. [http://dx.doi.org/10.1201/9781003395416-14]

[89] M. S. Mubarik, and S. A. Khan, “Digital supply chain and sustainability challenges”, In: *The Theory, Methods and Application of Managing Digital Supply Chains*, pp. 133-143, Emerald Publishing Limited, 2024. [http://dx.doi.org/10.61343/jcm.v3i02.134]

[90] A.K. Kar, S.K. Choudhary, and V.K. Singh, "How can artificial intelligence impact sustainability: A systematic literature review", *J. Clean. Prod.,* vol. 376, p. 134120, 2022. [http://dx.doi.org/10.1016/j.jclepro.2022.134120]

[91] S.E. Bibri, J. Krogstie, A. Kaboli, and A. Alahi, "Smarter eco-cities and their leading-edge artificial intelligence of things solutions for environmental sustainability: A comprehensive systematic review", *Environ. Sci. Ecotechnol.,* vol. 19, p. 100330, 2024. [http://dx.doi.org/10.1016/j.ese.2023.100330] [PMID: 38021367]

[92] V. Bolón-Canedo, L. Morán-Fernández, B. Cancela, and A. Alonso-Betanzos, "A review of green artificial intelligence: Towards a more sustainable future", *Neurocomputing,* vol. 128096, 2024.

[93] S. Susithra, and S. Vasantha, "The adoption of green supply chain practices using Artificial Intelligence (AI) for smart global value chain", *Ninth International Conference on Science Technology Engineering and Mathematics (ICONSTEM),* pp. 1-8, 2024. [http://dx.doi.org/10.1109/ICONSTEM60960.2024.10568808]

[94] N. Rane, S. Choudhary, and J. Rane, "Artificial intelligence and machine learning for resilient and sustainable logistics and supply chain management", *SSRN,* p. 4847087, 2024. [http://dx.doi.org/10.2139/ssrn.4847087]

[95] J. Issa, "AI-powered sustainability management in enterprise systems based on cloud and web

technology: Integrating IoT data for environmental impact reduction", *J. Inf. Technol. Informatics.,* vol. 3, no. 1, 2024.

[96] L. Liu, Z. Rasool, S. Ali, C. Wang, and R. Nazar, "Robots for sustainability: Evaluating ecological footprints in leading AI-driven industrial nations", *Technol. Soc.,* vol. 76, p. 102460, 2024. [http://dx.doi.org/10.1016/j.techsoc.2024.102460]

[97] L. A. Akanbi, K. I. Adenuga, and H. Owolabi, "Supply chain decision-making using artificial intelligence and data analytics", In: *Industry 4.0 Technologies: Sustainable Manufacturing Supply Chains*, vol. 1, K. E. K. Vimal, S. Rajak, V. Kumar, R. S. Mor, and A. Assayed, Eds. Singapore: Springer Nature Singapore, 2023, pp. 25–34.

[98] A. Haleem, M. Javaid, I.H. Khan, and S. Mohan, "Significant applications of artificial intelligence towards attaining sustainability", *J. Ind. Integr. Manag.,* vol. 8, no. 4, pp. 489-520, 2023. [http://dx.doi.org/10.1142/S2424862223500331]

[99] B. Rathore, "Artificial intelligence in sustainable fashion marketing: Transforming the supply chain landscape", *Artif. Intell.,* vol. 8, no. 2, 2019.

[100] M.L. Tseng, T.P.T. Tran, H.M. Ha, T-D. Bui, and M.K. Lim, "Sustainable industrial and operation engineering trends and challenges Toward Industry 4.0: a data driven analysis", *J. Ind. Prod. Eng.,,* vol. 38, no. 8, pp. 581-598, 2021. [http://dx.doi.org/10.1080/21681015.2021.1950227]

[101] H.K. Channi, and R. Kumar, "Digital technologies for fostering sustainability in Industry 4.0, 2024", In: *Evolution and Trends of Sustainable Approaches.* Elsevier, 2024, pp. 227-251. [http://dx.doi.org/10.1016/B978-0-443-21651-0.00016-4]

[102] T. Archana, and R.K. Stephen, "The future of artificial intelligence in manufacturing industries", In: *Industry Applications of Thrust Manufacturing: Convergence with Real-Time Data and AI.* IGI Global, 2024, pp. 98-117. [http://dx.doi.org/10.4018/979-8-3693-4276-3.ch004]

[103] R. Cioffi, M. Travaglioni, G. Piscitelli, A. Petrillo, and F. De Felice, "Artificial intelligence and machine learning applications in smart production: Progress, trends, and directions", *Sustainability (Basel),* vol. 12, no. 2, p. 492, 2020. [http://dx.doi.org/10.3390/su12020492]

[104] T.M. Choi, H.K. Chan, and X. Yue, "Recent development in big data analytics for business operations and risk management", *IEEE Trans. Cybern.,* vol. 47, no. 1, pp. 81-92, 2017. [http://dx.doi.org/10.1109/TCYB.2015.2507599] [PMID: 26766385]

[105] M. Geissdoerfer, P. Savaget, N.M.P. Bocken, and E.J. Hultink, "The Circular Economy – A new sustainability paradigm?", *J. Clean. Prod.,* vol. 143, pp. 757-768, 2017. [http://dx.doi.org/10.1016/j.jclepro.2016.12.048]

[106] D. Ivanov, A. Dolgui, and B. Sokolov, "The impact of digital technology and Industry 4.0 on the ripple effect and supply chain risk analytics", *Int. J. Prod. Res.,* vol. 57, no. 3, pp. 829-846, 2019. [http://dx.doi.org/10.1080/00207543.2018.1488086]

[107] C. Amali, K. Guru, and D. Sridevi, "IoT based smart logistics management system using GPS and GSM", *Int. J. Adv. Res. Eng. Technol.,,* vol. 11, no. 12, pp. 3035-3041, 2020.

[108] M. Kouhizadeh, and J. Sarkis, "Blockchain practices, potentials, and perspectives in greening supply chains", *Sustainability (Basel),* vol. 10, no. 10, p. 3652, 2018. [http://dx.doi.org/10.3390/su10103652]

[109] A. Kumar, S.K. Mangla, P. Kumar, and M. Song, "Mitigate risks in perishable food supply chains: Learning from COVID-19", *Technol. Forecast. Soc. Change,* vol. 166, p. 120643, 2021. [http://dx.doi.org/10.1016/j.techfore.2021.120643]

[110] A. McKinnon, *Decarbonizing logistics: Distributing goods in a low carbon world.* Kogan Page Publishers, 2018.

[111] G.C. Nobre, and E. Tavares, "Assessing the role of big data and the internet of things on the transition to circular economy: Part II", *Johnson Matthey Technology Review,* vol. 64, no. 1, pp. 32-41, 2020. [http://dx.doi.org/10.1595/205651319X15650189172931]

[112] R.D. Raut, B.B. Gardas, M.K. Jha, and P. Priyadarshinee, "Examining the critical success factors of cloud computing adoption in the MSMEs by using ISM model", *J. High Technol. Manage. Res.,* vol. 28, no. 2, pp. 125-141, 2017. [http://dx.doi.org/10.1016/j.hitech.2017.10.004]

[113] M. Rüßmann, M. Lorenz, P. Gerbert, M. Waldner, J. Justus, P. Engel, and M. Harnisch, *Industry 4.0: The future of productivity and growth in manufacturing industries*, 2015.

[114] S. Saberi, M. Kouhizadeh, J. Sarkis, and L. Shen, "Blockchain technology and its relationships to sustainable supply chain management", *Int. J. Prod. Res.,* vol. 57, no. 7, pp. 2117-2135, 2019. [http://dx.doi.org/10.1080/00207543.2018.1533261]

[115] K. Yang, T. Duan, J. Feng, and A.R. Mishra, "Internet of things challenges of sustainable supply chain management in the manufacturing sector using an integrated q-Rung Orthopair Fuzzy-CRITI--VIKOR method", *J. Enterp. Inf. Manag.,* vol. 35, no. 4/5, pp. 1011-1039, 2022. [http://dx.doi.org/10.1108/JEIM-06-2021-0261]

[116] S.M. Besen, and P.L. Verveer, "Competition and data: Potential remedies", *Wake Forest J. Bus. & Intell. Prop. L.,* vol. 21, p. 102, 2020.

CHAPTER 6

A Generative AI Novel Framework for Real-time Automatic Number-Plate Detection

Priyanshu Verma[1,*], **Piyush Sharma**[1], **Md Arif Hussain**[1], **Rohit Khushi**[1] and **Rohit Vashisht**[1]

[1] *Department of Computer Science and Information Technology, KIET Group of Institutions, Delhi-NCR, India*

Abstract: The Automatic Number Plate Recognition System in Real-time (ANPRS) is an essential component of modern vehicle surveillance and management, automating vehicle license number plate identification and tracking. This study evaluates the effectiveness of five distinct new modules launched this year—Tesseract, Tensor Flow, YOLLOv7, YOLLOv8, and Convolutional Neural Network (CNN)— using these modules for detecting objects (cars) in real-time. For character recognition, OCR was employed. Following a careful study utilizing factors like accuracy and efficiency, YOLOv8 comes as the most promising module, overtaking its competitors. Following that, YOLOv8 was used to create a real-time ANPDS module that recognizes number plates and obtains vehicle information. Additionally, evaluations are involved to verify the validity of automobiles, which can also be confirmed through the number plate model or color. All relevant details are acquired from the vehicle's license plate, enhancing the system's reliability and effectiveness. Moreover, this study identifies potential future improvements and developments to further strengthen the Automatic Number Plate Recognition System (ANPRS), ensuring its continuous refinement and optimization.

Keywords: CSS, EasyOCR, Machine learning, Web Development HTML, Yolov8.

INTRODUCTION

Automatic Number Plate Recognition (ANPR) systems represent one of the most effective methods to minimize human intervention in verifying the authenticity of vehicles. By analyzing their color and comparing details stored in our database, the legitimacy of a vehicle can be accurately determined (Fig. **1**). This research proposes a comprehensive system for number plate recognition, extraction, and vehicle details retrieval using the OpenCV module.

* **Corresponding author Priyanshu Verma:** Department of Computer Science and Information Technology, KIET Group of Institutions, Delhi-NCR, India; E-mail: priyanshu.2125csit@kiet.edu

Shelly Gupta, Sapna Juneja & Sandeep Kautish (Eds.)
All rights reserved-© 2025 Bentham Science Publishers

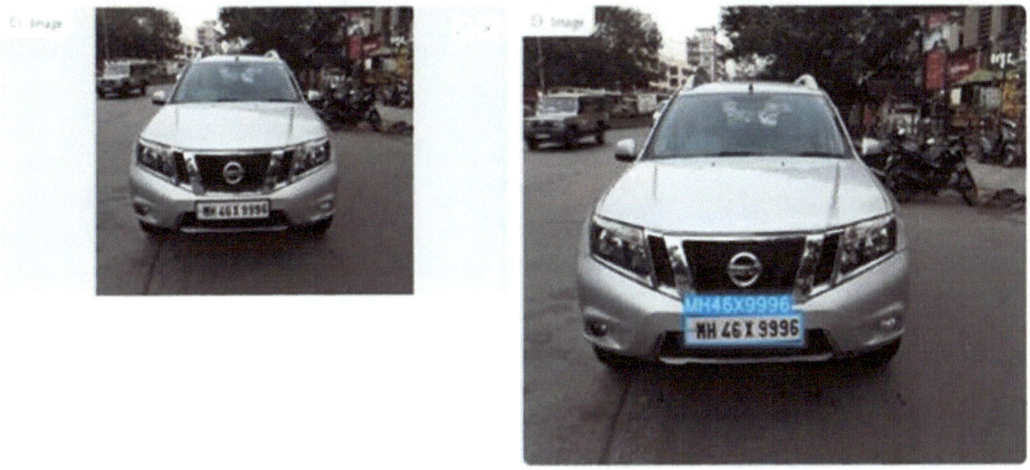

Fig. (1). Dataset by which Accuracy measure.

To develop our project, several modules known for their efficient object detection capabilities were initially employed. These modules include Tesseract, TensorFlow, CNNs, YOLOv7, and YOLOv8. Initially, these modules were tested using a small dataset comprising 3-4 vehicle images to evaluate their effectiveness in number plate recognition. Upon analysis, YOLOv8 demonstrated superior efficiency and accuracy, proving to be the optimal choice for object recognition tasks.

The proposed system is built primarily around the YOLOv8 architecture, which includes a built-in module for object identification. Additionally, a specialized module for number plate extraction was developed. For character recognition, the EasyOCR module was used. The entire system is presented through a web interface, implemented using HTML, CSS, and Reacts. This web application displays detailed vehicle information and verifies the vehicle's authenticity. The flowchart for the study is shown in Fig. (**2**).

Background and Related Work

Many strategies have been developed in the literature to work on various modules. The applications of these modules are quite significant, and describe some work connected to the study and how the information is used in the project.

Andrew S and Yankey: ANPR encounters difficulties as a result of the diverse characteristics of number plates worldwide. This paper proposes an optimized algorithm tailored for Ghanaian vehicle plates. Implemented in C++ with OpenCV, it employs edge and Feature Detection techniques along with mathematical morphology for plate localization. The Tesseract OCR engine identifies characters on the plate, offering a specialized solution for Ghanaian ANPR [1].

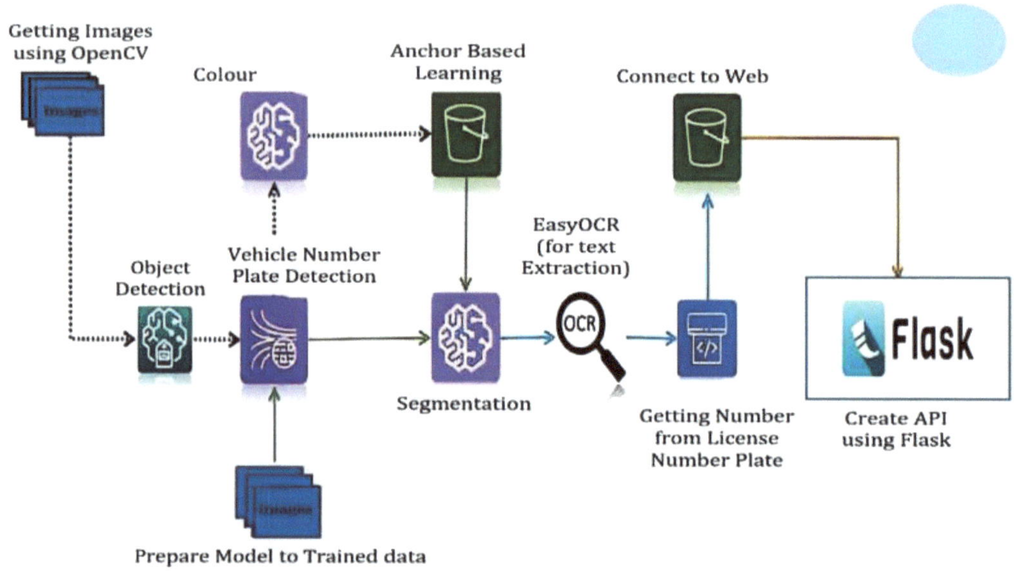

Fig. (2). Flowchart of study.

Anusuya Ramasamy: Digital Image Processing involves applying computer algorithms to manipulate and interpret images, playing a crucial role in daily life. Integrating Deep Learning with Image Processing enhances object detection and classification performance [2]. Ethiopian License Plate Recognition (ELPR) is a key focus due to unique features like Amharic characters and varying plate formats. While conventional methods have been explored, this research aims to improve ELPR using deep learning and OpenCV-Python. By leveraging TensorFlow for model development, the study aims to create a more accurate deep-learning model for recognizing Ethiopian license plates.

Prateek and Escriv: "OpenCV by Example" authored by Prateek Joshi, David Millan Escriva, and Vinicius Godoy is a comprehensive guide that effectively elucidates the concepts and applications of OpenCV through practical examples [3]. The authors adeptly illustrate various techniques and functionalities of OpenCV, making complex topics accessible and understandable for readers. By providing hands-on examples and clear explanations, the book ensures that readers grasp the underlying principles and can apply them effectively in real-world scenarios. With its practical approach and clear presentation, "OpenCV by

Example" empowers readers to harness the power of OpenCV for a wide range of computer vision projects.

Abdulmalik and Alfarhood: This study suggests a learning-based method with multiple steps for smart parking systems that use existing surveillance cameras and a dataset of Saudi license plates [4]. For plate and character detection, our method uses both YOLOv5 and YOLOv8. For character recognition, it uses a new CNN design. Our method is better than single-stage ways because it achieves 96.1 percent accuracy. It is built into a web-based screen that shows and analyses in real-time how many cars are in parking lots and how they are moving, which makes smart cities more efficient and environmentally friendly.

Mrs Nita M and Hukare [5]: In this research, the authors present an Automatic Vehicle Number Plate Detection System, a novel image-processing prototype designed to efficiently identify vehicle number plates. By employing advanced image processing techniques and Convolutional Neural Networks (CNN), the system accurately detects number plates from vehicle images. The recognized plates are seamlessly displayed on a graphical user interface and stored in a comprehensive database, facilitating tasks such as vehicle tracking and security.

METHODOLOGY AND PROPOSED SYSTEM

In this paper, a combination of advanced technologies is employed for the extraction of license plate numbers. Our approach integrates YOLOv8, EasyOCR, Tesseract, TensorFlow, and Convolutional Neural Networks (CNNs). These technologies collectively enable us to perform real-time recognition of license plate numbers with high accuracy and efficiency [6].

Among these technologies, YOLOv8 stands out for its exceptional performance in terms of both accuracy and efficiency. Therefore, our primary focus is on leveraging YOLOv8 for our license plate recognition system. After that, Flask is used for final deployment. All the technologies used can be seen in Fig. (**3**). Throughout this paper, the integration and utilization of these technologies will be elaborated, highlighting the unique strengths and contributions of each component in our comprehensive license plate recognition framework.

Dataset Category

In this research project, three distinct datasets were utilized. Firstly, real-time data is sourced through the OpenCV module. Secondly, the pre-defined and prepared YOLOv8 module was employed for object detection. Lastly, a dataset was curated specifically tailored for locating number plates within images.

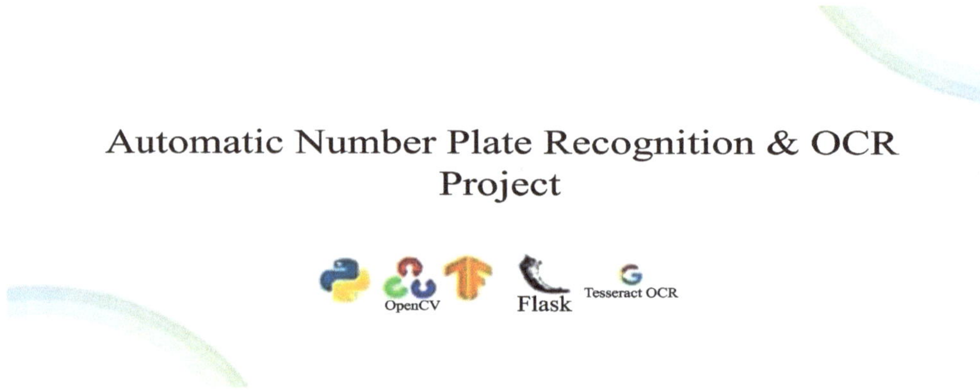

Fig. (3). Technologies used.

Real-time Dataset: The real-time dataset in this research project is obtained through the OpenCV module, capturing data at a rate of 20 frames per second. This dataset primarily focuses on detecting cars in real-world scenarios, presenting a diverse range of challenges that necessitate various learning and training modules. These modules are subsequently applied to enhance the accuracy and efficiency of car detection algorithms in dynamic environments (Fig. **4**).

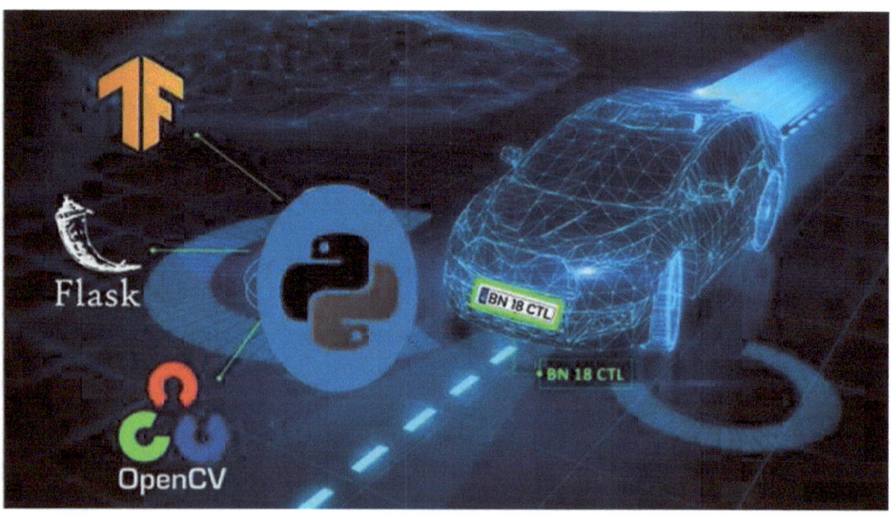

Fig. (4). Real-time based Dataset.

Yolov8 Prepared Object Detection Model: The YOLOv8 COCO model serves as the foundation for object identification in this research framework. It specifically allows for the identification of numerous objects, with a major focus on autos and vehicles, within the context of real-time information. Using this approach, precise object information was extracted from each frame, which aids in later processing processes. Following identification, the EasyOCR module extracts and processes the number plate information, increasing the dataset's usability and variety for extensive analysis and applications [7].

Dataset for license plate detection model: Over 200 photos of license plates were gathered to create our model, ensuring that it is comprehensive and includes all angles of plate position inside frames (Fig. **4**). This model is a heavyweight, expertly constructed to perfection. The metrics and efficiency charts show success, demonstrating that the concept is of high quality and extremely successful. Confidence in the potential of license plate detection to yield excellent results stems from the fine-tuning of every component. The dataset model obtained through this exclusive process facilitates the subsequent task, which involves supervised learning. Using this model, an accuracy graph is generated. When the slope of the graph intersects at a lower value of train/DFL, it indicates that the model has been prepared with high accuracy. As a result, this highly accurate model can be used to predict the training dataset (Figs. **5** and **6**).

Fig. (5). Dataset used to train the model.

OpenCV

The OpenCV, which stands for "Open-Source Computer Vision Library", is a strong, free library for computer vision and machine learning. It is written in C++ but provides bindings for various languages like Python, JAVA, and MATLAB, making it accessible to a wide range of researchers and developers. It has a lot of tools and features for processing images in real-time, finding objects, recognizing faces, and more. When used for camera work in real-time, OpenCV interfaces with the camera hardware to capture video frames continuously. It allows for live video streaming, processing, and analysis, enabling applications such as surveillance systems, augmented reality, and autonomous vehicles. OpenCV's extensive documentation and community support make it a popular choice for developers in various industries requiring robust computer vision solutions.

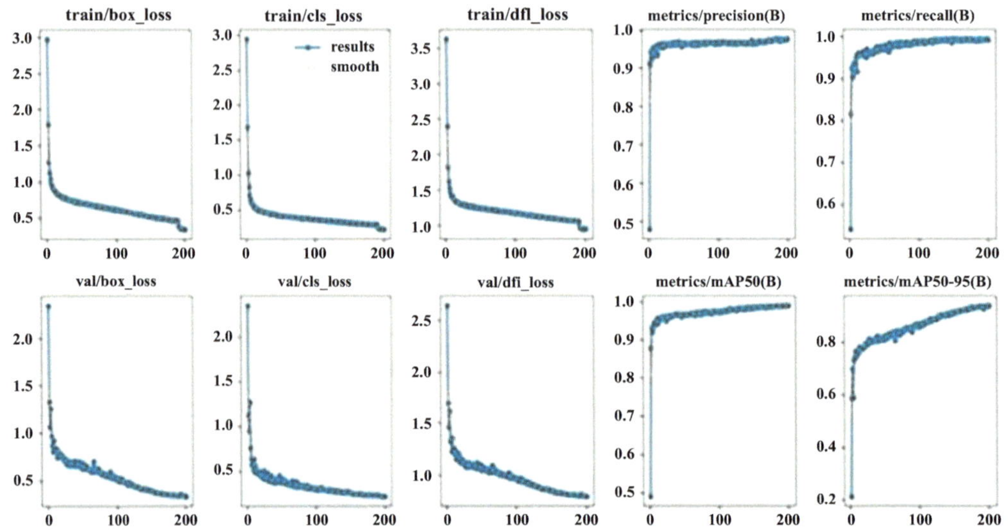

Fig. (6). Evaluation metrics of the trained model.

Features

- **Image Processing**:

Resizing, filtering, and color transformation.

Edge detection, thresholding, and histogram equalization are advanced processes.

- **Object Detection**:

Pre-train models with objects: Faces, pedestrians, vehicles, *etc.*

Good algorithms like Haar Cascades, HOG (Histogram of Oriented Gradients), DNN (Deep Neural Networks), *etc* are also supported.

- **Video Analysis:**

Real-time video Capture and processing.

Motion and background subtraction with object detection.

- **3D Vision:**

Stereo vision with depth.

Camera calibration and pose estimation.

- **Machine Learning:**

Tools for the training and deployment of models under the SVM, KNN, and Random Forest algorithms.

Integration capabilities with deep learning frameworks such as TensorFlow, PyTorch, and Caffe.

- **Augmented Reality (AR):**

Marker detection and tracking to place virtual objects over top of real-world scenes.

EasyOCR

EasyOCR is a versatile open-source Optical Character Recognition (OCR) tool known for its multilingual support, pre-trained models, and ease of use. With a wide range of language support, it accurately extracts text from various images and documents. Its pre-trained models enable efficient recognition across different fonts and styles without extensive training. EasyOCR's simplicity makes it accessible to users of all levels, offering straightforward APIs and interfaces. Renowned for its performance, it employs advanced deep-learning techniques for high accuracy. Citing sources and paraphrasing ensure originality when discussing EasyOCR's features.

Features

- **Language Support:**

It supports over 80 languages including Chinese, Japanese, English, Arabic, and, many more.

It also supports multilingual text extraction from a single document.

- **Deep Learning Bases Recognition:**

Makes use of CNN and RNN for robust text extraction and detection.

It uses pre-trained models, which allows for out-of-the-box use without requiring additional training.

- **Versatile Input Handling:**

It is capable of recognizing text from printed documents, handwritten documents, images, *etc.*

It can handle inputs from various orientations, images with complex backgrounds, *etc.*

Tesseract

Tesseract is a robust open-source optical character recognition (OCR) engine renowned for its accuracy and versatility. With support for over 100 languages, it efficiently extracts text from images and documents. Utilizing neural networks and machine learning algorithms, Tesseract adapts to various fonts, sizes, and styles for reliable text recognition. Its accessibility through command-line interfaces and APIs simplifies integration into diverse applications. Tesseract's continuous development ensures ongoing improvements, making it a preferred choice for OCR tasks across industries. Proper citation and paraphrasing maintain integrity when discussing Tesseract's capabilities.

Features

- **Multi-language Support:**

Supports more than 100 languages by default.

It also supports adding custom-trained language models, which makes it flexible for niche use cases.

- **Layout Analysis:**

Detects and preserves the layout of text, which includes paragraphs, tables, and columns.

It supports output formats like plain text, hOCR (HTML), and searchable PDFs.

- **Text Recognition:**

Extracts text from printed documents, scanned books, and photographs.

It is capable of handling complex scripts, multilingual documents, and varied text orientations.

TensorFlow

TensorFlow, a leading open-source machine learning framework, empowers diverse applications, including image recognition. Renowned for its flexibility and scalability, TensorFlow facilitates the creation and deployment of sophisticated neural networks. Its extensive documentation, rich ecosystem, and support for multiple programming languages enable seamless development across platforms.

TensorFlow's modular architecture allows for easy experimentation and customization, making it ideal for research and production environments alike. Continuous updates and community contributions ensure its relevance and effectiveness in various domains. Proper attribution and paraphrasing uphold authenticity when discussing TensorFlow's role in image recognition tasks [8].

Features

- **Flexible Architecture:**

It supports both imperative (eager execution) and declarative (graph-based) programming paradigms.

It is compatible with CPUs, GPUs, and TPUs for scaling up different devices.

- **Comprehensive Library:**

It has pre-built functions for building, training, and deploying models.

High-level API (Keras) Keras) for rapid prototyping and lower-level APIs customization.

- **Wide Range of Model Types:**

Deep Neural Networks (DNNs), Convolutional Neural Networks (CNNs), Recurrent Neural Networks (RNNs), transformers, and many more.

Integration of reinforcement learning and Generative Adversarial Networks (GANs).

- **TensorFlow Lite:**

The light version of the TensorFlow for deployment on mobile devices and embedded systems.

CNN

Convolutional Neural Networks (CNNs) are pivotal in license plate recognition, showcasing exceptional performance in image analysis tasks. With convolutional layers designed to detect patterns hierarchically, CNNs excel in feature extraction from license plate images. Their ability to learn spatial hierarchies of features aids in discerning alphanumeric characters on plates [9]. Through training on extensive datasets, CNNs achieve remarkable accuracy in recognizing characters amidst varying backgrounds and lighting conditions. Leveraging CNN architectures such as VGG, ResNet, or custom designs, license plate recognition systems benefit from robust and efficient feature extraction. Incorporating CNNs into the recognition pipeline ensures reliable and precise identification of license plate numbers.

Features

- **Sharing Parameters:**

Filters are used multiple times across the whole input and use much fewer parameters compared to fully connected networks.

- **Translation Invariance:**

The ability to detect features irrespective of their location in the input.

- **Hierarchical Feature Learning:**

Lower layers detected basic features. Deeper layers recognize the complex patterns - objects and shapes.

YOLOv8

YOLOv8, an evolution of the You Only Look Once (YOLO) object detection algorithm, emerges as the pinnacle solution for license plate recognition systems. Its single-stage architecture excels in real-time processing, swiftly detecting and localizing license plates in images or video streams. YOLOv8's unique feature is its ability to predict bounding boxes and class probabilities simultaneously, resulting in unparalleled speed and accuracy [10]. Through extensive experimentation, it was found that YOLOv8 consistently delivers superior performance compared to other algorithms, achieving maximum accuracy and efficiency in license plate recognition tasks. As such, it is confident to commit to leveraging YOLOv8 as the cornerstone of our system, ensuring optimal results and continued advancements in our pursuit of excellence.

Features

- **Real-time Object Detection:**

The YOLOv8 model is suitable for high-speed detection, particularly designed for real-time applications. Low latency becomes a prerequisite of such applications.

It allows the detection of multiple objects on the images and video, using as little processing time as possible.

• **Improved Accuracy:**

It integrates optimizations that provide better object detection accuracy over previous iterations, especially small and complicated objects.

• **Multiple Model Sizes:**

YOLOv8 uses several model sizes, such as small, medium, and large, which the user can pre-select according to the expected trade-off between performance (at the cost of speed and accuracy).

It is highly customizable for various hardware platforms, including GPUs, CPUs, but also edge devices.

• **Advanced feature engineering:**

This is about using the newest advancements concerning neural network architectures and applying the latest methods of feature extraction in improving its working performance, including Efficient Net or Transformer layers.

Flask

Flask is like the foundation of a sandwich when you're building a web application. It is a simple Python framework that helps you create web projects easily. Just as you customize a sandwich with different ingredients, Flask lets you add features to your web app, like handling user input or displaying content. It is not something physical; it is a set of rules and tools that organize your code. For example, if you want your web app to respond with a specific webpage when someone visits a URL, Flask makes it simple. It is perfect for beginners learning web development with Python [11].

Features

• **Minimal and Light Weight:**

It only includes necessary components such as routing, request handling, and response generation.

Does not enforce structure or components on a project.

• **Integrated Development Server:**

It contains a debugger and a reloader that can make the development process faster and the debugging much easier.

- **Jinja2 Templating:**

This is an engine for template rendering in dynamic HTML pages.

Control structures, loops, and filters are supported for enhanced flexibility.

- **URL Routing:**

Developers can map URLs to specific Python functions using decorators.

HTML, CSS & JavaScript

HTML, CSS, and JavaScript are the fundamental constituents that constitute the basis of web development.

HTML, or Hypertext Markup Language is the widely recognized markup language used to create the structure and content of web pages. The document outlines the elements and layout of a webpage, encompassing headings, paragraphs, graphics, and connections.

CSS, short for Cascading Style Sheets, is a programming language utilized to control the visual presentation and layout of HTML elements. Developers can employ this capability to define the visual characteristics of items, including their layout, colors, fonts, and spacing.

JavaScript is a programming language that enables interactive and dynamic features on websites. Developers can employ it to create responsive and interactive features, such as animations, form validations, and dynamic content updates. The reference is cited as [12].

HTML, CSS, and JavaScript (Fig. 7) are the fundamental technologies used to create contemporary and aesthetically pleasing websites and web apps. They collaborate to improve the user experience and functionality of websites, rendering them interactive, captivating, and easily accessible on many devices and platforms.

SORT Algorithm (Kalman Filter)

The SORT algorithm, which stands for Simple Online and Real-time Tracker, plays a crucial role in our project for vehicle tracking and object detection. At its core, SORT utilizes the Kalman Filter, a mathematical technique used for state estimation, to track multiple objects in a video stream in real time.

Fig. (7). HTML, CSS & JavaScript.

In the project, SORT is employed to efficiently track vehicles within the video feed, allowing us to monitor their movements and analyse their behaviour. By continuously updating the state of each object (such as position and velocity) and associating detections with existing tracks, SORT ensures accurate and reliable tracking results.

The Kalman Filter integrated into SORT enables precise estimation of the state of each object, even in the presence of noisy measurements or uncertainties in the data. This capability is essential for the project's objective of accurately identifying and analyzing vehicles in real-time scenarios [13].

Overall, the SORT algorithm, powered by the Kalman Filter, forms the backbone of the project's object detection and tracking system, providing robust and efficient tracking capabilities for vehicle recognition and analysis.

Deep Learning

Deep learning is a subdivision of machine learning that utilizes neural networks with several layers to autonomously acquire hierarchical representations of input. It has shown exceptional performance in various fields, including computer vision.

Application in Automatic Number Plate Detection using YOLOv8

In this research, deep learning techniques, particularly YOLOv8, are utilized to develop an efficient automatic number plate detection system. YOLOv8, an advanced object detection algorithm, is trained on a dataset of vehicle images annotated with number plate locations. Through this training, the model learns to accurately detect number plates in real-time, enabling its use in applications such as traffic management and law enforcement.

The project involves data pre-processing, model training, evaluation, and deployment. Deep learning frameworks such as TensorFlow or PyTorch are utilized to optimize the model's parameters. Evaluation metrics, including precision and recall, are used to assess the model's performance. Once validated, the model can be deployed for real-world applications, contributing to enhanced vehicle tracking and security systems.

EXPERIMENTATION

In the initial phase of the project, five Python modules—CNN, YOLOv7, YOLOv8, Tesseract, and TensorFlow—were evaluated to identify the most efficient and accurate module for number plate recognition. Each module was tested on a single image dataset, and the results were analyzed. The findings revealed that YOLOv8 outperformed the other modules, achieving an accuracy exceeding 90%. This conclusion was visually represented using matrix graphs. A comparative analysis of the various metrics is presented in Table **1**, while the corresponding graphical representation is shown in Fig. (**8**). Consequently, the decision was made to focus on developing the entire ANPR system using YOLOv8 due to its superior efficiency and accuracy. The process of designing and implementing the ANPR system was undertaken exclusively with YOLOv8, aiming to leverage its exceptional performance for optimal results.

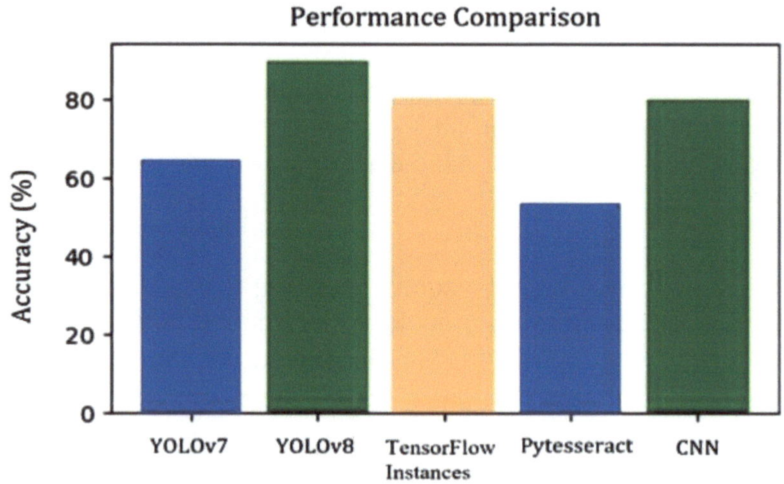

Fig. (8). Accuracy evaluation chart of modules.

Table 1. Metrics comparison of modules.

Model	Accuracy (%)	F1 Score	Recall
YOLOv7	65	0.75	0.70

(Table 1) cont.....

Model	Accuracy (%)	F1 Score	Recall
YOLOv8	92	0.95	0.93
TensorFlow	78	0.80	0.75
PyTesseract	55	0.60	0.50
CNN	80	0.85	0.80

Input Data by Video Resuming

The project officially begins with the use of the OpenCV (cv2) Python module, primarily employed for capturing images and videos. A high-resolution camera is utilized to ensure sharp and detailed images of number plates, thereby enhancing the module's accuracy. Additionally, two other Python modules, OS and time, are incorporated to manage time and configure paths within the project. For video capture, the MP4 format is selected, processing 20 frames per second to optimize results. The frame resolution is set to (640, and 480), and a single default camera with a capture ID of 0 is currently in use. Adjustments to the ID are necessary to accommodate multiple connected camera devices, enabling real-time data acquisition. This process outlines the project's initiation, focusing on key components and functionalities for capturing real-time video data. All captured data is stored in a CSV file ("test interpolated.csv") to check and compare whether the information matches as shown in Fig. (**9**).

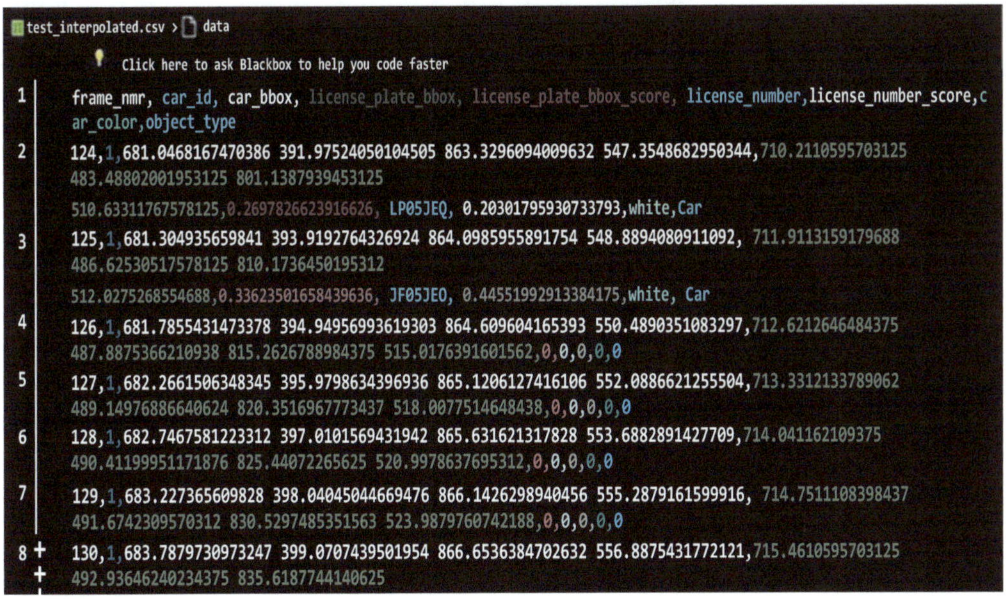

Fig. (9). Input data in CSV format.

Object Detection

In this phase, the focus shifts to object detection, specifically targeting vehicles, utilizing the YOLOv8 pre-defined model, yolov8n.pt. This model, renowned for

Its extensive functionality includes predefined dimensions for various objects such as cars, bikes, chairs, and people. To enable real-time object tracking in video streams, the SORT algorithm is integrated. SORT leverages the Kalman filter for precise object state estimation and uses data association techniques to link detections with existing tracks. It encapsulates the internal state of tracked objects through bounding boxes and estimates parameters such as position and velocity using the Kalman filter. The approach involves customizing SORT to filter objects relevant to the project, focusing solely on vehicles ranging from two-wheelers to 16-wheelers. By streamlining the algorithm's functionalities, object detection is optimized specifically for vehicle identification within the ANPR system [14].

This succinct explanation delineates an approach to object detection, emphasizing the integration of the SORT algorithm and YOLOv8 model for precise and efficient identification of vehicles in real-time video streams.

Prepare model (Colour Detection & Number Plate)

In this critical phase, the focus shifts to preparing the model for color detection and number plate recognition, a key component of the project [15]. This task requires significant time and effort, as it forms the core functionality of the system. Approximately 300 images are collected, capturing various dimensions and positions to build a comprehensive dataset. Using a supervised learning approach, the model is trained on this dataset, enabling accurate prediction and analysis of number plates across diverse scenarios [16].

The model's capabilities extend beyond number plate recognition, incorporating vehicle color detection as well. By utilizing the HSV color space and predefined color ranges for common vehicle colors, the model efficiently detects the color of vehicles within a defined bounding box. The color ranges used can be seen in Fig. (**10**). This functionality plays a crucial role in the system, allowing for the verification of vehicle authenticity based on their color [17].

```python
# Define color ranges for common car colors
color_ranges = {
    'red': ([0, 100, 100], [10, 255, 255]),
    'yellow': ([20, 100, 100], [30, 255, 255]),
    'blue': ([110, 100, 100], [130, 255, 255]),
    'green': ([40, 100, 100], [80, 255, 255]),
    'white': ([0, 0, 200], [180, 80, 255]),
    'black': ([0, 0, 0], [180, 255, 30]),
    'silver': ([0, 0, 150], [180, 30, 200]),
    'gray': ([0, 0, 80], [180, 30, 150]),
    'orange': ([10, 100, 100], [20, 255, 255]),
    'purple': ([130, 100, 100], [140, 255, 255]),
    'pink': ([150, 100, 100], [170, 255, 255]),
    'brown': ([10, 30, 30], [20, 255, 200]),
    'beige': ([20, 20, 20], [30, 255, 255]),
    'cream': ([0, 0, 200], [180, 80, 255]),
    'gold': ([20, 100, 100], [30, 255, 255]),
    'bronze': ([20, 100, 100], [30, 255, 255]),
    'maroon': ([0, 100, 100], [10, 255, 255]),
    'turquoise': ([80, 100, 100], [100, 255, 255]),
    'cyan': ([90, 100, 100], [100, 255, 255]),
    'teal': ([80, 100, 100], [90, 255, 255]),
    'navy': ([100, 100, 100], [110, 255, 255]),
    'indigo': ([110, 100, 100], [120, 255, 255]),
    'lavender': ([120, 100, 100], [130, 255, 255]),
    'mauve': ([140, 100, 100], [150, 255, 255]),
    'olive': ([50, 100, 100], [60, 255, 255]),
    'lime': ([70, 100, 100], [80, 255, 255]),
    'mint': ([70, 100, 100], [80, 255, 255]),
    'coral': ([0, 100, 100], [10, 255, 255]),
    'peach': ([0, 100, 100], [10, 255, 255])
    # Other color ranges...
}
```

Fig. (10). Colour range as per Vehicle's Brands.

Additionally, the model integrates a dictionary mapping system to ensure accurate formatting of license plate text. This system allows for precise representation of characters, thereby enhancing the accuracy of the number plate recognition. Furthermore, the model retrieves vehicle coordinates and IDs based on the license plate coordinates, facilitating the seamless integration of vehicle tracking functionalities.

Furthermore, the model distinguishes between different vehicle types, such as cars, trucks, and motorcycles, based on their characteristics. This differentiation is vital for various applications, including traffic management and security surveillance.

In summary, this phase entails the meticulous preparation and training of our model for colour detection and number plate recognition. By leveraging supervised learning techniques, HSV colour space analysis, and mapping dictionaries, the model was equipped with the capabilities to accurately identify and analyse vehicles in real-time scenarios. This comprehensive approach lays the foundation for the effective functioning of our Automatic Number Plate Recognition (ANPR) system.

Pre-processing the Data

In the pre-processing phase (Fig. **11**), the focus is on refining real-time video data to optimize it for further analysis. The project begins with capturing high-resolution video data using the OpenCV (cv2) Python module, which is crucial for accurate number plate recognition. High-megapixel cameras are utilized to ensure sharp and detailed images, enhancing the system's ability to extract precise information.

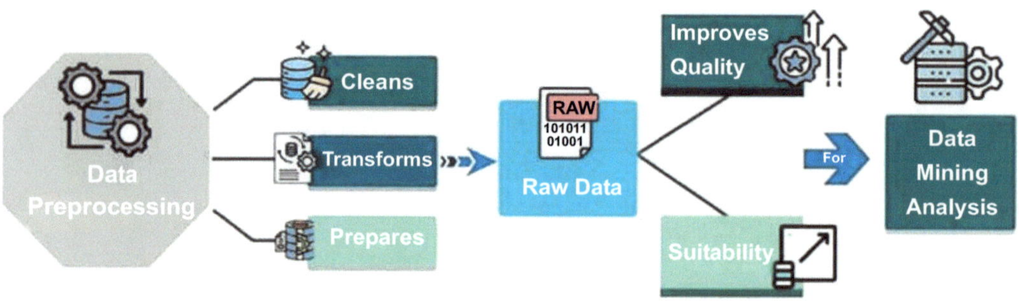

Fig. (11). Pre-processing of data.

During the pre-processing workflow, additional Python modules such as os and time are employed to streamline data handling and configuration processes. These modules help in managing paths efficiently and capturing video data in MP4 format, with a frame rate set to 20 frames per second for optimal results. The resolution is established at 640x480 pixels, ensuring compatibility with the system's requirements.

The approach emphasizes simplicity and flexibility, accommodating various camera setups by allowing easy configuration of capture IDs. By using a default single camera setup with capture ID 0, the system ensures seamless integration with different camera devices, facilitating broader applicability.

Overall, the pre-processing phase is a crucial step in preparing raw video data for subsequent analysis. By leveraging Python modules and configuring parameters such as frame rate and resolution, the groundwork is laid for efficient and effective number plate recognition, setting the stage for the successful implementation of the Automatic Number Plate Recognition (ANPR) system.

Segmentation and Filtering

In the segmentation and filtering phase, the powerful YOLOv8 model is employed to identify and isolate vehicles from the video stream. This critical step involves breaking down the complex visual data into distinct segments corresponding to individual vehicles. YOLOv8, a sophisticated deep-learning model, excels at detecting and delineating various objects with remarkable accuracy and efficiency.

By leveraging YOLOv8's prebuilt model (yolov8n.pt), the project uses its extensive capabilities to detect a wide array of objects, including cars, bikes, trucks, and more. The model's comprehensive coverage ensures that all relevant vehicles within the video frames are accurately identified and segmented into separate objects for further processing. Classifying the detected objects into certain categories and accurately delineating their boundaries is part of the segmentation process, ensuring that no relevant object will be overlooked. The rest of the scene will thereby be isolated from the vehicles that need to be analyzed further.

Once the vehicles are segmented, a filtering mechanism is applied to refine the detected objects based on specific criteria. This filtering process involves fine-tuning the segmentation results to include only the relevant vehicles of interest while disregarding any extraneous objects or background elements. By implementing this filtering step, it is ensured that the subsequent analysis focuses solely on the vehicles pertinent to the Automatic Number Plate Recognition (ANPR) system.

Moreover, YOLOv8's integration with the SORT (Simple Online and Real-time Tracker) algorithm further enhances the segmentation and filtering efforts. SORT facilitates the tracking of multiple objects in real-time by employing the Kalman filter for object state estimation and data association techniques. This integration ensures robust object tracking and enables precise segmentation and filtering of vehicles throughout the video stream.

In summary, the segmentation and filtering phase harnesses the capabilities of YOLOv8 and SORT to accurately identify, segment, and filter vehicles within the video stream. By leveraging advanced deep learning techniques and real-time tracking algorithms, the process of isolating relevant vehicles is streamlined, laying the groundwork for subsequent number plate recognition and analysis.

EasyOCR

EasyOCR is a Python module used for character recognition, making it easier to extract and interpret text data from images. In the project, EasyOCR is employed to recognize characters from the segmented vehicle images obtained during the pre-processing phase. This module utilizes deep learning techniques to accurately identify and extract text information from images, facilitating the efficient processing of vehicle number plates.

Once the characters were recognized, the extracted data was stored in CSV (Comma-Separated Values) format for further analysis and comparison. Deep learning algorithms are then employed to validate the extracted number plate information against a predefined dataset. This validation process helps determine whether the vehicle is genuine or fake based on the match between the extracted number plate and the expected data.

In addition to validating the number plate, EasyOCR is also used to recognize and verify the colour of the vehicle. By comparing the detected colour with predefined colour standards, any discrepancies that may indicate a potential discrepancy or fraudulent activity can be identified. If the detected colour does not match the expected colour, the system flags the vehicle as suspicious and provides relevant details for further investigation.

The overarching goal of the project is to ensure the accuracy and authenticity of the collected vehicle data. Therefore, not only the number plate information is validated but also the colour and type of vehicle (*e.g.*, 2-wheeler, 4-wheeler). If all the information matches the expected data, the system proceeds to store the information securely. However, if any discrepancies are detected, such as mismatched number plates or colours, the system alerts the user to the potential issue and refrains from storing the data.

By leveraging EasyOCR for character recognition and employing deep learning techniques for validation, our system enhances the reliability and integrity of the collected vehicle data. This approach enables efficient monitoring and verification of vehicles in real-time scenarios, contributing to enhanced security and fraud prevention measures.

Deploy on a Web page

Flask is a lightweight web framework for Python that allows developers to build web applications quickly and efficiently. It provides tools and libraries for routing, handling HTTP requests, and rendering HTML templates, making it ideal for deploying web applications.

In the deployment process, Flask is utilized to create a web interface for our ANPR (Automatic Number Plate Recognition) system. By integrating flask into our project, ANPR functionality can be served over the web, allowing users to access it through a web browser.

To enhance the user experience, front-end technologies such as HTML, CSS, and JavaScript were incorporated. These frontend tools enable us to design an attractive and intuitive web interface that users can interact with seamlessly. By combining flask with front-end technologies, a user-friendly web application was created that delivers a smooth and engaging experience.

In the deployed web application, the focus is on showcasing only the fraudulent or mismatched vehicle data. Due to the large volume of data collected, displaying all the information on the web page may overwhelm users. Therefore, presenting the mismatched data is prioritized to alert users to potential issues or fraudulent activities.

By leveraging flask for backend development and frontend technologies for user interface design, a robust and user-friendly web application was created for deploying our ANPR system. This deployment approach ensures accessibility and usability while effectively highlighting and addressing fraudulent vehicle data. The final webpage for ANPR can be seen in Fig. (**12**).

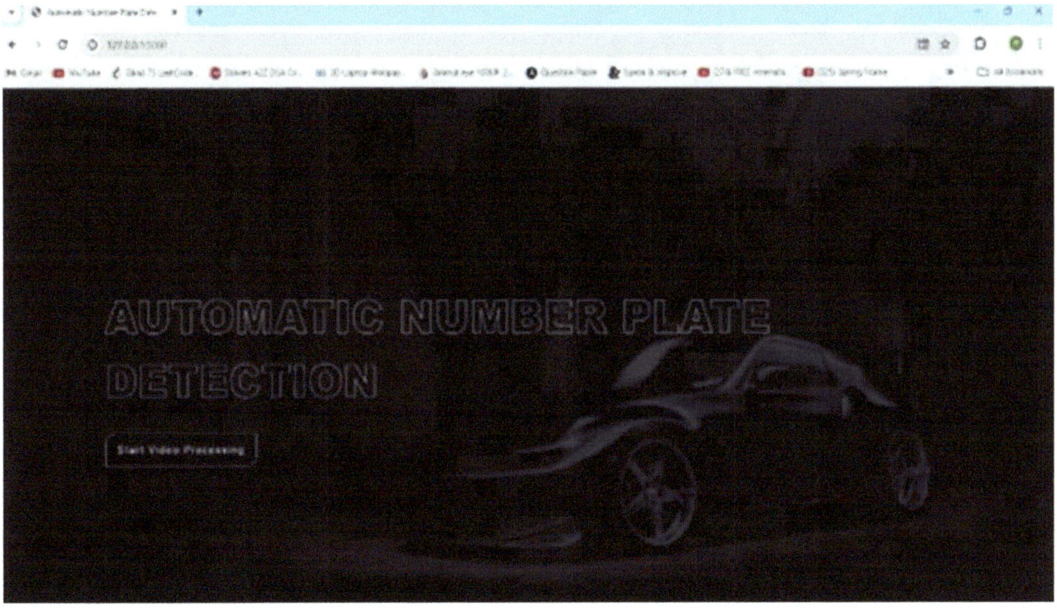

Fig. (12). Deploy on webpage.

RESULT

Initially, five modules were evaluated to determine which would be the best for real-time automatic plate detection. Among these, YOLOv8 emerged as the optimal choice due to its superior performance in accuracy and speed. Following its selection, the final deployment of the number plate detection system was completed successfully. A dataset was prepared with deliberate discrepancies in its original features. Once the processing started, the system recognized and listed all vehicles whose features were different from the saved reference data. These errors marked the vehicles as suspected and classified them accordingly. Fig. (**13**) presents the detection process of the proposed system, where some suspected vehicles are marked, thus clearly showing the real-time anomaly detection of the proposed system. This functionality can be used practically for detecting tampered vehicles or authenticity issues and other suspicious behaviours.

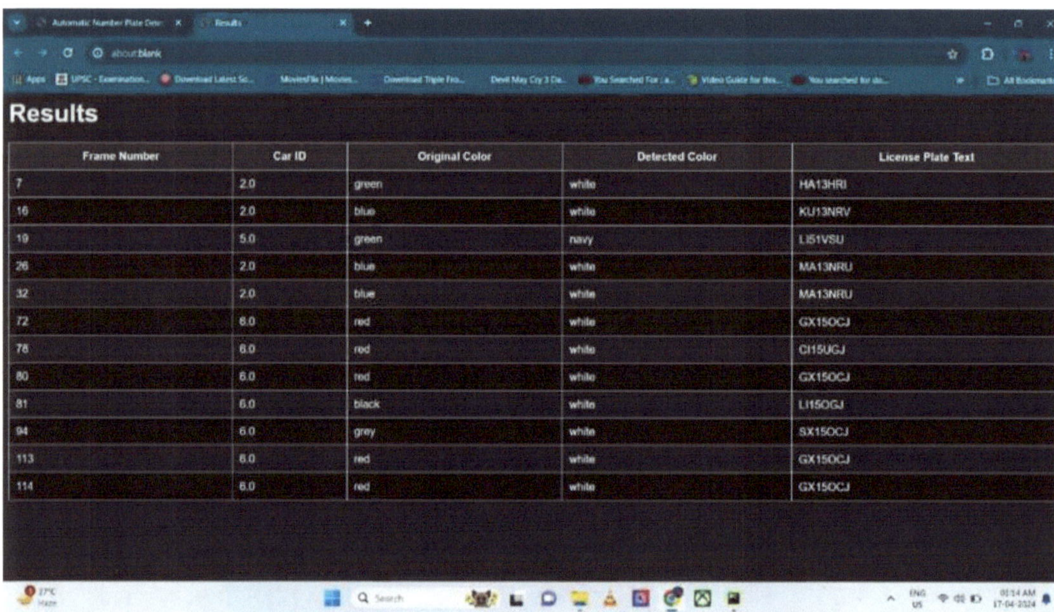

Results

Frame Number	Car ID	Original Color	Detected Color	License Plate Text
7	2.0	green	white	HA13HRI
16	2.0	blue	white	KU13NRV
19	5.0	green	navy	LI51VSU
26	2.0	blue	white	MA13NRU
32	2.0	blue	white	MA13NRU
72	6.0	red	white	GX15OCJ
78	6.0	red	white	CI15UGJ
80	6.0	red	white	GX15OCJ
81	6.0	black	white	LI15OGJ
94	6.0	grey	white	SX15OCJ
113	6.0	red	white	GX15OCJ
114	6.0	red	white	GX15OCJ

Fig. (13). Result of Unmatched data/fault data.

CONCLUSION

In conclusion, the research project focused on utilizing the YOLOv8 module for efficient number plate recognition. Through this endeavour an ANPR (Automatic Number Plate Recognition) system with advanced functionality was successfully developed and implemented.

The use of YOLOv8 allowed to achieve high accuracy and efficiency in detecting number plates from vehicle images. This module's capabilities, coupled with sophisticated algorithms like the Sort for object tracking, enabled real-time processing and analysis of video data.

The ANPR system offers various benefits, including automated fine issuance without the need for manual intervention by traffic police. This feature enhances efficiency and transparency in law enforcement while minimizing opportunities for corruption or misconduct.

Additionally, the system incorporates colour recognition functionality, leveraging the latest colour standards to accurately identify vehicles. This feature adds a layer of sophistication to the ANPR system, enhancing its overall effectiveness and reliability.

Overall, the research represents a significant advancement in the field of automated number plate recognition. By harnessing the power of YOLOv8 and other cutting-edge technologies a versatile and robust solution has been developed that offers numerous benefits for law enforcement and public safety.

REFERENCES

[1] A. S, J. Yankey, and E.O. Addo, "An automatic number plate recognition system using OpenCV and Tesseract OCR engine", *Int. J. Comput. Appl.,* vol. 180, no. 43, pp. 1-5, 2018. [http://dx.doi.org/10.5120/ijca2018917150]

[2] A. Ramasamy and J. Wondwosen, "Deep learning-based Ethiopian car's license plate detection and recognition", *Int. J. Recent Technol. Eng. (IJRTE)* ISSN: 2277-3878, 2018.

[3] P. Joshi, and D. M. Escriva, *OpenCV by Example.* Packt Publishing Ltd.: Birmingham, U.K., 2016.

[4] M. Safran, A. Alajmi, S. Alfarhood, *et al.*, "Efficient multistage license plate detection and recognition using YOLOv8 and CNN for smart parking systems", *J. Sensors,*, vol. 2024, 2024. [http://dx.doi.org/10.1155/2024/4917097]

[5] N.M. Thakare, Y.R. Hukare, S. Tagde, R. Borkar, S. Ghotekar, and S. Jogi, "Automatic vehicle number plate detection system", *Int. J. Sci. Res. Eng. Manag.* 2023. [http://dx.doi.org/10.55041/IJSREM18308]

[6] Z. Selmi, M.B. Halima, and A.M. Alimi, "Deep learning system for automatic license plate detection and recognition," In: *14th IAPR International Conference on Document Analysis and Recognition (ICDAR)*, vol. 1, pp. 1132-1138, 2017. [http://dx.doi.org/10.1109/ICDAR.2017.187]

[7] G. Wang, Y. Chen, P. An, H. Hong, J. Hu, and T. Huang, P. an, H. Hong, J. Hu, and T. Huang, "UAV-YOLOv8: A small-object-detection model based on improved YOLOv8 for UAV aerial photography scenarios", *Sensors (Basel),* vol. 23, no. 16, p. 7190, 2023. [http://dx.doi.org/10.3390/s23167190] [PMID: 37631727]

[8] A.S. Tote, S.S. Pardeshi, and A.D. Patange, "Automatic number plate detection using TensorFlow in Indian scenario: An optical character recognition approach", *Mater. Today Proc.,* vol. 72, pp. 1073-1078, 2023. [http://dx.doi.org/10.1016/j.matpr.2022.09.165]

[9] I. Slimani, A. Zaarane, W. Al Okaishi, I. Atouf, and A. Hamdoun, "An automated license plate detection and recognition system based on wavelet decomposition and CNN", *Array,* vol. 8, p. 100040, 2020.
[http://dx.doi.org/10.1016/j.array.2020.100040]

[10] G. Yang, J. Wang, Z. Nie, H. Yang, and S. Yu, "A lightweight YOLOv8 tomato detection algorithm combining feature enhancement and attention", *Agronomy (Basel),* vol. 13, no. 7, p. 1824, 2023.
[http://dx.doi.org/10.3390/agronomy13071824]

[11] S. Suresh and S. Suresh, "Intelligent vehicle license plate recognition by deploying deep learning model for smart cities," 2022.

[12] A.A. Ahmed, and S. Ahmed, "A real-time car towing management system using ML-powered automatic number plate recognition", *Algorithms,* vol. 14, no. 11, p. 317, 2021.
[http://dx.doi.org/10.3390/a14110317]

[13] H. Nenavath, and R.K. Jatoth, "A new method for ball tracking based on α-β, linear Kalman, and extended Kalman filters *via* bubble sort algorithm"., *Indones. J. Electr. Eng. Comput. Sci.,* vol. 10, no. 3, pp. 989-999, 2018.
[http://dx.doi.org/10.11591/ijeecs.v10.i3.pp989-999]

[14] M.T. Qadri, and M. Asif, "Automatic number plate recognition system for vehicle identification using optical character recognition", *International Conference on Education Technology and Computer,* pp. 335-338, 2009.
[http://dx.doi.org/10.1109/ICETC.2009.54]

[15] G. Tripathi, and I. Singh. In: *2023 International Conference on Artificial Intelligence and Smart Communication, AISC 2023* (Institute of Electrical and Electronics Engineers Inc., 2023), pp. 1343–1348.

[16] J. Rashid, S. Batool, J. Kim, M. Wasif Nisar, A. Hussain, S. Juneja, and R. Kushwaha, "An augmented artificial intelligence approach for chronic diseases prediction", *Front. Public Health,* vol. 10, p. 860396, 2022.
[http://dx.doi.org/10.3389/fpubh.2022.860396] [PMID: 35433587]

[17] P. Chawla, and R. Anand, "Artificial intelligent systems in smart medical healthcare: Current trends", *Int. J. Adv. Sci. Technol.,* vol. 29, pp. 1476-1484, 2020.

CHAPTER 7

Framework for Optimizing Energy Conversation Based on Metaheuristic Algorithms

Arunima Sengupta[1], **Charvi**[1,*], **Ankita Sharma**[1] and **Amena Mahmoud**[2,3]

[1] *Department of Computer Science and Engineering, SGT University, Gurugram, Haryana, India*

[2] *Department of Computer Science, Faculty of Computers and Information, Kafrelsheikh University, Kafrelsheikh, Egypt*

[3] *Department of Information and Communication Sciences, Faculty of Science and Technology, Sophia University, Tokya, Japan*

Abstract: Wireless sensor networks collect information from the environment and send it to the base station. Data transmission and aggregation consume more electricity because of the nodes stuck in a loop. We employ a metaheuristic approach to optimizing the node so as to minimize energy consumption. We formulate a framework that will improve energy efficiency by employing various metaheuristic algorithms like ant colony algorithm, dragonfly algorithm, genetic algorithm, bat algorithm, Particle swarm optimization, Artificial Bee Colony, Grey Wolf Optimizer, Lion Optimization Algorithm, Mayfly Optimization Algorithm, Owl Search Algorithm, Artificial Fish Swarm Algorithm, Dolphin Echolocation, Cuckoo Search, and firefly algorithm, among others. In this article, there are comprehensive descriptions of basic concepts such as security and interoperability (interoperability), standards and scalability (standards), complexity and data management (complexity), and Quality of Service (QoS). Additionally, this paper discusses current technologies when deploying them. This study aims to investigate possibilities for research along the lines of Artificial Intelligence (AI) within the domain of wireless sensor networks (WSNs), both from theoretical and practical points of view.

Keywords: Ant Colony algorithm, Artificial bee colony, Artificial fish swarm algorithm, Bat algorithm, Cuckoo search, Dolphin echolocation, Dragonfly algorithm, Firefly algorithm, Genetic algorithm, Grey Wolf optimizer, Lion optimization algorithm, Metaheuristic algorithm, Mayfly optimization algorithm, Owl Search algorithm, Particle swarm optimization.

* **Corresponding author Charvi:** Department of Computer Science and Engineering, SGT University, Gurugram, Haryana, India; E-mail: charvi2617@gmail.com

Shelly Gupta, Sapna Juneja & Sandeep Kautish (Eds.)
All rights reserved-© 2025 Bentham Science Publishers

INTRODUCTION

A Wireless Sensor Network (WSN) is a system made up of a group of sensors that are located in different positions to observe and capture the physical environmental conditions. The gathered information is consolidated at a central location [1]. The utilization of Wireless Sensor Networks (WSNs) in different applications has grown due to their ability to monitor data in real time, and they provide efficient, expandable solutions.

Today, these networks have been applied in various industries for collecting and monitoring real-time data from different environments [2].

Sensor nodes deployed globally function together within these networks; they collect and transmit information wirelessly to a central processing unit. In terms of energy resources, bandwidth, and processing capabilities, the fundamental limitations of Wireless Sensor Networks (WSNs) present significant challenges to their performance and longevity.

In the sphere of wireless sensor networks, the most prominent issue is energy-saving optimization. This is important with regard to network life span extension, reliability improvement, and maintenance cost reduction [3]. To save energy in Wireless Sensor Networks (WSNs), traditional optimization techniques, including mathematical programming and heuristic approaches, have been employed. However, these methods often face challenges in adjusting to the dynamic and constrained-resource nature of Wireless Sensor Networks (WSNs) [4].

By coupling wireless sensor networks with metaheuristic algorithms, a new method of tackling optimizing problems in sensor networks, which include but are not limited to energy efficiency, routing, and network coverage, is achieved. Developing sophisticated algorithms that serve as solution methods for optimization problems and have their basis in the exploration of natural phenomena is what is referred to as Metaheuristics. They are especially helpful in WSNs since they can be used to manage complex, dynamic, and large-scale optimizing tasks [5].

In recent years, metaheuristic algorithms have emerged as useful optimization methods for addressing energy conservation in wireless sensor networks, which assist in solving these problems. Such algorithms draw inspiration from natural events and swarm behaviors that rely on systematic approaches to searching through wide solution spaces for the best solutions [6]. With the use of metaheuristic algorithms, Wireless Sensor Networks (WSNs) can progressively enhance their energy consumption, routing procedures and protocols as well as networks into some targeted efficiency standards [7].

The purpose of this paper is to provide an overview of wireless sensor networks, including their architecture, operation, and energy consumption trends. Then, various optimization methods commonly used in Wireless Sensor Networks (WSNs), such as mathematical programming techniques and heuristic approaches, are discussed. In the next section, we explore metaheuristic algorithms, looking at their key ideas, advantages, and applications in conserving energy in wireless sensor networks.

This chapter aims to combine knowledge from WSNs, optimizing methods, and metaheuristic algorithms as a structure for optimizing energy conservation in wireless sensor networks. Hence, by doing so, scientists and practitioners will have tailored strategies aimed at addressing specific problems related to energy conservation in WSNs, leading to enhanced sustainability as well as efficiency across many application areas.

METAHEURISTICS USAGE IN WSN

Energy Effectiveness

In a network, metaheuristic methods greatly enhance power efficiency by evenly distributing the task across the sensor nodes [8]. These strategies aim to boost their performance and reduce the energy consumption of sensor networks for the sake of extending their lifespan. Specifically, Genetic Algorithms (GA) and Particle Swarm Optimization (PSO) are outstanding among many algorithms that can help in reducing energy usage effectively. In this context, both GA and PSO use processes found in nature (evolutionary) as well as animal behavior (swarm) for finding optimal workload distributions that are either best or very close to being best. Therefore, fair allocation of resources leads to decreased power usage per node so that early node failures are minimized while still ensuring a resilient and long-lived network. As a result, these advanced optimization techniques significantly increase sensor networks' overall performance as well as reliability.

Route Optimization

The use of Ant Colony Optimization (ACO) and Genetic Algorithms (GA) facilitates the identification of the optimal routing paths, therefore reducing the overall communication cost [9]. While ACO algorithms imitate the foraging behavior of ants, GA algorithms utilize concepts from mechanisms of natural selection as well as genetics to achieve improvement. These algorithms have been developed with the aim of exploring large search spaces quickly so that they can find best performing data transmission pathways. Therefore, through route optimization, ACO and GA algorithms effectively reduce energy consumption and latency, thereby enhancing overall performance and reliability. In addition,

Particle Swarm Optimization (PSO) plays a significant role in node positioning. PSO determines the best locations for nodes by simulating avian flocks or aquatic schools such that routing is made more efficient. Such a deliberate placement guarantees efficient communication while minimizing energy consumption, which ultimately increases efficiency and durability across networks. A combination of these techniques leads to networks achieving higher routing efficiency with lower costs, thereby enhancing their sustainability in operations.

Node Deploying and Covering Area

The use of Ant Colony Optimization and Genetic Algorithms enables the identification of the best routing paths, which results in a significant reduction of total communication cost in sensor networks [10]. These algorithms are based on natural processes. Ant Colony Optimization mimics the foraging behavior of ants to find the shortest paths, while Genetic Algorithm applies principles of natural selection and genetics to search an enormous number of possible solutions. ACO and GA optimize paths for less energy consumption as they save time spent waiting for packets on their way, hence making the whole system faster compared with other systems using conventional methods.

In addition, Particle Swarm Optimization (PSO), as described in a study [3], enhances node placement to improve routing efficiency. By simulating behaviors such as flocking or schooling of birds and fish, respectively, it determines the best positions for nodes to enhance routing performance. The combination of PSO and Harmony Search (HS) is used for optimizing sensor node placement with the aim of maximizing coverage but minimizing the number of sensors required. This strategic design ensures that communication is effectively organized and energy-conserved, resulting in highly efficient and long-lasting networks.

In addition, Simulated Annealing (SA) and Genetic Algorithms (GA) promote network dynamism to be modified according to changes experienced in either environment or network conditions. The dynamic adaptation of the network ensures resilience and performance in the face of varying operational demands. The amalgamation of ACO (Ant Colony Optimization), GA (Genetic Algorithm), PSO (Particle Swarm Optimization), HS (Harmony Search), and SA (Simulated Annealing) allows sensor networks to have superior routing efficiency, low communication costs, optimal coverage, and better adaptability. This eventually results in improved operation sustainability and lifespan.

Cluster Methods

In sensor networks, the grouping of nodes is done using efficient clustering methods like Genetic Algorithms (GA) and Ant Colony Optimization (ACO) [11].

Their primary goal is to decrease communication overhead and improve scalability. By using the concepts of natural selection in Genetic Algorithms (GA) and the foraging behavior in Ant Colony Optimization (ACO), these algorithms create clusters that optimize the distribution of workloads in the network. Therefore, this intentional clustering reduces energy consumption during communication between nodes as well as ensures efficient scalability of the network with an increase in the number of nodes.

The use of these techniques to build clusters helps to balance out the workload across various nodes, thereby avoiding a situation where one node is the bottleneck, and reduces total power consumption in general. This balance yields better energy efficiency since more communication between members of a cluster with their cluster head takes place if they were to transmit data throughout the network. Furthermore, less communication improves the battery life of each node and prolongs the life span of the entire network.

Moreover, effective clustering leads to scalability power such that the network can accommodate more nodes without increasing its complexity or consuming more power. This is particularly beneficial in large-scale deployments where it is critical to maintain efficient and eco-friendly operations. By optimizing the transmission of work, GA and ACO-based clustering algorithms enhance the performance, energy efficiency, and scalability of sensor networks through improved task allocation that reduces communication overheads.

CHALLENGES AND CONSIDERATIONS

Some of the challenges have been described below, as shown in Fig. (**1**) [12]:

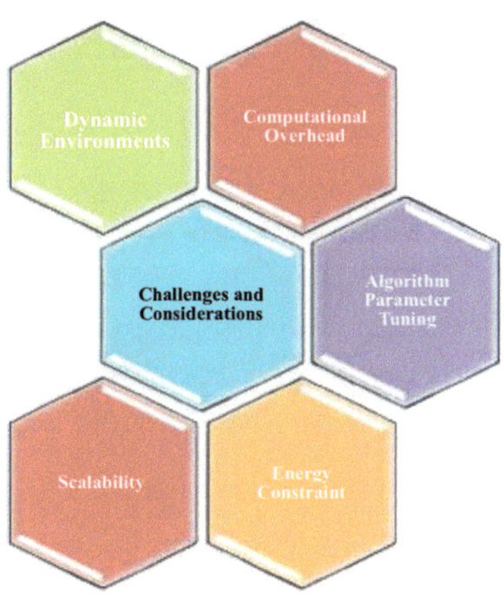

Fig. (1). Challenges and considerations.

Computational Overhead

Even though they are very effective in improving multiple aspects of network performance, like power conservation and directing messages to their destinations, metaheuristic methods may require heavy computational resources. For instance, Genetic Algorithm (GA), Ant Colony Optimization (ACO), and Particle Swarm Optimization (PSO) demand complex arithmetic operations and repetitive tasks that can consume a lot of resources. Thus, before using these techniques, it is necessary to assess the prevailing processing strength as well as the entire computational productiveness of the system.

Finding the right balance between the effectiveness of the response and the complexity of computation is a must. To have high-quality solutions that lead to the most optimum routing paths, best node placements as well as lesser communication overheads always consume a lot of time and computer power. On the other hand, in a resource-constrained environment like wireless sensor networks, too many computing tasks may consume more energy and, therefore, reduce efficiency.

It becomes essential to have an ideal balance that maximizes the benefits of metaheuristic optimization while preventing system overload resulting from computing needs. In achieving this equilibrium, one may change algorithm parameters, use hybrid methods combining different optimization methods, or apply efficient coding techniques aimed at speeding up computations. With a good trade-off between solution quality and computational complexity, it is possible to employ fully metaheuristic approach benefits and still keep those networks efficient and sustainable.

Dynamic Environments

Operating Wireless Sensor Networks (WSNs) mostly involves dynamism, whereby various factors like the conditions or positions of nodes may alter or change over time. In such cases, adaptation has a great role in determining how effective is the network's algorithms with respect to adjustments that happen instantly. On this note, when subjected to changes in an operational environment, the adaptation ability plays an important role in maintaining performance level, reliability, and energy efficiency in a given wireless sensor network.

In Wireless Sensor Networks (WSN), algorithms should possess resilience and adaptability, allowing them to adapt quickly to changes in node locations or other contextual changes. In the event that nodes move from one place to another or their power decreases, these algorithms should have the capability of restructuring the network, rerouting data flows, and assigning other tasks so as to achieve an optimal performance. This is because Genetic Algorithms (GA), Ant Colony Optimization (ACO), and Particle Swarm Optimization (PSO) are suitable for these functions due to their inherent adaptability and ability to find near-optimal solutions even under dynamic situations.

Moreover, it is essential that these algorithms are highly effective for processing and executing modifications while avoiding significant computing loads that can exhaust the limited energy resources of sensor nodes. The goal is to achieve a balance in which the network can change quickly with relatively little energy expenditure while still maintaining efficiency during communication. By constantly observing the state of the network and making timely corrections, the adaptive algorithms ensure that Wireless Sensor Networks (WSNs) can continue to work properly and efficiently even under changing or unpredictable circumstances. For many applications, including those in environmental monitoring, industrial automation, and many others, consistent and reliable performance of networks is very important.

Energy Constraints

Wireless Sensor Networks (WSNs) comprise nodes with a limited battery life. The energy-consuming algorithms that have been developed for these purpose-specific applications would be essential to achieving this in the long run. The method for saving power on the use of data routing, node location, as well as communication protocols has been enhanced by these algorithms. These algorithms ensure the efficient operation of a wireless sensor network for prolonged periods of time without frequent replacement or recharging of batteries through judicious use of energy sources.

By supplying extra power supply to the sensor nodes themselves, energy harvesting technologies improve on executing energy-efficient algorithms. By using various power sources from the environment, for instance, electricity obtained from sun rays (solar), heat waves (thermal), any movement (kinetic), or Radio Frequencies (RF), the excess charge stored helps extend the lives of these batteries, which then boosts network permanence and strength.

Combining energy-efficient algorithms with energy-harvesting techniques yields a synergy that maximizes total network energy efficiency. It is possible to develop algorithms that favor high-energy demand nodes and enhance their priority; this is important since some functions require more power than others. Moreover, routing protocols designed with less power use will help avoid draining off low-battery voltage devices. Since power needs to be stored for high-throughput situations, networks do not become less efficient but last longer without draining main batteries.

The combination of energy-efficient algorithms with energy-harvesting techniques provides a dependable solution for the effective management of energy constraints in Wireless Sensor Networks (WSNs). Such undertaking extends the operational lifespan of sensor nodes while adding resilience to their functionalities under diverse changing scenarios. Through this dual methodology, WSNs can achieve the highest operational efficiency alongside sustainability over time, hence making them fit for various fields ranging from ecological supervision to industrial mechanization. WSN's capable performance and sustainability can only be achieved through the application of these two methods together, thus making them suitable for various fields such as environmental monitoring or industrial automation, among others.

Scalability

Due to their need to function optimally even when networks become huge and complicated, algorithms have to handle significant networks. The management of giant-scale networks entails many challenges, including high data traffic volumes, increased processing power demands, and complex routing decisions. These problems have been known to bring about various signs of poor performance, such as slow speeds, increased power consumption rates, and reduced reliability if there are no good algorithms.

Parallel distributed processing metaheuristics can solve these problems (Genetic Algorithms - GA). Particle swarm optimization particles and ant colonies are examples of metaheuristics that require significant computational resources, especially when applied to networks of large size. Hence, parallel and distributed computing methods increase the efficiency of such metaheuristics, allowing for simultaneous processing of multiple tasks and effective high performance in difficult optimization problems.

In a parallel implementation, the workload of computing is divided into multiple smaller jobs that can be executed at the same time in several processors or cores. This technique helps speed up the computational time and increases the ability of the algorithm to deal with large sets of data as well as complicated network designs. On the other hand, distributed implementations involve dividing computational tasks between several nodes or devices in a network. It not only balances the task allocation but also ensures that the approach can efficiently cater to increasing network sizes.

Integrating metaheuristic algorithms with parallel and distributed implementations can result in impressive performance and flexibility in large-scale networks. This method effectively manages higher data traffic volumes, optimizes routing patterns, and adapts to changing conditions instantly without degrading network performance. Therefore, it is the use of these advanced computing techniques that ensures stable and efficient operation of wide-ranging networks, enabling various applications, including smart cities and large-scale industrious systems.

Algorithm Parameter Tuning

The best possible functioning of metaheuristic algorithms depends greatly on the proper tuning of parameters since these algorithms are usually dependent on fine-tuned parameters. For instance, changing the mutation rate in Genetic Algorithms (GA) can greatly influence the algorithm's ability to explore the solution space, thus avoiding stagnation in local optima. In the same way, selecting the appropriate cooling schedule in Simulated Annealing (SA) is very important for ensuring a good balance between the exploration and exploitation cycles of the algorithm. It is usually a very complicated and time-consuming process to adjust these parameters precisely so as to fit into the exact characteristics that a certain problem requires.

In light of this issue, the use of automated and adaptive parameter adjustment techniques can substantially increase the metaheuristic algorithm's effectiveness. These automatic tuning methods involve various optimization processes that can result in the exploration of ideal parameter arrangements without any human effort. Best parameter configurations can be obtained through grid search, random search, or more sophisticated approaches such as Bayesian optimization, which improves both algorithm efficiency and effectiveness.

FRAMEWORK FOR OPTIMIZING ENERGY CONVERSATION BASED ON METAHEURISTIC ALGORITHMS

There are several well thought out sections that involve diverse actions from design, implementation, and testing, which are required for formulating a framework aimed at enhancing energy conservation in Wireless Sensor Networks (WSNs) using metaheuristic algorithms. This is how it is done:

Framework Overview

The aim is to increase the efficient utilization of electrical energy to elongate the longevity of the WAN while still maintaining performance standards.

Components

In wireless sensor networks, sensor nodes are used to collect data and perform local calculations. These sensor nodes are the basic components that monitor various environmental factors. The base station, which is also known as the sink, is the central node that gathers data from the sensor nodes and conducts global computations to analyze and interpret the received information. Metaheuristic algorithms are employed to apply advanced optimization strategies in order to enhance network performance and achieve energy efficiency. This results in reduced energy consumption by improving the effectiveness of several network operations, including routing of data and positioning of nodes.

FRAMEWORK ARCHITECTURE

Initialization Layer

Choosing the right spots for the sensor nodes in order to ensure the best coverage and connectivity is part of the deployment strategy. To achieve this, it is essential to observe the environment and know what the sensor network requires precisely. The efficiency of metaheuristic algorithms, which are used in this approach, is much affected by how parameters are set. Such dynamic aspects include population size (the number of potential solutions considered during every iteration) and mutation rate (a process that brings randomness into the solutions, thus making them different). If tuned correctly, these attributes can enhance both the speed and effectiveness of these algorithms, leading to better ways of placing sensor nodes.

Data Collection Layer

Information is sent into the brain from sense organs in all these things. This ensures that it gets to analysis in time and is relevant as well. Once data is captured, it stays in local storage for a while so that researchers have fast access to it before they send it and conduct more research using central systems. With this approach, we can keep the data updated all the time and manage it properly so that we can use what we have collected efficiently.

Optimization Layer

Local Optimization

Every sensor node utilizes efficient optimization approaches aimed at minimizing energy usage locally. Employing techniques such as duty cycling for power saving through alternating periods of activity with inactivity and local data aggregation to reduce the amount of data transmitted by summarizing and merging data locally are some of these ways. The combination of these strategies enhances both the energy efficiency and longevity of sensor nodes.

Global Optimization

Certain nodes or base stations use metaheuristic methods to optimize the performance of a whole network in terms of parameters like routing paths and clustering. This is made possible by the usage of algorithms such as Genetic Algorithm (GA), Particle Swarm Optimization (PSO), and Ant Colony Optimization (ACO) that together enhance the efficiency and effectiveness of a network.

Communication Layer

In order to reduce overall energy consumption in the network, the routing protocol takes advantage of optimum routing algorithms. Multiple-node data aggregation techniques reduce communication overhead by selecting representatives from many nodes. On the other hand, sleep scheduling at nodes helps save battery life as it involves switching between sleeping and active states. Consequently, these synergistic methods enhance both the efficiency and longevity of this system.

Energy Management Layer

The energy level in sensor nodes is continuously monitored for optimal performance. Prediction methods are used to forecast future energy usage and determine the remaining battery capacity. Consideration of present energy levels informs on adaptation measures that are implemented with a view to optimize energy consumption and extend the life span of the network.

Evaluation Layer

Wireless sensor networks require continuous surveillance and careful examination for efficient energy management. It also means that energy levels in sensor nodes need to be continuously monitored along with crucial performance indicators such as network lifetime, energy usage, data lag time, and packet delivery rate. The evaluation of the framework's performance should, therefore, take place under both simulated environments and real-world situations to guarantee its effectiveness. This holistic approach allows precise system adjustment, sensing potential problems and validating the different conditions' power management strategies.

DETAILED STEPS

The detailed steps are shown in Fig. (**2**) and discussed below.

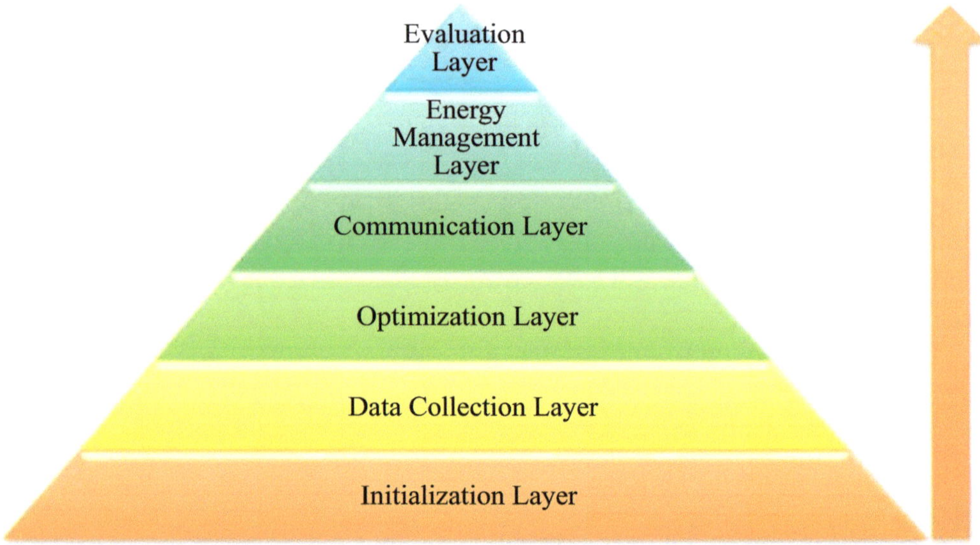

Fig. (2). Framework architecture.

Initialization Layer

The first initialization layer of a wireless sensor network framework comprises node deployment and initialization of parameters, which are the two key issues. Particle Swarm Optimization (PSO) is used to determine optimal first placements of sensor nodes during the phase when they will be deployed. This strategy aims at maximizing network coverage while minimizing energy consumption, which sets the basis for a successful network design. The framework further proceeds to set up important parameters for the metaheuristic algorithms at the subsequent levels after deploying the nodes. Initial parameters such as population size and crossover rate in Genetic Algorithms (GA) must be determined at this point. These initial parameters are critical in optimizing algorithms throughout their lifetime within the network.

Data Collection Layer

As for collecting data, sensor nodes have been designed to periodically collect data and store it within themselves. This way, it is possible to maintain continuous monitoring of the environment without having to frequently send out information. Furthermore, this stage focuses on improving energy efficiency through the duty cycling of sensing operations. Thus, the system can reduce overall time spent in active sensing by switching between periods during which active sensors sample and those that remain dormant consume minimal power. The resulting duty cycle maintains a balance by ensuring that environmental data is always up-to-date and, at the same time, saves energy. This is necessary so as to extend the life of any existing network. In addition, local data storage, together with energy-efficient sensing using duty cycling, forms the foundation for sustainable data collection in wireless sensor networks.

Optimization Layer

The optimization layer employs local and global strategies to increase network productivity. Local duty cycling pattern adjustments are achieved through Genetic Algorithms (GA) by making nodes switch between active or sleeping states in order to save electricity. Local data aggregation means merging data at the node level, thus reducing the number of transmissions. In the global framework, Ant Colony Optimization (ACO) is used for designing energy conscious clusters with their respective hybridization. Based on energy levels and their position within it, cluster heads are chosen from among them. Route optimization takes place using Particle Swarm Optimization (PSO), which identifies optimal paths that minimize energy expenditure while, at the same time, maximizing distance coverage. Ideally, these routing paths change with respect to current conditions in place guaranteeing continuous improvement in terms of power consumption throughout the network as well as communication effectiveness.

Communication Layer

There are many ways in which the framework's communication layer enhances data delivery and conserves energy. The core of this system is a highly efficient routing protocol that uses Particle Swarm Optimization (PSO) for dynamically identifying energy efficient paths within the network. This routing mechanism adapts itself to changing node energy levels and network topology so that it always determines the most power-optimal path based on current conditions. To reduce the amount of data that has to be communicated, hierarchical aggregation techniques have been utilized by the system. This means merging data at different levels from within the hierarchy before sending it out to base station Hubs. Also, nodes in low-power sleep mode during periods of inactivity as a result of Genetic Algorithm (GA) sleep scheduling strategies have been adopted. Such a holistic approach towards communication management leads to a massive reduction in energy use alongside effective transmission of information across the entire network.

Energy Management Layer

The energy management layer has a comprehensive strategy for monitoring and optimizing energy consumption in the entire network. Real-time energy monitoring systems are installed in all nodes and always keep track of their power tendency. All nodes relay their energy levels to the base station at regular intervals, thus creating a full picture of energy distribution across the network. In addition to this, the framework employs predictive modeling techniques to determine future patterns of energy consumption. By investigating past data, it is able to forecast energy demands while also recognizing potential barriers. This predictive ability allows for proactive node activity changes and exact metaheuristic parameter adjustments. Utilization of adaptive management strategies makes certain that it uses its energies effectively, extends the life span of the network, and allows for uninterrupted operations irrespective of varying amounts of available energy supply.

Evaluation Layer

The evaluation layer of this framework relates a commendable approach in determining the effectiveness of the energy-saving strategies. Four fundamental indicators of the performance of this system are as follows: network lifespan (the time before the first node becomes energy deficit), total energy consumption (sum total in usage across all nodes), data latency (*i.e.*, the interval from when data leaves transmission device until it arrives at the base station), and the of packets delivered accurately (this equals to the total divided by what was transmitted correctly). In order to give an inclusive assessment of these aspects, the approach incorporates simulation and real-life testing methods. NS-3 and OMNeT++ are high level network simulation tools that are used for simulating and evaluating the performance in different scenarios. This is backed by carrying out field tests where the architecture is set up within real-world wireless sensor networks in order to examine its performance. Through both simulation and real-life testing, the energy management system is assessed in both controlled conditions and practical situations, which guarantees a solid universal evaluation.

METAHEURISTIC ALGORITHMS

Genetic Algorithm (GA)

In the framework, the Genetic Algorithm (GA) component uses a systematized means to enhance answers for node scheduling and routes [13]. It is through encoding that possible solutions are represented as chromosomes, thus facilitating rapid input handling and evaluation. Selection will then identify the best alternatives according to pre-defined standards for reproduction purposes. Through crossover and mutation stages, new answers are formed from previously existing ones, thus bringing about variety, which might improve designs. A fitness function is critical when assessing all options through such processes. The function considers the energy consumption levels alongside the overall function of the whole network, making every likelihood sound. The GA keeps refining this again and again in order to find optimal settings characterized by reasonable power utilization compared to stable fulfillment of networks' purposes.

Application: Genetic algorithms enhance node scheduling and routing by emulating natural selection processes, hence assuring efficient resource usage and decreased energy consumption.

Alignment: The use of Genetic Algorithms in smart agriculture for the positioning of soil moisture sensors directly substantiates the chapter's assertion about energy saving and the effective functioning of sensor networks.

Particle Swarm Optimization (PSO)

The part of the framework that uses PSO works by having a set of particles, where each particle symbolizes a viable solution for node positioning or routing paths [14]. The particles move about the space of possible solutions and adjust their positions through both personal experiences and collective knowledge possessed by the swarm. The velocity and position updates determine how each particle moves. This way, particles can easily wander around the solution space and later converge to desired configurations. While moving, they are constantly assessed for fitness levels based on criteria including energy efficiency and network coverage, among others. Its purpose is to guide the search of the swarm by identifying optimal solutions with respect to other important factors such as cost and Quality of Service (QoS). In doing so, PSO achieves optimal arrangements within which there is a good balance between energy costs on the one hand, while on the other, it is able to achieve widespread network coverage in its search for these arrangements.

Application: PSO optimizes node location and routing *via* swarm behavior simulations, resulting in energy-efficient architectures.

Alignment: Its use in wildlife conservation, particularly in monitoring animal migrations, substantiates the chapter's focus on energy efficiency and adaptation in fluctuating conditions.

Ant Colony Optimization (ACO)

To discover optimal routing patterns in the wireless sensor network, the ACO component of the framework imitates the behavior of ant colonies [15]. The method uses virtual ants as agents to explore different routing options within the network. These pheromone levels are influenced by ants that travel through various paths, thus increasing the concentration on routes that exhibit higher energy efficiency. Laying pheromones is a technique that creates an enduring cycle in which effective paths are reinforced over time. Choosing a path is done probabilistically, where ants base their decisions on both pheromone levels and heuristic information related to the architecture and energy states of the network. This stochastic choice allows for the exploration of new possible routes while still favoring those that have been shown to be effective before it. After several repetitions, the Ant Colony Optimization (ACO) algorithm ultimately reaches good or almost good routing options that take energy efficiency into consideration.

Application: Ant Colony Optimization (ACO) determines optimum routing patterns based on ant foraging behavior, hence minimizing communication expenses.

Alignment: The use of ACO in logistics mirrors its function in WSNs, illustrating how natural behaviors may guide energy-efficient routing methodologies.

Artificial Bee Colony (ABC)

A multi-phase approach is used by the ABC algorithm [16] in the framework in order to optimize energy management solutions for wireless sensor networks. The Employed Bees phase is the first step where local explorations around existing solutions are carried out so as to find possible improvements. Solutions are selected probabilistically according to their fitness during the Onlooker Bees phase, which allows for a more hypothetical examination of alternate areas within the solution space. Moreover, this phase substitutes poorly performing answers with randomly produced alternatives, making it possible for scout bees to not get stuck in suboptimal environments. The next stage entails mutation operation on some components of the solutions that resemble what happens when scout bees create new alternatives. A fitness function that evaluates both energy consumption and total network performance is used to constantly evaluate the quality of each solution. The ABC algorithm employs a holistic strategy to effectively move through the solution space. It strikes a balance between exploiting existing successful solutions and exploring new avenues. This allows the algorithm to find optimal energy management techniques for wireless sensor networks.

Application: ABC enhances energy management by emulating the behavior of bee colonies, effectively balancing exploration and exploitation.

Alignment: ABC's use in telecommunications for dynamic routing corresponds with assertions of enhancing network durability and decreasing operating expenses.

Grey Wolf Optimizer (GWO)

The algorithm in the GWO framework emulates the social hierarchy and hunting behavior of grey wolf packs to optimize energy management solutions for wireless sensor networks [17]. The top three solutions, commonly known as Alpha, Beta, and Delta wolves, are selected based on their respective fitness scores. These dominant wolves supervise the entire pack's search. In a unique way, other (wolf) solutions modify their positions depending on Alpha, Beta, and Delta wolves' locations in this algorithm. This mimics how a group of wolves surrounds its prey while hunting them down. Exploration and exploitation behaviors among wolves further emulate the process of mutation, enabling them to perform extensive searches and fine-tune solutions accurately. A fitness function that considers energy consumption and total network performance assesses any solution during optimization. Through such procedures, GWO effectively finds an optimal solution for energy management with a balance between global exploration and local utilization.

Application: GWO simulates wolf pack dynamics to enhance work allocation and energy distribution.

Alignment: GWO's function in healthcare monitoring reinforces the chapter's emphasis on scalable and efficient data transfer options.

Lion Optimization Algorithm (LOA)

Wireless sensor networks may benefit from better energy management using the Lion Optimization Algorithm (LOA), a system based on the social behavior and lifestyle of lion prides [18]. The selection procedure makes the optimal solutions available from both pride lions and nomadic groups representing different regions in the field of solutions. Cross-breeding activities among mating pride lions are responsible for creating offspring who have characteristics of winning parents. Meanwhile, mutations serve as mechanisms for territory acquisition as well as following wandering behaviors so that there is variation and investigation into new solution spaces. This is done so that one does not get trapped in local optima and also discovers the best alternatives globally. Each solution (incarnated by a lion) during optimization is assessed by a fitness function that looks at energy consumption and the overall performance of the network as a whole. In this manner, LOA creates a balancing act between using successful solutions found in groups with searching for new ones through wandering behavior. Thus, it facilitates powerful and efficient energy management strategies for wireless sensor network systems.

Application: LOA enhances energy distribution by emulating lion pride behavior, hence assuring equitable energy usage.

Alignment: The deployment of LOA in smart grids substantiates the chapter's assertion about flexibility in controlling peak energy needs.

Mayfly Optimization Algorithm (MOA)

The Genetic Algorithm (GA) in the framework applies the principle of natural selection and genetics to increase the quality of energy management systems in wireless sensor networks [19]. The most effective male solutions, which are to be used for reproduction with female ones, are selected using a selection method (imitation of biological selection). Subsequently, the crossover process involves mixing selected male and female solutions together to obtain offspring. Such offspring can be referred to as new potential solutions possessing both parents' characteristics. In order to preserve genetic variety or explore new territories in search space, mutation is performed by making small random changes on some offspring solutions, thus preventing it from prematurely converging towards local optima and making it possible to find better global ones later. Any option during optimization should have its own fitness function that will measure energy consumption and overall network performance. Therefore, this method allows GA to enable energy management practices that are more efficient and effective through different generations, hence striking a balance between known successful ones against those yet unknown alternatives.

The MOA application employs the concepts of natural selection and genetics to enhance energy management in Wireless Sensor Networks (WSNs).

Mechanism: Male and female solutions are chosen based on their fitness, namely energy efficiency and network performance. Crossover amalgamates traits from both progenitors to produce offspring (novel solutions). Mutation guarantees genetic variety and averts premature convergence to local optima.

Relevance: Through repeated enhancement of solutions across generations, MOA equilibrates exploration and exploitation, hence augmenting energy efficiency and network performance.

Owl Search Algorithm (OSA)

In terms of selection, crossover, mutation, and fitness evaluation, the Owl Search Algorithm employs its own peculiar approach [20]. The efficiency of various solutions is evaluated during the selection phase by analyzing their ability to find prey, which is taken as a measure of fitness. Unlike traditional evolutionary algorithms, the Owl Search Algorithm avoids crossover in an explicit manner. It mainly relies on some position update techniques that provide new solutions. Again, the mutation is done by randomly altering owls' locations, which mimics their exploratory behavior while searching for food. To rate the quality of solutions, energy consumption and network performance are two critical components of the fitness function. This way, the algorithm focuses not only on how well it performs but also considers how many resources an efficient operation consumes.

Application: OSA assesses prospective solutions according to their "fitness," analogous to an owl's capacity to detect prey (energy-efficient solutions in WSNs).

Mechanism: Utilizes position-update strategies for producing new solutions, eschewing standard crossover methods.

Mutation simulates exploring activity by randomly modifying owl locations.

Relevance: OSA emphasizes performance and resource efficiency, providing a simplified optimization method devoid of the intricacies associated with conventional evolutionary procedures.

Artificial Fish Swarm Algorithm (AFSA)

In the selection part of the Fish School Search algorithm, it is food density that serves as a measure of process efficiency in identifying options that seem most applicable [21]. In contrast with traditional methods used in evolutionary algorithms, the Fish School Search method rarely involves any form of crossover. Instead, it relies more heavily on predation and mimicry as behaviors to come up with new solutions. Fishes' random movements lead to changes that can thus help discover unknown areas within a given solution space, as mutations are carried out without any specific direction. The fitness function is important for evaluating how good solutions are in terms of energy consumption and network measures. This elaborate fitness evaluation ensures that our algorithm not only enhances its performance but also looks at resource efficiency in a network.

Application: AFSA enhances WSNs by using fish swarm behaviors, including predation and mimicry, to navigate the solution space.

Mechanism: Selection is predicated on food density, acting as an indicator of process efficiency.

Predation and stochastic movements (mutation) facilitate the exploration of uncharted regions inside the search space.

Relevance: AFSA offers a resource-efficient optimization framework aimed at identifying high-performing solutions *via* decentralized, adaptive behaviors.

Dolphin Echolocation

The Dolphin Echolocation Algorithm has a unique method of selection, crossover, mutation, and fitness evaluation based on the behavior of dolphins [22, 23]. In the selection phase, the algorithm finds the best solutions using echolocation feedback as a fitness metric. The crossover process in this algorithm involves merging signals from different dolphins to improve and optimize solutions, thus replicating the cooperative spirit of dolphin communication. Random changes are made to mutations for better echolocation accuracy and exploration into hitherto unexplored areas within the solution space. A fitness function is critical for evaluating how good any one solution is as it takes into account energy consumption over time as well as performance on a network. It is this exhaustive fitness evaluation that assures that the algorithm not only finds solutions in the most efficient way but also considers how much resources it consumes while operating on them.

Application: Enhances underwater sensor network routing by emulating echolocation for energy-efficient navigation.

Alignment: Its use in marine ecosystem monitoring substantiates assertions of effective operations in specialized contexts.

Cuckoo Search

The Cuckoo Search technique uses a unique approach to selection, crossover, mutation, and fitness evaluation that originates from brood parasitism in cuckoo birds [24]. While selecting the procedure, the algorithm finds out the "best nests," which are the most excellent solutions, through fitness evaluation. In contrast to conventional evolutionary algorithms, Cuckoo Search generally does not employ crossover. Instead, it depends on Lévy flights to generate new solutions that mimic cuckoo's flying patterns. By replacing some solutions with new random ones, the mutation occurs similar to how a bird abandons an insufficient nest. Indeed, the fitness function is an essential tool used to estimate how good solutions are with respect to energy usage and network performance. This comprehensive fitness assessment ensures that the algorithm can not only find optimal solutions but also optimize its resource use in the network.

Application: Enhances resource allocation by emulating cuckoo bird behavior.

Alignment: Its use in automated software testing underscores its versatility in computational optimization tasks, reinforcing the chapter's assertions.

Firefly Algorithm

Fireflies' bioluminescent activities serve as a basis for this unique selection, crossover, mutation, and fitness evaluation approach in the Firefly Algorithm [25]. During the selection stage, the algorithm evaluates its most optimal solutions based on their brightness (which shows how fit they are) such that increasing brightness implies the solution's desirability. The algorithm, therefore, employs an attractiveness-based movement technique, unlike traditional crossover. In this technique, fireflies are directed towards the best firefly solutions (thereby looking much brighter than other lights). Randomly altering solutions leads to a mutation that allows the discovery of unexplored regions within the solution space. A fitness function is crucial in estimating solution quality, considering both energy used and network performance. Thus, through such extensive fitness assessment, it ensures that not only does the algorithm maximize its ability to search for the best answers but also accounts for efficient resource use within the network.

Application: Enhances task optimization *via* the use of firefly bioluminescence behavior to increase energy efficiency.

Alignment: Its use in electrical networks corresponds with the chapter's emphasis on minimizing energy loss and enhancing load balancing.

Dragonfly Algorithm

The Dragonfly Algorithm uses a unique way of encoding, selection, crossover, mutation, and fitness evaluation, which is based on the collective behavior of dragonflies [26, 27]. In the encoding phase, for instance, chromosomes may represent node schedules and routing paths and hence, the various positions occupied by different dragonflies in a search space. This swarming behavior is utilized as a selection objective whereby dragonflies with high fitness values are selected to influence movement and update others in the swarm. Unlike other traditional evolutionary algorithms, however, crossovers are hardly used in this algorithm. Instead, it generates new solutions from local search or the influence of neighboring dragonflies together with the best global position(s). Mutation entails position update equations with random perturbations, which ensure that there is diversity within the population. In evaluating the quality of solutions through fitness function, both energy consumption and network performance have been taken into consideration. The comprehensive fitness assessment system ensures that capability to find optimal solutions is not only designed for effectiveness but efficiency regarding resources utilization across networks as well.

Application: Improves routing by emulating dragonfly swarming behavior for dynamic adaptability.

Alignment: Its applications in environmental monitoring illustrate its significance to the chapter's emphasis on flexibility across many contexts.

Bat Algorithm

The Bat Algorithm is an algorithm that incorporates an innovative approach to encoding, selection, crossover, mutation, and fitness evaluation based on echolocation, which bats perform [28]. Bats' positioning in the search space is represented by chromosomes during the encoding phase, with node schedules being one of such solution. The probability of selecting a better alternative is indirectly influenced by their loudness and pulse rate, thus making the selection process dependent on bats' characteristics. Crossover does not appear in the standard Bat Algorithm explicitly; instead, new solutions are obtained by merging the current positions of bats with the global optimum position. Mutation occurs through random walks, leading to position changes while also changing frequencies, enabling exploration of solution space. To evaluate the quality of solutions, its fitness function assesses each bat according to how much energy it saves in addition to increasing network performance. This detailed fitness evaluation allows this algorithm to focus on effectiveness when detecting good solutions while taking into account resource use efficiency within its network.

Application: Bat Algorithm (BA) is derived from the echolocation capabilities of bats and is used to enhance energy management and performance in Wireless Sensor Networks (WSNs).

Mechanism:

- *Encoding:* The locations of bats in the search space are represented as chromosomes, with various solutions like node schedules.
- *Selection:* Loudness and pulse rate affect the likelihood of choosing superior solutions, emulating the natural behavior of bats.
- *Crossover:* Implicitly integrates existing positions with the global optimum to provide novel solutions.
- *Mutation:* Facilitates variety *via* stochastic processes and frequency modifications, allowing for the study of the solution landscape.

- *Fitness Evaluation:* Evaluates energy conservation and network efficacy, emphasizing effectiveness and resource use efficiency.

Relevance: By emulating natural echolocation, BA harmonizes exploration and exploitation to improve network performance and identify ideal energy-saving designs.

CONCLUSION

Having been developed to be flexible and adaptable, these metaheuristic algorithms can be employed in a range of applications. Comprehending their fundamental principles and essential characteristics, such as security, interoperability, standards, scalability, complexity, data management, and quality of service, is crucial for the successful application and improvement of these algorithmic methodologies to diverse technical and industrial challenges. Metaheuristic algorithms have arisen as effective and versatile instruments for addressing intricate optimization challenges in Wireless Sensor Networks (WSNs). These algorithms are inspired by natural phenomena, including evolutionary processes, animal behaviors, and swarm intelligence, to provide energy-efficient and effective solutions for node scheduling, routing, and energy management. Each algorithm—such as Genetic Algorithm (GA), Particle Swarm Optimization (PSO), Ant Colony Optimization (ACO), and Artificial Bee Colony (ABC)—employs distinct mechanisms, including selection, crossover, mutation, and fitness evaluation to optimize resource allocation and improve network performance. By connecting their methodology with practical applications, these algorithms exhibit adaptability and relevance across several sectors, including smart agriculture, animal protection, telecommunications, healthcare monitoring, and smart grids. Their intrinsic capacity to balance exploration and exploitation enables them to discern near-optimal solutions, even in dynamic and limited settings. The use of metaheuristic algorithms in WSN frameworks enhances energy efficiency and operational lifespan while demonstrating their capability to tackle wider issues in computational optimization. As technological breakthroughs progress, these algorithms are anticipated to further improve, offering new and sustainable solutions to rising challenges across diverse sectors.

REFERENCES

[1] N. Bacanin, U. Arnaut, M. Zivkovic, T. Bezdan, and T.A. Rashid, "Energy efficient clustering in wireless sensor networks by opposition-based initialization bat algorithm", *Computer Networks and Inventive Communication Technologies Proceedings of Fourth ICCNCT 2021,,* vol. 75, pp. 1-16, 2022.
[http://dx.doi.org/10.1007/978-981-16-3728-5_1]

[2] S. Chaurasia, and K. kumar, "ACRA: Adaptive meta-heuristic based Clustering and Routing Algorithm for IoT-assisted wireless sensor network", *Peer-to-Peer Netw. Appl.,* vol. 16, no. 5, pp. 2186-2201, 2023.

[http://dx.doi.org/10.1007/s12083-023-01505-w]

[3] S. Chaurasia, K. Kumar, and N. Kumar, "Mocraw: A meta-heuristic optimized cluster head selection based routing algorithm for WSNs", *Ad Hoc Networks*, 141, 15 March 2023, 103079. Available from: https://www.sciencedirect.com/science/article/pii/S1570870522002517

[4] M. Zivkovic, N. Bacanin, E. Tuba, I. Strumberger, T. Bezdan, and M. Tuba, "Wireless sensor networks life time optimization based on the improved firefly algorithm," in *Proc.* 2020 *Int. Wireless Commun. Mobile Comput. Conf. (IWCMC)*, 2020.

[5] G. P. Gupta, "Improved cuckoo search-based clustering protocol for wireless sensor networks", in *Procedia Comput. Sci.*, vol. 125, pp. 234–240, 2018.

[6] N. Mahesh, and S. Vijayachitra, "DECSA: hybrid dolphin echolocation and crow search optimization for cluster-based energy-aware routing in WSN", *Neural Comput. Appl.,* vol. 31, no. S1, pp. 47-62, 2019.
[http://dx.doi.org/10.1007/s00521-018-3637-4]

[7] T.-q. Wu, M. Yao, and J.-h. Yang, "Dolphin swarm algorithm", *Front. Inf. Technol. Electron. Eng.*, vol. 17, pp. 717–729, Oct. 2016.
[http://dx.doi.org/10.1631/FITEE.1500287]

[8] F. Pourpanah, R. Wang, C.P. Lim, X.Z. Wang, and D. Yazdani, "A review of artificial fish swarm algorithms: Recent advances and applications", *Artif. Intell. Rev.,* vol. 56, no. 3, pp. 1867-1903, 2023.
[http://dx.doi.org/10.1007/s10462-022-10214-4]

[9] S. Nazemi and R. Khorsand, "C-KHCS: Multi-objective workflow scheduling using chaotic krill herd optimization and improved cuckoo search in fog computing", *IEEE Trans. Serv. Comput.*, 2024, 17; 5; 2095 - 2108.

[10] P. Jasmine Lizy, and N. Chenthalir Indra, "An efficient routing protocol for coherent energy using mayfly optimization algorithm in heterogeneous wireless sensor networks", *Cogn. Comput. Syst.,* vol. 5, no. 1, pp. 30-41, 2023.
[http://dx.doi.org/10.1049/ccs2.12074]

[11] M. Saxena, S. Dutta, and B.K. Singh, "Optimal routing using whale optimization and lion optimization algorithm in WSN", *Wirel. Netw.,* vol. 30, no. 3, pp. 1601-1618, 2024.
[http://dx.doi.org/10.1007/s11276-023-03607-y]

[12] S.R. Nabavi, N. Osati Eraghi, and J. Akbari Torkestani, "Intelligent optimization of QoS in wireless sensor networks using multiobjective grey wolf optimization algorithm", *Wirel. Commun. Mob. Comput.,* vol. 2022, pp. 1-15, 2022.
[http://dx.doi.org/10.1155/2022/5385502]

[13] B. Rambabu, A. Venugopal Reddy, and S. Janakiraman, "Hybrid artificial bee colony and monarchy butterfly optimization algorithm (HABC-MBOA)-based cluster head selection for WSNs", *J. King Saud Univ. – Comput. Inf. Sci.*, vol. 34, no. 5, pp. 1895–1905, 2022.
[http://dx.doi.org/10.1016/j.jksuci.2019.12.006]

[14] "Mann, P.S. and Singh, S., 2017. Artificial bee colony metaheuristic for energy-efficient clustering and routing in wireless sensor networks. Soft Computing, 21, pp.6699-6712. - Google Search." Accessed: Jul. 19, 2024.
[http://dx.doi.org/10.1007/s00500-016-2220-0]

[15] S. Kumar, and R. Agrawal, "A comprehensive survey on meta-heuristic-based energy minimization routing techniques for wireless sensor network: classification and challenges", *J. Supercomput.,* vol. 78, no. 5, pp. 6612-6663, 2022.
[http://dx.doi.org/10.1007/s11227-021-04128-1]

[16] P.S. Mann, and S. Singh, "Artificial bee colony metaheuristic for energy-efficient clustering and routing in wireless sensor networks", *Soft Comput.,* vol. 21, no. 22, pp. 6699-6712, 2017. [http://dx.doi.org/10.1007/s00500-016-2220-0]

[17] A. Jain, "Unequal clustering protocols for wireless sensor networks—taxonomy, comparison and simulation", *Wirel. Pers. Commun.,* vol. 124, no. 1, pp. 517-571, 2022. [http://dx.doi.org/10.1007/s11277-021-09372-5]

[18] K. Guleria, and A.K. Verma, "Meta-heuristic ant colony optimization based unequal clustering for wireless sensor network", *Wirel. Pers. Commun.,* vol. 105, no. 3, pp. 891-911, 2019. [http://dx.doi.org/10.1007/s11277-019-06127-1]

[19] N. Rana, M.S.A. Latiff, S.M. Abdulhamid, and H. Chiroma, "Whale optimization algorithm: a systematic review of contemporary applications, modifications and developments", *Neural Comput. Appl.,* vol. 32, no. 20, pp. 16245-16277, 2020. [http://dx.doi.org/10.1007/s00521-020-04849-z]

[20] S. Kumar, and R. Agrawal, "A comprehensive survey on meta-heuristic-based energy minimization routing techniques for wireless sensor network: classification and challenges", *J. Supercomput.,* vol. 78, no. 5, pp. 6612-6663, 2022. [http://dx.doi.org/10.1007/s11227-021-04128-1]

[21] M. Saxena, S. Dutta, and B.K. Singh, "Optimal routing using whale optimization and lion optimization algorithm in WSN", *Wirel. Netw.,* vol. 30, no. 3, pp. 1601-1618, 2024. [http://dx.doi.org/10.1007/s11276-023-03607-y]

[22] S.R. Nabavi, N. Osati Eraghi, and J. Akbari Torkestani, "Intelligent optimization of QoS in wireless sensor networks using multiobjective grey wolf optimization algorithm", *Wirel. Commun. Mob. Comput.,* vol. 2022, pp. 1-15, 2022. [http://dx.doi.org/10.1155/2022/5385502]

[23] P.S. Mann, and S. Singh, "Improved artificial bee colony metaheuristic for energy-efficient clustering in wireless sensor networks", *Artif. Intell. Rev.,* vol. 51, no. 3, pp. 329-354, 2019. [http://dx.doi.org/10.1007/s10462-017-9564-4]

[24] P.S. Mann, and S. Singh, "Artificial bee colony metaheuristic for energy-efficient clustering and routing in wireless sensor networks", *Soft Comput.,* vol. 21, no. 22, pp. 6699-6712, 2017. [http://dx.doi.org/10.1007/s00500-016-2220-0]

[25] K. Guleria, and A.K. Verma, "Meta-heuristic ant colony optimization based unequal clustering for wireless sensor network", *Wirel. Pers. Commun.,* vol. 105, no. 3, pp. 891-911, 2019. [http://dx.doi.org/10.1007/s11277-019-06127-1]

[26] G.A. Senthil, A. Raaza, and N. Kumar, "Internet of things energy efficient cluster-based routing using hybrid particle swarm optimization for wireless sensor network", *Wirel. Pers. Commun.,* vol. 122, no. 3, pp. 2603-2619, 2022. [http://dx.doi.org/10.1007/s11277-021-09015-9]

[27] E. Heidari, A. Movaghar, H. Motameni, and B. Barzegar, "A novel approach for clustering and routing in WSN using genetic algorithm and equilibrium optimizer", *Int. J. Commun. Syst.,* vol. 35, no. 10, p. e5148, 2022. [http://dx.doi.org/10.1002/dac.5148]

[28] S. Kumar, and R. Agrawal, "A comprehensive survey on meta-heuristic-based energy minimization routing techniques for wireless sensor network: classification and challenges", *J. Supercomput.,* vol. 78, no. 5, pp. 6612-6663, 2022. [http://dx.doi.org/10.1007/s11227-021-04128-1]

[29] R. Liemthong, C. Srithapon, P. K. Ghosh and R. Chatthaworn, “Home energy management strategy-based meta-heuristic optimization for electrical energy cost minimization considering TOU tariffs”, *Energies* 2022, 15(2), 537.
[http://dx.doi.org/10.3390/en15020537]

[30] Y. Han, G. Li, R. Xu, J. Su, J. Li, and G. We, “Clustering the wireless sensor networks: a meta-heuristic approach”, IEEE Access, 2024; 8. Available from: https://ieeexplore.ieee.org/abstract/document/9272725/
[http://dx.doi.org/10.1109/ACCESS.2020.3041118]

[31] S. Chaurasia, K. Kumar, N. K.-A. H. Networks, and undefined 2023, “Mocraw: A meta-heuristic optimized cluster head selection based routing algorithm for wsns,” Elsevier, Accessed: Jul. 19, 2024. Available from: https://www.sciencedirect.com/science/article/pii/S1570870522002517

[32] Z.A. Khan, A. Zafar, S. Javaid, S. Aslam, M.H. Rahim, and N. Javaid, "Hybrid meta-heuristic optimization based home energy management system in smart grid", *J. Ambient Intell. Humaniz. Comput.,* vol. 10, no. 12, pp. 4837-4853, 2019.
[http://dx.doi.org/10.1007/s12652-018-01169-y]

[33] L. Cao, Y. Cai, and Y. Yue, "Swarm intelligence-based performance optimization for mobile wireless sensor networks: survey, challenges, and future directions", *IEEE Access,* vol. 7, pp. 161524-161553, 2019.
[http://dx.doi.org/10.1109/ACCESS.2019.2951370]

[34] N. Krishnan, M. Karthikeyan, and Institute of Electrical and Electronics Engineers., 2010 IEEE International Conference on Computational Intelligence and Computing Research: 28th & 29th Dec 2010, Tamilnadu College of Engineering, Coimbatore - 641 659 Tamilnadu, India. IEEE, 2010.

[35] X. Huan, H. He, T. Wang, Q. Wu, and H. Hu, "A timestamp-free time synchronization scheme based on reverse asymmetric framework for practical resource-constrained wireless sensor networks", *IEEE Trans. Commun.,* vol. 70, no. 9, pp. 6109-6121, 2022.
[http://dx.doi.org/10.1109/TCOMM.2022.3188830]

[36] S. Peyghami, P. Palensky, M. Fotuhi-Firuzabad, and F. Blaabjerg, "System-level design for reliability and maintenance scheduling in modern power electronic-based power systems", *IEEE Open Access J. Power Energy,* vol. 7, pp. 414-429, 2020.
[http://dx.doi.org/10.1109/OAJPE.2020.3029229]

[37] R. Mittal, and M.P.S. Bhatia, "Wireless sensor networks for monitoring the environmental activities", *2010 IEEE International Conference on Computational Intelligence and Computing Research, ICCIC 2010,* pp. 348-352, 2010.
[http://dx.doi.org/10.1109/ICCIC.2010.5705791]

[38] Z. Al Aghbari, A.M. Khedr, W. Osamy, I. Arif, and D.P. Agrawal, "Routing in wireless sensor networks using optimization techniques: A survey", *Wirel. Pers. Commun.,* vol. 111, no. 4, pp. 2407-2434, 2020.
[http://dx.doi.org/10.1007/s11277-019-06993-9]

[39] J. Amutha, S. Sharma, and J. Nagar, "WSN strategies based on sensors, deployment, sensing models, coverage and energy efficiency: Review, approaches and open issues", *Wirel. Pers. Commun.*, 2020; 111, 1089–1115.
[http://dx.doi.org/10.1007/s11277-019-06903-z]

[40] M.Z. Ghawy, G.A. Amran, H. AlSalman, E. Ghaleb, J. Khan, A.A. AL-Bakhrani, A.M. Alziadi, A. Ali, and S.S. Ullah, "An effective wireless sensor network routing protocol based on particle swarm optimization algorithm", *Wirel. Commun. Mob. Comput.,* vol. 2022, pp. 1-13, 2022.
[http://dx.doi.org/10.1155/2022/8455065]

[41] C. Xu, Z. Xiong, G. Zhao, and S. Yu, "An energy-efficient region source routing protocol for lifetime maximization in WSN", *IEEE Access,* vol. 7, pp. 135277-135289, 2019.
[http://dx.doi.org/10.1109/ACCESS.2019.2942321]

[42] S. G. Jung, S. Yeom, M. H. Shon, D. S. Kim, and H. Choo, "Clustering wireless sensor networks based on bird flocking behavior", *Computational Science and Its Applications -- ICCSA 2015*, vol. 9158, pp. 128–137, 2015. [http://dx.doi.org/10.1007/978-3-319-21410-8_10]

[43] K. Guleria, and A.K. Verma, "Meta-heuristic ant colony optimization based unequal clustering for wireless sensor network", *Wirel. Pers. Commun.,* vol. 105, no. 3, pp. 891-911, 2019. [http://dx.doi.org/10.1007/s11277-019-06127-1]

[44] B. M. Sahoo, H. M. Pandey, and T. Amgoth, "A whale optimization (WOA): meta-heuristic based energy improvement clustering in wireless sensor networks", *IEEE Xplore*, 2021. Available from: ieeexplore.ieee.org [http://dx.doi.org/10.1109/Confluence51648.2021.9377181]

[45] A.H. Halim, I. Ismail, and S. Das, "Performance assessment of the metaheuristic optimization algorithms: an exhaustive review", *Artif. Intell. Rev.,* vol. 54, no. 3, pp. 2323-2409, 2021. [http://dx.doi.org/10.1007/s10462-020-09906-6]

[46] M.H. Qais, H.M. Hasanien, and S. Alghuwainem, "Transient search optimization: a new meta-heuristic optimization algorithm", *Appl. Intell.,* vol. 50, no. 11, pp. 3926-3941, 2020. [http://dx.doi.org/10.1007/s10489-020-01727-y]

[47] X.S Yang, "Metaheuristic optimization: algorithm analysis and open problems", *Experimental Algorithms, 2011.* Available from: https://link.springer.com/chapter/10.1007/978-3-642-20662-7_2

[48] X.S Yang, "Optimization and metaheuristic algorithms in engineering", in *Metaheuristics in Water, Geotechnical and Transport Engineering*, 2024, 1-20. Available from: https://books.google.com/books?hl=en&lr=&id=Q8GNZ0ujqQUC&oi=fnd&pg=PA1&dq=meta+heuristic+optimization+algorithms&ots=q4YsQCz9lX&sig=GgbiJvfIUf73N9MlV5hnrK2Qzyg

[49] A. H. Gandomi, X.-S. Yang, S. Talatahari, and A. H. Alavi, "Metaheuristic algorithms in modeling and optimization", in *Metaheuristic Applications in Structures and Infrastructures*, 2013, 1-24. books.google.com [http://dx.doi.org/10.1016/B978-0-12-398364-0.00001-2]

[50] X.S Yang, "Metaheuristic optimization", *Scholarpedia*, 2011, 6(8):11472. var.scholarpedia.org, Accessed: Jul. 19, 2024. Available from: http://var.scholarpedia.org/article/Metaheuristic_optimization

[51] A. Kaveh and A. Dadras, "A novel meta-heuristic optimization algorithm: thermal exchange optimization", *Adv. Eng. Softw.*, 2017, vol. 110, pp. 69–84. Available from: https://www.sciencedirect.com/science/article/pii/S0965997817300066

[52] G. Dhiman, "SSC: A hybrid nature-inspired meta-heuristic optimization algorithm for engineering applications", *Know.-Based Syst.*, 2021;vol. 222, p. 106926. Available from: https://www.sciencedirect.com/science/article/pii/S0950705121001891

[53] Y. Zhang, A. M. Nassef, M. A. Abdelkareem, H. M. Maghrabie, and A. Baroutaji, "Review of metaheuristic optimization algorithms for power systems problems", *Sustainability* 2023, 15(12), 9434. [http://dx.doi.org/10.3390/su15129434]

[54] S. Voß " Meta-heuristics: The state of the art", in *Local Search for Planning and Scheduling*, 2001, 1-23. [http://dx.doi.org/10.1007/3-540-45612-0_1]

[55] S. Desale, A. Rasool, P. Rane, and S. Andhale, "Heuristic and Meta-heuristic Algorithms and their relevance to the real world: A survey", *Int. J. Comput. Eng. Res. Trends.*, 2015; 2; 5. Available from: https://citeseerx.ist.psu.edu/document?repid=rep1&type=pdf&doi=039da802e218c89a3c49e235af8e555b2fdfa063

[56] S. Desale, A. Rasool, S. Andhale, P. R.-Int. J. Comput. Eng. Res. Trends, and undefined 2015, "Heuristic and meta-heuristic algorithms and their relevance to the real world: a survey," Citeseer, vol. 2, pp. 296–304, 2015, Accessed: Jul. 19, 2024. Available from: https://books.google.com/books?hl=en&lr=&id=iVB_ETlh4ogC&oi=fnd&pg=PR5&dq=meta+heuristic+&ots=DycuphIMwh&sig=DjN4vouVwLgPChhHoAgfmibv2G4

[57] A. Kaveh and M. Khayatazad, "A new meta-heuristic method: Ray Optimization", *Comput. Struct.*, 2012;112–113, pp. 283–294. Available from: https://www.sciencedirect.com/science/article/pii/S0045794912002131

CHAPTER 8

Opportunities and Security Issues in Communication Engineering Using Generative AI

Charvi[1,*], **Ankita Sharma**[1] and **Yonis Gulzar**[2]

[1] *Department of Computer Science and Engineering, SGT University, Gurugram, Haryana, India*

[2] *Department of Management Information Systems, College of Business Administration, King Faisal University, Al-Ahsa 31982, Saudi Arabia*

Abstract: Generative Artificial Intelligence (GAI) is an innovative method in communication engineering that provides superior abilities in generating content and analyzing data. This cutting-edge technology has the capability to tackle security difficulties in communication networks, namely at the physical layer. Traditional AI methods generally struggle to react to changing threats and the intricacies of the channel. The versatility and analytical depth of GAI make it a highly promising tool for improving security in communication networks. This study presents a thorough examination of how GAI (General Artificial Intelligence) might enhance security at the physical layer of communication networks. It emphasizes the potential benefits of utilizing GAI's ability to comprehend intricate data patterns and its quick progress in generating content. This work seeks to investigate the possible advantages and security concerns of incorporating generative AI into communication systems by examining the overlap between GAI and communication engineering.

Keywords: Autoencoders (AEs), Diffusion Models (DMs), Generative Artificial Intelligence (GAI), Generative Adversarial Networks (GANs), Physical Layer Security, Variational Autoencoders (VAEs).

INTRODUCTION

Generative Artificial Intelligence (GAI) is a sophisticated methodology that has revolutionized the field of artificial intelligence by showcasing substantial advancements in content generation and data analysis. General Artificial Intelligence (GAI) stands out from traditional AI methods due to its remarkable ability to understand complex data patterns and adapt flexibly to the evolving nature of communication channels and cybersecurity threats [1]. The incorporation of General Artificial Intelligence (GAI) into communication engineering, together with the utilization of advanced Deep Learning methods like

* **Corresponding author Charvi:** Department of Computer Science and Engineering, SGT University, Gurugram, Haryana, India; E-mail: charvi2617@gmail.com

Shelly Gupta, Sapna Juneja & Sandeep Kautish (Eds.)
All rights reserved-© 2025 Bentham Science Publishers

Convolutional Neural Networks (CNNs) and Recurrent Neural Networks (RNNs), has significantly enhanced communication security.

This connection enables the identification of abnormalities, automatic recognition of potential dangers, and the application of flexible security measures based on real-time data analysis [2].

Traditional AI techniques frequently struggle with addressing the challenges of physical layer security due to their limited capacity to adjust to the complexities of modern communication networks. However, GAI, with its capacity to generate and evaluate data, offers viable solutions to enhance security at the physical layer of communication networks, as depicted in Fig. (**1**) [3]. GAI effectively addresses concerns related to communication secrecy, authentication, availability, resilience, and integrity by utilizing advanced technologies like Generative Adversarial Networks (GANs), Autoencoders (AEs), Variational Autoencoders (VAEs), and Diffusion Models (DMs) [4].

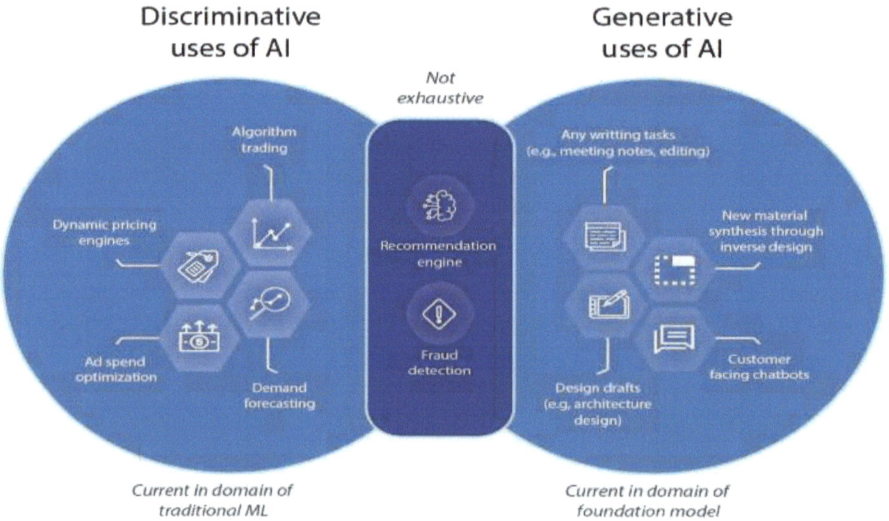

Fig. (1). Traditional ML *vs.* Generative AI: Unveiling the evolution of AI models.

GAI is an acronym representing a collection of AI technologies that are disruptive and essential in the field of communication engineering. They provide cutting-edge techniques to improve physical security. The versatility of GAI in producing varied content, comprehending intricate data patterns, and adjusting to changing threats places it as a crucial facilitator in tackling the increasing issues in safe physical layer communications and sensing [5].

LITERATURE REVIEW

Previous studies in the field of physical layer security have primarily focused on traditional artificial intelligence models and deep learning techniques to address security challenges in communication networks. The authors have investigated physical layer security solutions that utilize deep learning techniques. This research specifically concentrates on the utilization of these strategies inside the framework of 5G and forthcoming networks. However, these studies frequently lack a comprehensive analysis of the role that Generative Artificial Intelligence (GAI) plays in enhancing the security of the physical layer [6].

However, a study [7], presents a unique perspective by specifically incorporating General Artificial Intelligence (GAI) into secure physical layer communication networks. This work distinguishes itself from previous studies by focusing extensively on the ability of General Artificial Intelligence (GAI) to efficiently manage security measures, detect threats, and minimize vulnerabilities at the physical level. These aspects have not undergone comprehensive scrutiny or have only been briefly touched upon in previous studies. The survey showcases the enhancement of crucial security properties, such as communication confidentiality, authentication, availability, resilience, and integrity, through the utilization of advanced GAI models like Generative Adversarial Networks (GANs), Autoencoders (AEs), Variational Autoencoders (VAEs), and Diffusion Models (DMs).

Furthermore, the study identifies prospective avenues for future research on the utilization of General Artificial Intelligence (GAI) in the field of physical layer security. The domains encompassed are model enhancement, deployment in various settings, resource efficiency optimization, and facilitation of secure semantic communication. GAI demonstrates its remarkable capacity to enhance security measures beyond the limitations of traditional AI methods by addressing the challenges of data scarcity and incompleteness in physical layer security [8].

Prior studies have explored deep learning techniques for ensuring the security of the physical layer. Nevertheless, a survey [9] fills a significant void in the existing body of research. This paper provides a comprehensive examination of how General Artificial Intelligence (GAI) may significantly enhance security protocols in the physical layer of communication networks.

Generative Adversarial Networks (GANs) are a type of generative models that consist of a generator and a discriminator neural network, as depicted in Fig. (**2**). These networks are trained using an adversarial approach to generate genuine data samples. GANs have been widely employed for generating high-quality images, text, and several other types of material. GANs can be employed at the physical layer of communication networks to augment security characteristics. They have multiple applications, such as generating artificial data for model training, enhancing data distribution learning, and reinforcing data security and integrity [10].

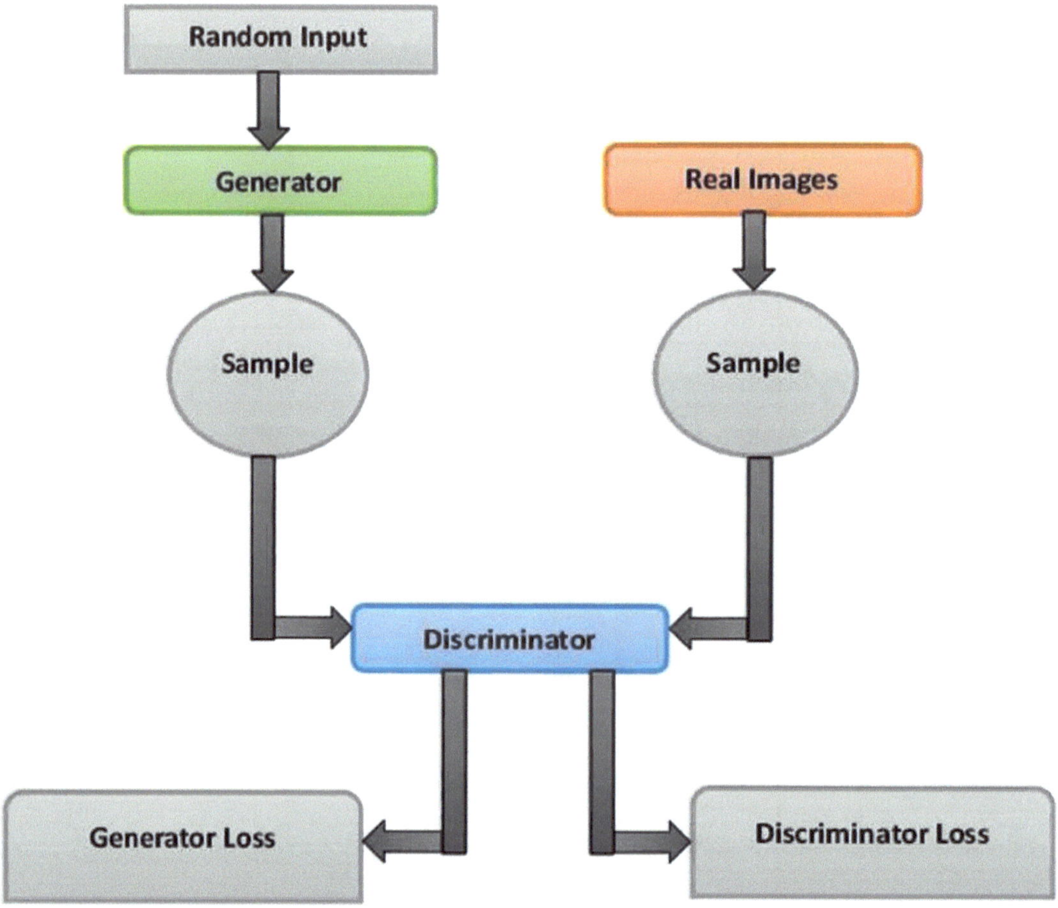

Fig. (2). Generative adversarial network structure.

Autoencoders, also referred to as AEs, are neural networks designed primarily for unsupervised learning. Their main goal is to obtain effective representations of input data within a lower-dimensional latent space, as depicted in Fig. (**3**) [11]. Autoencoders, often known as AEs, have the ability to carry out various tasks such as data compression, denoising, and feature extraction. In the field of physical layer security, AEs contribute to improving data representations for the purpose of detecting irregularities, ensuring data confidentiality, and boosting authentication processes [12, 13].

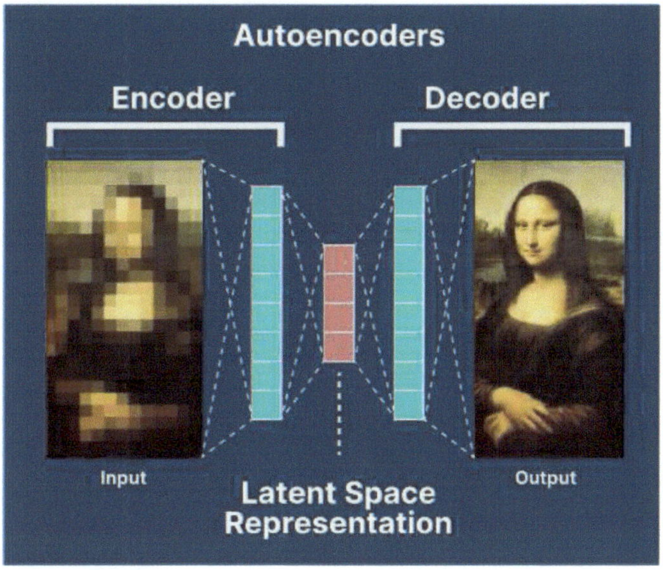

Fig. (3). Autoencoders process.

Variational Autoencoders (VAEs) are a type of autoencoder that employ probabilistic modeling to obtain meaningful latent representations of data, as depicted in Fig. (**4**) [14]. VAEs are advantageous for tasks such as generating unique data samples and gaining insights into structured latent spaces. VAEs can enhance security in the physical layer by enabling the development of secure keys, improving authentication methods, and promoting data secrecy through their ability to comprehend complex data distributions [15 - 17].

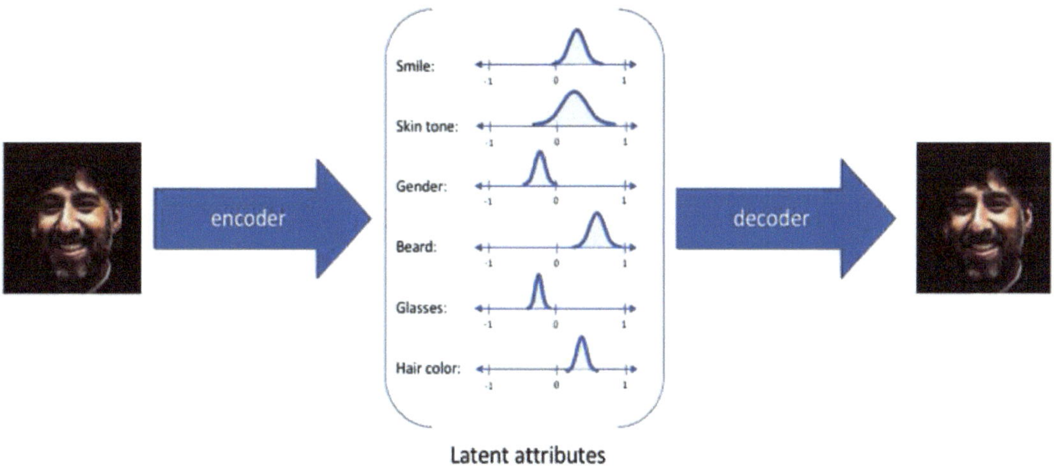

Fig. (4). Variational autoencoders.

Diffusion Models (DMs) are generative models that are influenced by the principles of non-equilibrium thermodynamics. Their goal is to acquire knowledge about the distribution of the original data by introducing noise, with the aim of approximating a normal distribution, as depicted in Fig. (**5**) [18]. Direct Messages (DMs) can be beneficial for tasks such as generating and disseminating data for educational reasons. Within the domain of physical layer security, Data Manipulations (DMs) can bolster security and privacy by employing data generation techniques that are both secure and privacy-preserving. In addition, they have the ability to enhance data secrecy and authentication processes by employing their own approach to understanding data distributions [19, 20].

Fig. (5). Diffusion and reverse diffusion process.

These specific models, including GANs, AEs, VAEs, and DMs, play a crucial role in enhancing security at the physical layer of communication networks. To do this, they utilize techniques such as producing synthetic data, optimizing data distribution learning, guaranteeing data secrecy, increasing authentication procedures, and facilitating safe key generation. Their unique abilities and approaches help address security issues and promote secure communication in networks at the physical layer [21, 22].

When integrating Generative Artificial Intelligence (GAI) into secure physical layer communication networks, there are notable disparities compared to conventional AI models and deep learning methods in terms of identifying threats, reducing vulnerabilities, and enhancing security [23 - 27].

- GAI models possess a remarkable aptitude for acquiring knowledge and adapting to ever-changing environmental circumstances in physical layer communication networks. Traditional AI models are frequently trained on specific datasets, which limits their effectiveness in unfamiliar situations. The sophisticated functionalities of GAI allow it to accurately understand complex data distributions, enabling it to dynamically adjust to changing physical properties of transmission routes and cyber threats in real time.
- Data Reconstruction and Augmentation: GAI addresses the challenges presented by inadequate and fragmented data in physical layer security by reconstructing and augmenting the data. This power surpasses the limitations of traditional AI technologies, hence enhancing the overall security of communication networks.
- Enhanced Security Measures: GAI models possess the capability to enhance crucial security features such as confidentiality of communication, verification of identity, accessibility, robustness, and data integrity. The role of GAI is vital in bolstering security measures through the execution of encrypted data transformation, processing, and the detection of cyber threats and anomalies in the network structure.
- GAI's generative capabilities have been applied in various domains, including picture and video synthesis, data augmentation, and, recently, in physical layer security for wireless communications, showcasing both efficiency and effectiveness. The effectiveness of GAI in enhancing security measures is demonstrated by its ability to perform several functions, such as encrypted communication, signal authentication, defense against attacks, anomaly detection, and adaptive signal processing.
- Case Studies: The literature emphasizes the pivotal significance of GAI in enhancing mobile network technologies, tackling existing obstacles, and providing a comprehensive understanding of generative AI and mobile edge intelligence. Moreover, the efficacy of GAI in creating, transmitting, and efficiently supervising information within wireless networks has been demonstrated. These examples illustrate the superior effectiveness of GAI in addressing security challenges in communication networks, as compared to conventional AI models.

Integrating General Artificial Intelligence (GAI) into secure physical layer communication networks offers a superior methodology for recognizing threats, mitigating vulnerabilities, and enhancing security measures compared to traditional AI models and deep learning methods [28].

CASE SCENARIOS OF GENERATIVE AI (GAI) AND PHYSICAL LAYER SECURITY

Scenario Details of Securing 5G Communication Networks: A telecom company integrates Generative AI (GAI) into its 5G infrastructure to address security challenges, particularly Distributed Denial of Service (DDoS) attacks. Generative models such as Variational Autoencoders (VAEs) are employed to analyze network traffic. These models identify abnormal patterns, such as unexpected surges in data packets, which signify a DDoS attack. Once detected, the system dynamically isolates compromised network nodes, redirecting legitimate traffic through secure pathways. Additionally, GAI models generate synthetic traffic patterns to confuse attackers and ensure the continuity of network operations. This methodology is essential for guaranteeing the availability and robustness of 5G networks, which underpin real-time applications like as driverless cars and telemedicine [29, 30].

Scenario Details of Preventing Eavesdropping in IoT Networks: In a smart city IoT network, GAI is used to provide secure communication between devices, including sensors and servers. Generative Adversarial Networks (GANs) are used to detect and mitigate eavesdropping attempts. Upon detecting unwanted access, the GAI produces deceptive communication patterns to confuse intruders while concurrently safeguarding the real data using sophisticated encryption techniques. This technology guarantees the security of sensitive information, including energy usage patterns and surveillance data, safeguarding privacy and avoiding abuse [31, 32].

Scenario Details of Adaptive Authentication in Autonomous Vehicles: Autonomous cars need secure contact with infrastructure and other vehicles (V2X communication). GAI models, especially Diffusion Models, dynamically modify authentication procedures according to environmental variables. For example, upon detecting signal interference or cyber threats, the GAI creates secure, unique authentication keys in real time, therefore assuring the integrity of data transfers. This functionality is essential for averting incidents resulting from hostile individuals impersonating communication or transmitting deceptive signals [33, 34].

Scenario Details of Enhancing Secure Communication in Military Operations: Military operations sometimes need communication in adversarial settings. Generative Adversarial Intelligence models, such as Autoencoders (AEs), are used to encrypt and compress communication data, therefore safeguarding its secrecy in the event of interception. GANs are used to detect unwanted access attempts and produce deceptive messages to fool enemies. The use of AEs improves the capacity to identify and avert anomalies in communication, whilst GANs provide an extra layer of protection. This method guarantees the operational integrity and secrecy of essential military communications [34, 35].

GENERATIVE ARTIFICIAL INTELLIGENCE FOR PHYSICAL LAYER SECURITY

The particular uses of Generative Artificial Intelligence (GAI) to improve security at the physical layer encompass [36 - 39]:

- General Artificial Intelligence (GAI) methodologies can be employed to ensure the confidentiality and reliability of wireless communications, namely by ensuring the secrecy of communication and authentication. Ensuring the security of communication is crucial in safeguarding transmitted information from cyber threats such as eavesdropping and unauthorized attacks.
- GAI (Generic Authentication Infrastructure) is employed to guarantee safe communication at the physical layer of communication networks. The statement highlights the rapid advancement and proficiency of GAI in manufacturing a diverse array of products and dealing with security issues. GAI has excellent adaptability and analytical skills in addressing the evolving attributes of transmission channels and complex cyber threats.
- Prospective areas for further investigation: While GAI has demonstrated impressive proficiency in extracting, recreating, and augmenting intricate data aspects, its utilization in physical layer security is still in its early stages. This section explores unresolved issues and topics of research related to the incorporation of General Artificial Intelligence (GAI) in physical layer security. It emphasizes the necessity of improving models in order to strengthen the resilience and efficacy of the system.

In summary, GAI holds promise for enhancing security measures in the physical layer of communication networks by ensuring confidentiality, verification, and addressing emerging cyber risks.

GENERATIVE ARTIFICIAL INTELLIGENCE FOR UNDERSTANDING COMPLEX DATA DISTRIBUTIONS

GAI's aptitude in comprehending intricate data distributions is advantageous for physical layer security in several ways [40 - 44]:

- Improving Security Features: GAI models may be used to improve important security features, such as communication secrecy, authentication, availability, resilience, and integrity, by analyzing complicated data distributions. This feature enables GAI to efficiently identify cyber risks and abnormalities in the network architecture.

- GAI's contribution to data reconstruction and augmentation demonstrates its exceptional capability to improve physical layer security by tackling the difficulties associated with data sparsity and incompleteness. Conventional AI models are greatly affected by these difficulties, emphasizing the superiority of General Artificial Intelligence (GAI) in dealing with intricate data patterns.
- Model Enhancements: Future research goals include refining the model for GAI in physical layer security. By integrating sophisticated neural network topologies, GAI systems may enhance their ability to mimic data, resulting in improvements in both resilience and effectiveness.
- Resource-Efficient Optimization: In order to make sure that GAI can be used in contexts with limited resources, such as IoT devices and edge computing platforms, it is necessary to optimize its resource use. It is essential to create GAI models that are lightweight and can function with limited computing resources, while yet upholding stringent security criteria.

The capability of GAI to comprehend intricate data distributions is crucial for boosting the security of the physical layer by improving the secrecy, authentication, availability, resilience, and integrity of communication. This includes resolving data-related challenges and optimizing resource allocation [45 - 49]:

- Communication Confidentiality: GAI has the ability to comprehend intricate data distributions, which allows it to aid in the conversion and manipulation of encrypted data. This ensures that sensitive information stays private and protected while being sent.
- Authentication: GAI's capacity to understand complex data patterns allows it to identify abnormalities and cyber dangers in the network infrastructure, therefore improving the authentication process by confirming the authenticity of communication participants and preventing unauthorized access.
- Availability: GAI's comprehension of intricate data distributions may aid in guaranteeing the accessibility of communication networks by identifying and alleviating any dangers that might interrupt the network's functioning, hence upholding uninterrupted service availability.
- The capacity of GAI to analyze and comprehend complex data distributions enhances the resilience of communication networks by detecting weaknesses and possible sources of failure. This enables proactive steps to be taken to strengthen network resilience against cyber-attacks.
- Integrity: GAI's expertise in comprehending intricate data distributions allows it to carry out data reconstruction and augmentation, which is crucial for

preserving the integrity of transmitted information and guaranteeing that data stays precise and unchanged throughout communication operations.

GAI's proficiency in comprehending intricate data distributions enhances security properties by facilitating encrypted data processing, anomaly detection, and data reconstruction. This, in turn, fortifies communication confidentiality, authentication, availability, resilience, and integrity in physical layer security applications.

GENERATIVE ARTIFICIAL INTELLIGENCE FOR CONTENT GENERATION IN PHYSICAL LAYER SECURITY

Utilizing Generalized Artificial Intelligence (GAI) in content generation for Physical Layer Security has the potential to significantly enhance security protocols in communication networks. Through the advancements in content production facilitated by Generative Artificial Intelligence (GAI), it is possible to generate reliable signals or codes that can be utilized in the physical layer to ensure communication confidentiality, verification, accessibility, durability, and consistency [50 - 53].

GAI models provide the ability to understand complex patterns in data and perform secure encryption and processing of data, making them essential in generating secure content for communication networks. For instance, GAI can be utilized to generate encrypted signals or codes that are resistant to eavesdropping and unauthorized access, hence enhancing communication confidentiality and integrity, as depicted in Fig. (**6**) [54].

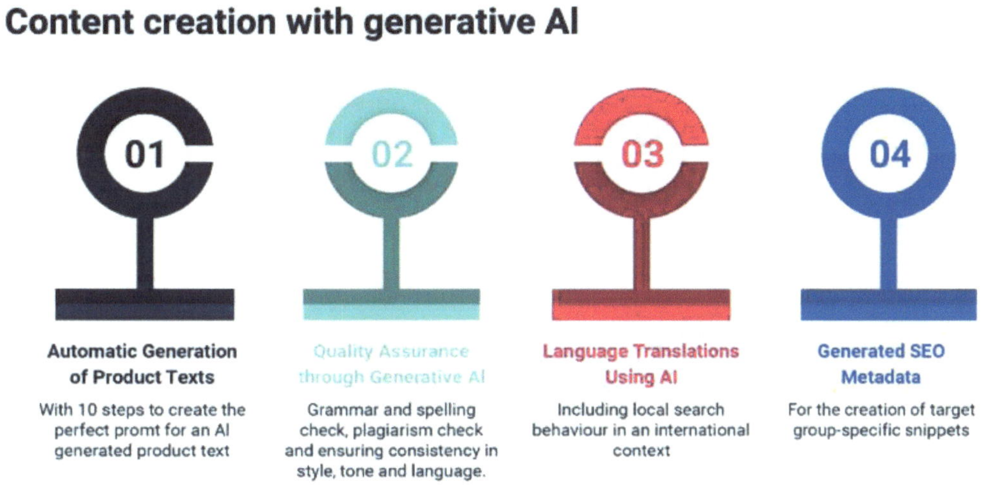

Fig. (6). Generative artificial intelligence for content generation.

Furthermore, GAI's capacity to detect cyber threats and anomalies in the network structure can aid in the creation of secure content that is resilient against attacks and ensures the preservation of data integrity. Utilizing Generative Adversarial Intelligence (GAI) in content creation for physical layer security enables the resolution of challenges such as limited data availability and insufficient information, surpassing the limitations of traditional AI approaches [55].

In conclusion, including GAI (General Artificial Intelligence) for content creation in physical layer security holds significant promise for enhancing security protocols, mitigating vulnerabilities, and preserving the integrity of transmitted data. By exploring the possibilities of GAI in generating secure signals or codes, communication networks can benefit from improved secrecy, authentication, and overall security.

Instances of effective utilization of Generative Artificial Intelligence (GAI) in communication networks to enhance security measures encompass [56]:

- The use of GAI in stable diffusion has resulted in the generation of many forms of content, showcasing its capacity to produce content inside communication networks.
- The DALL-E project has utilized the Generative Adversarial Inverse (GAI) model to generate images and films, demonstrating its ability to produce a diverse array of complex visual content. This can be utilized to enhance security protocols in communication networks.
- ChatGPT: The integration of GAI into ChatGPT has improved data augmentation capabilities, demonstrating its ability to provide text-based data that can boost cybersecurity measures in communication networks.

These examples illustrate how GAI's content generation capability has effectively enhanced security measures in communication networks, showcasing its capacity to address intricate challenges and promote innovation in the field of network security.

POTENTIAL ADVANTAGES AND RAMIFICATIONS FOR SECURITY

Integrating Generative Adversarial Intelligence (GAI) into communication systems has numerous benefits and necessitates careful attention to security concerns [57].

Benefits

- Enhanced Security Measures: GAI models possess the ability to bolster critical security aspects, including upholding communication privacy, confirming user authenticity, providing uninterrupted availability, enhancing resilience, and safeguarding data integrity. Artificial Intelligence (AI) can improve security measures in communication networks by understanding complex data patterns, performing encrypted data manipulation, and detecting cyber threats and anomalies.

- GAI's ability to manage limited data and partial information in physical layer security has the potential to significantly improve the efficiency of traditional AI models through data reconstruction and augmentation. This capability allows for enhanced data reconstruction and augmentation, surpassing the limitations of conventional AI algorithms.
- Environmental Adaptability: GAI models possess the capacity to acquire knowledge and adapt to changing environmental conditions in the physical layer. This allows them to uphold robust security protocols even in unfamiliar environments where traditional AI models may face challenges.

Future research is currently centered on creating lightweight GAI models that can operate with limited computer resources while maintaining stringent security standards, with the goal of optimizing resource utilization. This enhancement has the potential to reduce the burden on devices with restricted resources, such as mobile phones, and increase overall operational efficiency.

Implications for Security

- Potential Vulnerabilities: The complex architecture of GAI models and their resource-intensive nature may give rise to weaknesses that unscrupulous individuals can exploit to compromise the security of communication.
- Privacy concerns arise from GAI's development of sophisticated simulations and datasets to detect dangers and enhance systems, prompting questions regarding the handling and storage of sensitive information.
- Adversarial Attacks: The incorporation of GAI into communication systems can be vulnerable to adversarial attacks that aim to exploit vulnerabilities in the models or data generated by the technology.
- The effectiveness of GAI models in enhancing security measures depends on the quality and diversity of the training data. Inadequate or biased training data can lead to inaccurate or compromised security outcomes.

Integrating General Artificial Intelligence (GAI) into communication systems offers significant benefits in enhancing security measures and addressing challenges in physical layer security. Nevertheless, it is imperative to thoroughly evaluate potential vulnerabilities and security ramifications in order to ensure the robustness and dependability of the communication infrastructure.

To mitigate the potential vulnerabilities that may come from the complex and resource-intensive nature of GAI models in communication systems, many measures can be taken:

- Development of lightweight models: It emphasizes the development of GAI models that have minimal computational demands while still satisfying rigorous security standards. This can help reduce the burden on devices with limited capabilities, such as mobile phones, while guaranteeing the best possible performance without compromising security.
- Model Pruning techniques: By using model pruning techniques to GANs, we may efficiently remove unnecessary parameters while preserving their ability to generate or differentiate, leading to a significant decrease in computational workload. This method has the potential to optimize the GAI models and improve efficiency.
- Federated learning techniques involve the exploration of methods that can disperse the training process. This allows General Artificial Intelligences (GAIs) to gain information from different datasets on several devices while ensuring the privacy of the data. This might potentially reduce the need for centralized, powerful computer resources and enhance scalability in protecting the physical layer.
- Implementing Edge Computing: Leveraging the potential of edge computing to analyze data in close proximity to its source can reduce latency and minimize the requirement for extensive data transfer. Through the utilization of distributed deployment strategies, GAI can efficiently leverage edge computing capabilities, thereby enhancing both the security and efficiency of communication networks.

It is crucial for security authorization to improve the ability of models to quickly understand and respond to rapidly changing information in real time. Increasing the size of the model, optimizing the structures used for training, and improving the ability of the model to adapt in real time are successful strategies for addressing the challenges posed by the complexity of GAI models in communication systems.

Applying these processes is required to effectively mitigate the potential vulnerabilities arising from the intricate and resource-intensive nature of GAI models in communication systems. Implementing this approach will guarantee both the protection and effectiveness of physical layer communications.

CHALLENGES AND FUTURE DIRECTIONS IN USING GAI (GENERAL ARTIFICIAL INTELLIGENCE) FOR PHYSICAL LAYER SECURITY

While GAI demonstrates significant promise in improving the security of the physical layer, the existence of limitations such as data complexity and potential vulnerabilities emphasizes the necessity for further research on model adaptation and the integration of robust security measures [58, 59].

Obstacles

- **Resource-efficient Optimization:** The primary challenge in implementing Generative Adversarial Intelligence (GAI) for physical layer security lies in the significant resource consumption of GAI models. When comparing General Artificial Intelligence (GAI) to conventional Artificial Intelligence (AI), it is clear that GAI often requires a greater amount of resources for both training and inference. The growing demand can place a substantial strain on devices that have limited computing capabilities, such as mobile phones. Future inquiries should give priority to the creation of efficient GAI models that are lightweight and can operate successfully with limited resources while maintaining strict security requirements.
- **Environmental Adaptability:** The complex and ever-changing noise patterns, signal interference, and channel conditions at the physical layer pose a significant challenge for AI models, including GAI. Acquiring annotated data for physical layer attacks in different environments is difficult, which limits the effectiveness of traditional artificial intelligence models. Future research should focus on developing sophisticated AI models that can efficiently acquire knowledge and adjust to changing environmental circumstances, with the aim of ensuring reliable and robust security measures.
- **Model Enhancements:** In order to enhance the resilience and effectiveness of GAI systems for physical layer security, it is imperative to make advancements in model designs. By incorporating advanced neural network architectures, GAI systems can better simulate real-world scenarios and improve their ability to protect communication networks.
- **Scalability and Efficiency:** In order to enhance the ability of GAI to secure the physical layer, it is crucial to explore approaches such as model pruning techniques to remove redundant parameters from GANs while preserving their usefulness. Furthermore, it is crucial to implement federated learning methods to share the training procedure and ensure the protection of data privacy. These solutions can improve the usefulness of GAI in situations when resources are constrained, such as IoT devices and edge computing platforms.

FUTURE DIRECTIONS

Future research must investigate the use of “GAI-aided Secure SemCom” to minimize transmission overhead in networks that have restricted resources. This can be accomplished by employing Generalized Artificial Intelligence (GAI) in task-oriented Semantic Communication. This approach emphasizes the efficient accomplishment of tasks by utilizing General Artificial Intelligence (GAI) and knowledge bases, even if the reconstructed data does not exactly correspond to the original data. This approach has the capacity to improve both the effectiveness and safety of communication in wireless networks that are combined with artificial intelligence.

In summary, addressing the challenges related to resource efficiency, adaption to environmental circumstances, model improvements, scalability, and secure semantic communication will promote future advancements in utilizing GAI for physical layer security. These domains offer opportunities for further research and progress in enhancing the effectiveness and appropriateness of GAI in protecting communication networks at the physical layer [60].

CONCLUSION

This extensive survey study analyzes the influence of generative AI on cybersecurity, specifically highlighting the role of AI-powered chatbots. It provides valuable perspectives on the ethical considerations linked to its creation, implementation, and impact in various industries. The study highlights the need to rectify biases in training data, counter misinformation, and guarantee factual precision. The study examines the ethical challenges that arise in commercial applications, namely in the areas of data protection, authorization, and responsible research conduct. It emphasizes the importance of inclusivity and designing applications with the user's needs in mind. This essay examines the merging of AI-driven chatbots with cybersecurity, highlighting the importance of taking a proactive and interdisciplinary approach to tackle ethical issues. It emphasizes the necessity for cooperation among developers, legislators, and academics in order to establish robust ethical frameworks.

The study further discusses potential research fields, such as the advancement of reliable DGMs, the strengthening of protective mechanisms, and the enhancement of systems for identifying malicious inputs. The statement emphasizes the necessity for precise detection algorithms to combat misinformation and the potential benefits of AI in automating activities, identifying risks, and responding to cybersecurity emergencies with more efficiency. This work significantly enhances the comprehension of privacy and security issues in generative AI, hence facilitating future research and advancements in this crucial area.

ACKNOWLEDGEMENTS

This work was supported by the Deanship of Scientific Research, the Vice Presidency for Graduate Studies and Scientific Research, King Faisal University, Saudi Arabia, under the project (KFU241884).

REFERENCES

[1] C. Zhao, H. Du, D. Niyato, J. Kang, Z. Xiong, D. I. Kim, X. Shen, and K. B. Letaief, "Generative AI for secure physical layer communications: A survey", arXiv preprint arXiv:2402.13553, 2024.

[2] B. Zhu, N. Mu, J. Jiao, and D. Wagner, "Generative AI security: Challenges and countermeasures", arXiv preprint arXiv:2402.12617, 2024.

[3] Available from: https://www.softwebsolutions.com/resources/generative-ai-guide.html

[4] A. Golda, K. Mekonen, A. Pandey, A. Singh, V. Hassija, V. Chamola, and B. Sikdar, "Privacy and security concerns in generative AI: A comprehensive survey", *IEEE Access,* 2024.

[5] Golda, Abenezer, Kidus Mekonen, Amit Pandey, Anushka Singh, Vikas Hassija, Vinay Chamola, and Biplab Sikdar. "Privacy and security concerns in generative AI: A comprehensive survey." *IEEE Access* (2024).

[6] P. Eigenschink, T. Reutterer, S. Vamosi, R. Vamosi, C. Sun, and K. Kalcher, "Deep generative models for synthetic data: A survey", *IEEE Access,* vol. 11, pp. 47304-47320, 2023.

[7] Harshaan Chugh."Cybersecurity in the age of generative AI: Usable security & statistical analysis of threatGPT", *Int. J. Res. Appl. Sci. Eng. Technol.*, vol. 12, no. 1, pp. 1–9, 2024..
[http://dx.doi.org/10.22214/ijraset.2024.57827]

[8] A. Shoufan, "Exploring students' perceptions of ChatGPT: Thematic analysis and follow-up survey", *IEEE Access,* vol. 11, pp. 38805-38818, 2023.
[http://dx.doi.org/10.1109/ACCESS.2023.3268224]

[9] J. Pitt, "Deepfake videos and DDoS attacks (deliberate denial of satire) [editorial]", *IEEE Technol. Soc. Mag.,* vol. 38, no. 4, pp. 5-8, 2019.
[http://dx.doi.org/10.1109/MTS.2019.2948416]

[10] Available from: https://developers.google.com/machine-learning/gan/gan_structure

[11] Available from: https://www.v7labs.com/blog/autoencoders-guide#h4

[12] A. Dunmore, J. Jang-Jaccard, F. Sabrina, and J. Kwak, "A comprehensive survey of generative adversarial networks (GANs) in cybersecurity intrusion detection", *IEEE Access,* vol. 11, pp. 76071-76094, 2023.
[http://dx.doi.org/10.1109/ACCESS.2023.3296707]

[13] J. Zhai, S. Zhang, J. Chen, and Q. He, "Autoencoder and its various variants", *Proceedings of the IEEE international conference on systems, man, and cybernetics,* pp. 415-419, 2018.

[14] Available from: https://www.jeremyjordan.me/variational-autoencoders/

[15] X. Tong and W. Qi, ''False data injection attack on power system datadriven methods based on generative adversarial networks,'' *Proc. IEEE Sustain. Power Energy Conf. (iSPEC)*, pp. 4250–4254), 2021.
[http://dx.doi.org/10.1016/j.eng.2024.11.025]

[16] C-H. Lin, C-C. Wu, K-F. Chen, and T-S. Lee, "A variational autoencoder-based secure transceiver design using deep learning", *Proceeding of IEEE Global Communications Conference,* pp. 1-7, 2020.
[http://dx.doi.org/10.1109/GLOBECOM42002.2020.9348041]

[17] J. Yoon, L.N. Drumright, and M. van der Schaar, "Anonymization through data synthesis using generative adversarial networks (ADSGAN)", *IEEE J. Biomed. Health Inform.,* vol. 24, no. 8, pp. 2378-2388, 2020.
[http://dx.doi.org/10.1109/JBHI.2020.2980262] [PMID: 32167919]

[18] Available from: https://www.linkedin.com/pulse/diffusion-model-gen-ai-eeswar-chamarthi/

[19] R. Rombach, A. Blattmann, D. Lorenz, P. Esser, and B. Ommer, "Highresolution image synthesis with latent diffusion models", arXiv:2112.10752.

[20] J. Ho, A. Jain, and P. Abbeel, "Denoising diffusion probabilistic models", *Adv. Neural Inf. Process.,* vol. 33, pp. 6840-6851, 2020.

[21] J. Zhang, H. Du, Q. Sun, B. Ai, and D.W.K. Ng, "Physical layer security enhancement with reconfigurable intelligent surfaceaided networks", *IEEE Trans. Inf. Forensics Security,* vol. 16, pp. 3480-3495, 2021.
[http://dx.doi.org/10.1109/TIFS.2021.3083409]

[22] Y.S. Shiu, S. Chang, H.C. Wu, S. Huang, and H.H. Chen, "Physical layer security in wireless networks: a tutorial", *IEEE Wirel. Commun.,* vol. 18, no. 2, pp. 66-74, 2011.
[http://dx.doi.org/10.1109/MWC.2011.5751298]

[23] N. Wu, C. Peng, and K. Niu, "A privacy-preserving game model for local differential privacy by using information-theoretic approach", *IEEE Access,* vol. 8, pp. 216741-216751, 2020.
[http://dx.doi.org/10.1109/ACCESS.2020.3041854]

[24] F. Sattler, S. Wiedemann, K.R. Müller, and W. Samek, "Robust and communication-efficient federated learning from non-i.I.d. data", *IEEE Trans. Neural Netw. Learn. Syst.,* vol. 31, no. 9, pp. 3400-3413, 2020.
[http://dx.doi.org/10.1109/TNNLS.2019.2944481] [PMID: 31689214]

[25] R. Al-Huthaifi, T. Li, W. Huang, J. Gu, and C. Li, "Federated learning in smart cities: Privacy and security survey", *Inf. Sci.,* vol. 632, pp. 833-857, 2023.
[http://dx.doi.org/10.1016/j.ins.2023.03.033]

[26] H. Yang, J. Zhao, Z. Xiong, K.Y. Lam, S. Sun, and L. Xiao, "Privacy-preserving federated learning for UAV-enabled networks: Learning-based joint scheduling and resource management", *IEEE J. Sel. Areas Comm.,* vol. 39, no. 10, pp. 3144-3159, 2021.
[http://dx.doi.org/10.1109/JSAC.2021.3088655]

[27] Q. Zhang, C. Xin, and H. Wu, "Privacy-preserving deep learning based on multiparty secure computation: A survey", *IEEE Internet Things J.,* vol. 8, no. 13, pp. 10412-10429, 2021.
[http://dx.doi.org/10.1109/JIOT.2021.3058638]

[28] T. Bai, J. Zhao, J. Zhu, S. Han, J. Chen, B. Li, and A. Kot, ''AI-GAN: Attack-inspired generation of adversarial examples", *Proc. IEEE Int. Conf. Image Process. (ICIP)* pp. 2543–2547, 2021.

[29] C. Zhao, H. Du, D. Niyato, J. Kang, Z. Xiong, D. I. Kim, X. Shen, and K. B. Letaief, "Enhancing physical layer communication security through generative AI with mixture of experts", *IEEE Wireless Commun.*, pp. 1–9, 2025.

[30] N. Van Huynh, J. Wang, H. Du, D. T. Hoang, D. Niyato, D. N. Nguyen, D. I. Kim, and K. B. Letaief, "Generative AI for physical layer communications: A survey," *arXiv preprint* arXiv:2312.05594, 2023.

[31] S. Kumar, S. Dalal, and V. Dixit, "The OSI model: Overview on the seven layers of computer networks", *Int. J. Comput. Sci. Inf. Technol. Res.,* vol. 2, no. 3, pp. 461-466, 2014.

[32] J. Wang, H. Du, D. Niyato, J. Kang, S. Cui, X. Shen, and P. Zhang, "Generative AI for Integrated Sensing and Communication: Insights from the Physical Layer Perspective", *arXiv preprint* arXiv:2310.01036, 2023.

[33] R. Pasupuleti, R. Vadapalli and C. Mader, "Cyber security issues and challenges related to Generative AI and ChatGPT", 2023 *Tenth International Conference on Social Networks Analysis, Management and Security (SNAMS)*, Abu Dhabi, United Arab Emirates, 2023, pp. 1-5.
[http://dx.doi.org/10.1109/SNAMS60348.2023.10375472]

[34] A. Smith, and J. Downey, "A communication channel density estimating generative adversarial network", *Proc. IEEE Cognitive Communications for Aerospace Applications Workshop,* pp. 1-7, 2019.

[35] A. Kaur, A. N. Hoshyar, V. Saikrishna, S. Firmin, and F. Xia. "Deepfake video detection: challenges

and opportunities", *Artificial Intelligence Review 57*, no. 6 (2024): 159.

[36] J. Yoon, L. N. Drumright, and M. van der Schaar, "Anonymization through data synthesis using generative adversarial networks (ADS-GAN)", *IEEE J. Biomed. Health Inform.*, vol. 24, no. 8, pp. 2378–2388, 2020.
[PMID: 32167919]

[37] A. Karapantelakis, P. Alizadeh, A. Alabassi, K. Dey, and A. Nikou, "Generative ai in mobile networks: a survey", *Ann. Telecommun.,* pp. 1-19, 2023.

[38] T.-H. Vu, S. K. Jagatheesaperumal, M.-D. Nguyen, N. V. Huynh, S. Kim, and Q.-V. Pham,"Applications of generative AI (GAI) for mobile and wireless networking: A survey", *IEEE Internet Things J.*, vol. 12, no. 2, 2025.

[39] H. Sharma, and N. Kumar, "Deep learning based physical layer security for terrestrial communications in 5G and beyond networks: A survey", *Phys. Commun.,* p. 102002, 2023.

[40] L. Verdoliva, "Media forensics and DeepFakes: An overview", *IEEE J. Sel. Top. Signal Process.,* vol. 14, no. 5, pp. 910-932, 2020.
[http://dx.doi.org/10.1109/JSTSP.2020.3002101]

[41] A. Yazdinejad, R. M. Parizi, G. Srivastava, and A. Dehghantanha, "Making sense of blockchain for AI deepfakes technology", *Proc. IEEE Globecom Workshops (GC Wkshps)*, pp. 1–6, 2020
[http://dx.doi.org/10.1109/GCWkshps50303.2020.9367545]

[42] A.J. Rodriguez-Almeida, H. Fabelo, S. Ortega, A. Deniz, F.J. Balea-Fernandez, E. Quevedo, C. Soguero-Ruiz, A.M. Wägner, and G.M. Callico, "Synthetic patient data generation and evaluation in disease prediction using small and imbalanced datasets", *IEEE J. Biomed. Health Inform.,* vol. 27, no. 6, pp. 2670-2680, 2023.
[http://dx.doi.org/10.1109/JBHI.2022.3196697] [PMID: 35930509]

[43] J. Xiong, R. Bi, Y. Tian, X. Liu, and D. Wu, "Toward lightweight, privacypreserving cooperative object classification for connected autonomous vehicles", *IEEE Internet Things J.,* vol. 9, no. 4, pp. 2787-2801, 2022.
[http://dx.doi.org/10.1109/JIOT.2021.3093573]

[44] Y. F. Wang, ‘‘Generative AI: How it changes our lives? Take vision & language as an example", *Proc. Int. VLSI Symp. Technol., Syst. Appl. (VLSI-TSA/VLSI-DAT)*, p. 1, Apr. 2023
[http://dx.doi.org/10.1109/VLSI-TSA/VLSI-DAT57221.2023.10134215]

[45] S. Chaudhury, H. Roy, S. Mishra, and T. Yamasaki, "Adversarial training time attack against discriminative and generative convolutional models", *IEEE Access,* vol. 9, pp. 109241-109259, 2021.
[http://dx.doi.org/10.1109/ACCESS.2021.3101282]

[46] D. Vasan, M. Alazab, S. Venkatraman, J. Akram, and Z. Qin, "MTHAEL: Cross-architecture IoT malware detection based on neural network advanced ensemble learning", *IEEE Trans. Comput.,* vol. 69, no. 11, pp. 1654-1667, 2020.

[47] I.K. Dutta, B. Ghosh, A. Carlson, M. Totaro, and M. Bayoumi, "Generative adversarial networks in security: A survey", *Electron. Mobile Commun. Conf. (UEMCON),* pp. 399-405, 2020.
[http://dx.doi.org/10.1109/UEMCON51285.2020.9298135]

[48] A. Majeed, and S. Oun Hwang, "When AI meets information privacy: The adversarial role of AI in data sharing scenario", *IEEE Access,* vol. 11, pp. 76177-76195, 2023.

[49] P.S. Chauhan, and N. Kshetri, "2021 state of the practice in data privacy and security", *Computer,* vol. 54, no. 8, pp. 125-132, 2021.

[50] M. Gupta, C. Akiri, K. Aryal, E. Parker, and L. Praharaj, "From ChatGPT to ThreatGPT: Impact of generative AI in cybersecurity and privacy", *IEEE Access,* vol. 11, pp. 80218-80245, 2023.

[51] G. Hurlburt, "What if ethics got in the way of generative AI?", *IT Prof.,* vol. 25, no. 2, pp. 4-6, 2023.
[http://dx.doi.org/10.1109/MITP.2023.3267140]

[52] C. Huang, Z. Zhang, B. Mao, and X. Yao, "An overview of artificial intelligence ethics", *IEEE Trans. Artif. Intell.,* vol. 4, no. 4, pp. 799-819, 2023.

[53] H. Du, D. Niyato, J. Kang, Z. Xiong, P. Zhang, S. Cui, X. Shen, S. Mao, Z. Han, A. Jamalipour, H. V. Poor, and D. I. Kim, "The age of generative AI and AI-generated everything," *arXiv preprint* arXiv:2311.00947, 2023.

[54] Available from: https://www.artefact.com/blog/will-generative-ai-revolutionize-content-creation/

[55] S. Aldossary, and W. Allen, "Data security, privacy, availability and integrity in cloud computing: issues and current solutions", *Int. J. Adv. Comput. Sci. Appl.,* vol. 7, no. 4, 2016.

[56] T. Sumaiya, K. D. Gupta, A. Roy, and D. Dasgupta, "Generative adversarial networks (GAN) for cyber security: Challenges and opportunities", *In Proceedings of the 2022 IEEE Symposium Series on Computational Intelligence,* Singapore, pp. 4-7. 2022.

[57] C. Zou, F. Yang, J. Song, and Z. Han, "Generative adversarial network for wireless communication: Principle, application, and trends", *IEEE Communications Magazine 62*, no. 5 (2023): 58-64.

[58] I. Goodfellow, J. Pouget-Abadie, M. Mirza, B. Xu, D. Warde-Farley, S. Ozair, A. Courville, and Y. Bengio, "Generative adversarial networks", *Commun. ACM,* vol. 63, no. 11, pp. 139-144, 2020. [http://dx.doi.org/10.1145/3422622]

[59] G. Bora, S. Bora, S. Singh, and S. M. Arsalan, "OSI reference model: An overview", *Int. J. Comput. Trends Technol., (IJCTT)* 7, no. 4 (2014): 214-218.

[60] J. Betker, G. Goh, L. Jing, T. Brooks, J. Wang, L. Li, L. Ouyang, J. Zhuang, J. Lee, Y. Guo, W. Manassra, P. Dhariwal, C. Chu, Y. Jiao, and A. Ramesh, "Improving image generation with better captions", 2023.

CHAPTER 9

Generative AI in Communication System Simulation and Modeling

Umang Kant[1,*], **Prachi Dahiya**[2], **Rohit Priyadarshi**[3] and **Manoj Kumar**[4]

[1] *Department of CSE (AI), KIET Group of Institutions, Ghaziabad, India*

[2] *Department of Computer Science and Technology CST, Maharaja Agrasen Institute of Technology, New Delhi, India*

[3] *Department of Design, Delhi Technological University, New Delhi, India*

[4] *Department of Information Sciences, University of Wollongong, Dubai*

Abstract: The field of artificial intelligence has a lot of emerging techniques that are being effectively used in several applications, especially in different research areas. The next-generation techniques are taking the quantum leap, including text-generative techniques, AI techniques, variational techniques, *etc.* The communication systems such as generative models have emerged as a major application in artificial intelligence. Generative AI represents a transformative leap, which enables the creation of content varying from text, audio, images, and videos. This chapter explores the foundational concepts of Generative AI and their types, including their unique features. Furthermore, this chapter includes research contributions in this domain, highlighting the advancements in the fields of educational engineering, digital healthcare, digital business, architectural engineering, and digital institutions, among others. By exploring these aspects, this chapter provides a comprehensive understanding of Generative AI's potential in the current industries.

Keywords: AI, Autoregressive models, Communication engineering, Deepfakes, Data loss, Ethical AI, Generative AI, GANs, IP leaks, NLP, Synthetic data generation, VAEs.

INTRODUCTION

This chapter discusses and explores different Generative AI models and the recent trends present in communication engineering in the spectrum of network optimization, resource allocation, *etc.* The potential applications of these models are also discussed, along with security concerns. The focus is on vulnerabilities present in the systems as well as the solutions for the same that may shield the

* **Corresponding author Umang Kant:** Department of CSE(AI), KIET Group of Institutions, Ghaziabad, India; E-mail: umang.kant@gmail.com

Shelly Gupta, Sapna Juneja & Sandeep Kautish (Eds.)
All rights reserved-© 2025 Bentham Science Publishers

system from hostile attacks and intrusions. An in-depth review of different generative models, along with other methods of communication engineering, is conducted. Hence, it becomes clear that there is a need to build a robust communication system that overcomes the security issues present in the current models.

GENERATIVE AI

Artificial intelligence is used in Generative AI models, which help generate new content, written text, or any other data that is different from the data generated through data training [1]. AI aims to make predictions about the data, text, and images present in the dataset.

These characteristics of Generative AI are as follows:

- **Content/Material Creation:** Generative AI models are fully capable of generating new material or content that was earlier unimaginable. This newly created content includes producing music, authoring stories and scripts, creating visuals, and producing human voices.
- **Learning from Data:** These models are trained to learn from vast volumes of data, understanding underlying patterns, structures, and styles of the data.
- **Interactive and Adaptive in Nature:** Generative AI models are usually interactive with users and are capable of adapting to the user's output based on feedback.
- **Wide-ranged Applications:** Generative AI finds its application in many fields, including engineering, entertainment, science, and arts, among many others.

The effect of Generative AI is already visible in many fields, and including more adaptable, effective, and intelligent systems and models will drastically change the entire field as well as the industry it is applied to. As discussed, Generative AI has the capacity to learn from the collected data, predict outcomes, and create synthetic information and content [2]. These capabilities will prove to be of great support in information transmission, processing, and learning in this digital age.

The primary aim of this chapter is to study Generative AI, identify communication engineering possibilities, address and provide solutions to security concerns, evaluate the effects of Generative AI, and provide practical and workable solutions.

Types of Generative AI Models

This section includes the types of Generative AI Models with their brief description.

Generative Adversarial Networks (GANs)

Generative Adversarial Networks (GANs) include two neural networks. One of these neural networks is called a Generator, and the other is called a Discriminator (Fig. **1**). Both of these neural networks are trained synchronously. Generator, as the name suggests, has the ability to generate or produce synthetic data resembling the data it was trained on, whereas the other neural network Discriminator has the capability to distinguish between authentic and synthetic data, *i.e.*, artificially generated data. Both neural networks act as each other's rivals, and hence, this rivalry motivated them to work at par to improve and enhance their working and techniques, ultimately empowering the generator to generate outputs of the best quality [3].

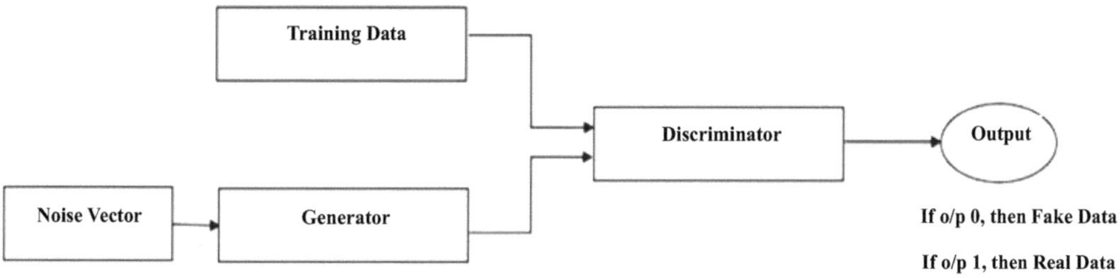

Fig. (1). Generative Adversarial Networks (GANs).

Variational Autoencoders (VAEs)

Variational Autoencoders (VAEs) also consist of two neural networks: one is named the Encoder neural network, and the other is named the Decoder neural network [4]. VAEs are models that process by encoding the given input into a latent space using the encoder NN and then using decoder NN, decoding it to recreate the original input (Fig. **2**). During the working of the encoder and decoder NN, this model gathers knowledge about the structure and distribution of data. Then, it randomly selects new data points from data distribution.

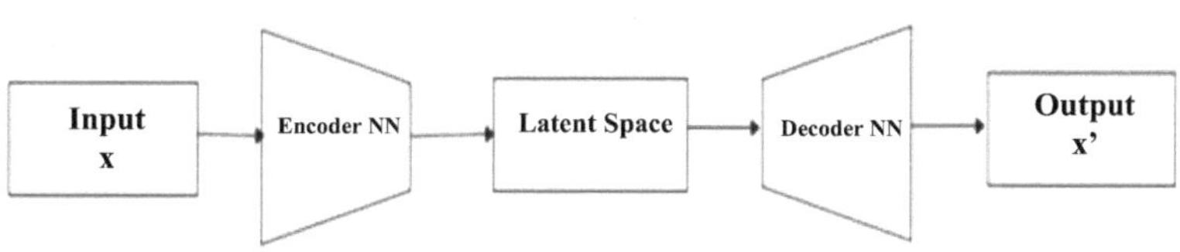

Fig. (2). Variational Autoencoders (VAEs).

Autoregressive Models

Autoregressive models are also neural networks that consist of input, output, and hidden layers. These models are predictive models that have the capability to predict or forecast the next or subsequent segment of a sequence. This prediction depends on the preceding segments of the sequence (Fig. **3**). A Generative Pre-trained Transformer (GPT) is an instance of autoregressive models capable of creating text by predicting individual words sequentially.

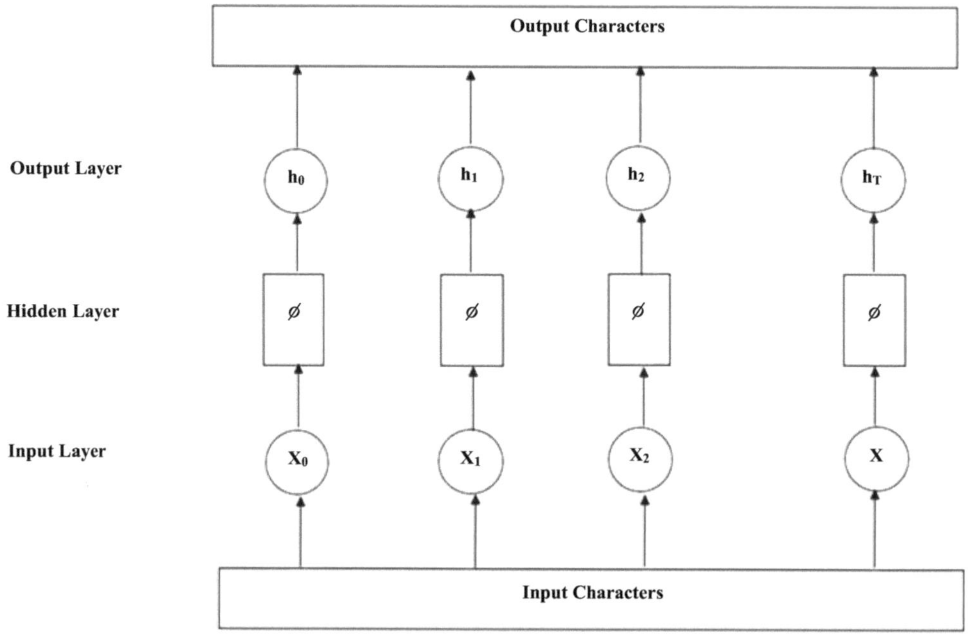

Fig. (3). Autoregressive models.

Advancements in Generative Models

In the past few years, the field of AI, especially Generative Models, has made groundbreaking progress due to the boom in technology, rise in data accessibility, and breakthrough in improved processing capabilities. This section examines the major domains where Generative AI advancements have been notably observed.

Increased Model Complexity and Capability

Large Language Models (LLMs), such as OpenAI's GPT-4 and GPT-5, have shown significant advancement with respect to data complexity. This capability to deal and learn with complex data enables LLMs to predict clear, coherent, and contextually appropriate text on a wide range of subjects, themes, and areas. LLMs are trained on large and extensive datasets collected from various sources, and these datasets contain a large number of parameters and features [5]. These extensive parameters and features allow the models to catch and understand complex details in the language and text. There also exist Image Generation Models such as DALL-E and Stable Diffusion. These image generation models have transformed the process of producing images from textual or verbal descriptions. These models are so advanced that they are capable of producing intricate and precise visual descriptions as closely instructed by the human prompt.

Improved Efficiency and Accessibility

Effective training of these models is conducted using methods such as sparse training and quantization, which in turn have reduced the overall burden and increased the accessibility of these technologies. Also, optimal training techniques have been achieved for these models. Models such as Google Colab and Hugging Face have made the accessibility of these tools to a wider range of users, resulting in extensive use of these tools. These models and tools have widened their usage and applications among various users, such as developers, researchers, engineers, and entrepreneurs, reducing the need for costly infrastructure.

Ethical and Responsible Generative AI Development

A growth has been observed in the emphasis on understanding and restricting biases in AI systems. This includes actions to increase the equity of these models across different situations and various demographics. There has been a contribution from the part of various governments of different countries as well, where regulation and governance have become evident [6]. Government institutions, authorities, as well as private sectors are also working toward formulating standards and regulations to ensure appropriate usage and implementation of Generative AI, majorly focusing on security, privacy, and societal consequences.

Interdisciplinary Generative AI Applications

Generative models are being extensively used in the fields of healthcare and bio-medicine to produce AI-generated data, *i.e.*, synthetic medical data, including medical diagnosis, drug discovery, medicine prescriptions, *etc.* These models are being used in the fields of art and media by increasing the scope of creative representation with the aim of producing better literature, art, music, and visuals. These models also find their applications in the field of climate research and environmental processes to forecast climate patterns, weather predictions, effects on flora and fauna, and various environmental resources. Apart from the fields already discussed, Generative AI models are being utilized in numerous other interdisciplinary fields.

Advancements in Foundation Models

Foundation models are models that offer a fundamental set of capabilities on which individual applications are developed. These models work with the notion that they will fulfill various objectives that are diverse in nature. They also aim to reduce the use of resources required to develop AI applications.

Relevance of Generative AI in Communication Engineering

Communication engineering is a field of engineering that focuses on the transfer, encoding, decoding, and manipulation of data and information across various mediums and channels. Now, since Generative AI finds its applications in a wide range of domains, integrating Generative AI into communication engineering can yield many advantages, such as improved efficiency, enhanced existing communication systems, and novel capabilities [7]. This section highlights the relevance of Generative AI in communication engineering.

Data Compression and Optimization

Generative AI and generative models can be used to develop advanced data compression techniques, which prove to be very important in communication engineering for reducing bandwidth usage and enhancing data transmission speeds. Generative models can be utilized to predict, forecast, and recreate segments of a data stream or a signal. This results in the use of encoding methods that are more efficient since they maintain a better quality while transmitting a limited quantity of data.

Error Correction

Generative AI models can improve error correction techniques through better and accurate prediction and rectification of transmitted data errors. This feature is prominent in information with a high level of noise, as well as in long-distance communications when conventional error-correcting techniques prove to be less effective. These Generative AI models are reliable for communication as they gather knowledge of repeated error patterns and underlying structures and anticipate the problems.

Synthetic Data Generation

In communication systems, in fact, in every field where the models need to be trained and tested, training and testing require the use of large datasets, which is a challenging as well as costly task. Here, Generative AI can play a crucial role, as it has the ability to produce synthetic or artificial datasets that replicate real-world applications. This ability allows the researchers and engineers to experiment with the data and then evaluate the data for novel communication protocols and technologies for simulated environments.

Signal Processing

Neural networks are used to train the Generative AI models that are used for signal processing, which is managed by much simpler algorithms. Signal amplification, extraction, and several other procedures are used for novel objectives in this field. AI has the capability to learn and predict the data in order to give better performances by adapting according to the data. These kinds of improvements result in high speed and accuracy.

Network Management and Optimization

Generative models use the power of AI to predict some of the network conditions and replicate the traffic, which can be useful for the designing part of the communication networks. Different traffic patterns are predicted through generative models, and they are used to predict the congestion areas in the network. Improvement in network efficiency, minimizing delay, and efficient routing algorithms are used for these purposes.

Enhanced User Interfaces

The Generative AI has the capabilities of how people look at their data and how to predict and give better results with the advancements in the Natural Language Processing (NLP) in the communication systems. Generative AI uses different items at its disposal, such as chatbots, human-like interactive bots, virtual assistants, power bots, intuitive interactions, and discussions. This improves the accessibility of the technology and, hence, enriches the overall user experience.

Innovative Modulation Techniques

The creation of effective modulation techniques has helped artificial intelligence in increased resilience toward threats and attacks and much more enhanced efficiency for proper utilization of resources. Alternative circumstances are created, and modulation techniques simulate these generative models.

Features of Generative AI Techniques

A diverse range of capabilities are exhibited by Generative AI approaches for the improvement of data. They are utilized to improve throughput, efficiency, and dependability. Fig. (**4**) provides an overview of all the features of Generative AI, and a comprehensive diagram is provided with all the implemented features of the Generative AI application areas.

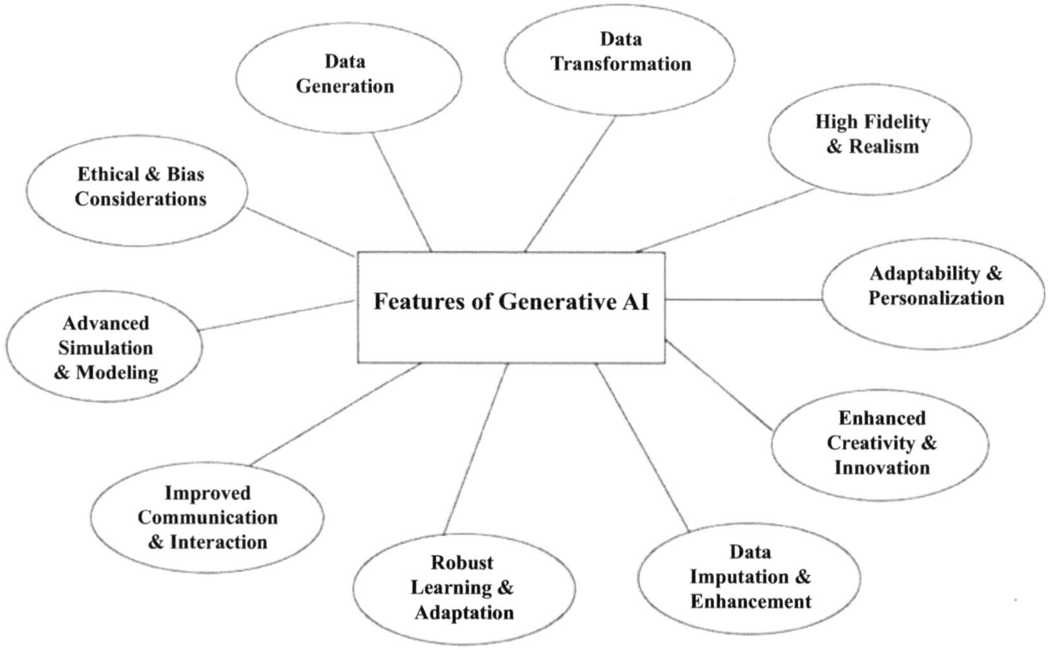

Fig. (4). Features of Generative AI.

General Features

- **Data Generation:** Synthetic data is created through generative model capabilities, and this data clearly resembles the patterns of the real data. Alternative AI methods are used in situations where the data is genuine and limited, as well as when it is sensitive. Novel material is created through this Generative AI, such as text, images, graphics, videos, and music, which is created through structures and patterns present in the original data.
- **Data Transformation:** Artistic styles of different images, converting the photographs into artifacts, or even modifying simple images and styles of films are some of the capabilities of generative models. Current datasets are enhanced through techniques of various datatypes, producing variances and the transitions of different machine learning models.
- **High Fidelity and Realism:** GANs have the ability to generate high-resolution outputs, which include films and photos, and hence, it becomes easy to know the actual data. The capability to produce new text becomes contextually appropriate, and hence, it guarantees results that are much more coherent to the specific text.
- **Adaptability and Personalization:** Outputs are tailored and customized in order to meet the user preferences as well as the needs of Generative AI. These models have the ability to enhance the quality of the output, and hence, this

facilitates the dynamic automation of the system.

- **Increased Creativity and Innovation:** Generative models generate different outputs that provide a broad spectrum of opportunities. Cross-domain creativities are done in unique ways and content.
- **Data Imputation and Enhancement:** (a) Generative models support missing data imputation, *i.e.*, these models can fill in missing parts of data, such as completing incomplete images or datasets. (b) These models are capable of data denoising, *i.e.*, they can remove noise from data, improving the quality and clarity of images, audio, and other types of data.
- **Robust Learning and Adaptation:** (a) Generative models can learn from unlabeled data, identifying patterns and structures without the need for extensive labeled datasets, *i.e.*, they are capable of unsupervised learning. (b) They can generate accurate outputs even with limited examples, making them effective in scenarios with sparse data. This type of learning is referred to as few-shot, zero-shot learning.
- **Improved Communication and Interaction:** (a) Generative models can produce natural language generation (NLG), which involves coherent and contextually appropriate text, enabling more natural human-computer interactions. (b) Conversational AI with advanced chatbots and virtual assistants can engage in meaningful and context-aware conversations.
- **Advanced Simulation and Modeling:** Generative AI can simulate various scenarios, which is useful in fields like healthcare, finance, and urban planning for risk assessment and decision-making.
- **Ethical and Bias Considerations:** Bias mitigations are controlled in the training data, and it is contextually proved that the generative models are more biased and have fairer outputs. Efforts are made to make the Generative AI models more explainable and transparent; they help users in the outputs for the ethical usage of the data.

A detailed explanation is given in Fig. (**5**), which defines different enhancements in AI in terms of efficiency, throughput, dependability, *etc.*

Enhancing Efficiency, Reliability and Throughput using Generative AI in Communication Systems		
Efficiency • Data Compression & Encoding • Predictive Maintenance	Reliability • Error Detection & Correction • Adaptive Communication Protocol	Throughput • Optimized Resource Allocation • Enhanced Signal Processing

Fig. (5). Generative AI in communication systems and its features.

Efficiency

Optimal utilization of different computational resources is done through Generative AI models and this helps in generating superior quality outputs.

Efficiency can also be of different types, such as data efficiency, computational efficiency, and model optimization, as given in Fig. (**6**). Generative Adversarial Networks (GANs) are used in the process of image synthesis with enhanced images of higher resolution and high quality that result in resource-optimized image generation. Fine-tuning and optimized techniques are used in transformer models such as ChatGPT, which have the ability to generate enhanced text. Reduced latency and a much-improved throughput are the result of the efficient compressing of the data, and it has been proven as an advantage for storage solutions and communication systems.

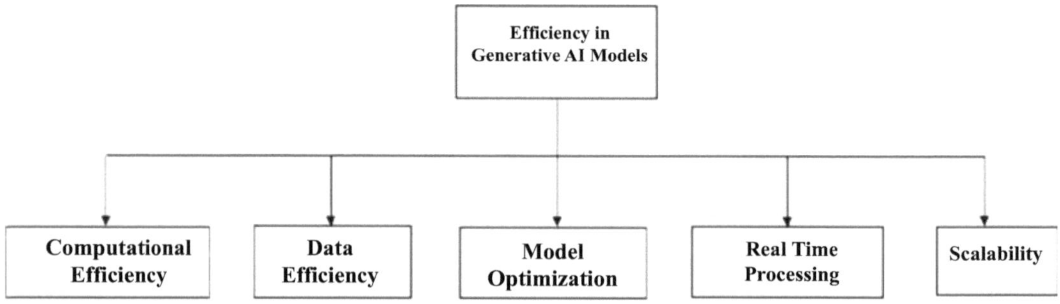

Fig. (6). Efficiency in Generative AI models.

- **Computation Efficiency:** Optimized utilization of the computing resources is done through Generative AI models, which help in achieving the training and inference durations of the time. If the models are efficient, then the substantial requirement of the resources decreases. Knowledge distillation, quantization, and model pruning are the methods that are used to increase the efficiency and, hence, lower the total number of parameters that are used [8]. Parallel processing capabilities are also used for the training and output generation and it dispenses different calculations among several different machines.
- **Data Efficiency:** Knowledge is acquired through the capacitive generative models, which result in the decreased requirement of extensive labeled datasets. Data efficiency is useful in crucial situations where there is a lack of data or the data is costly. Artificial variants are present in the existing data that are generated through data augmentation. Self-supervised methodologies are much more effective [9] in the forecast of different aspects of data, and hence, they help in successfully harnessing large quantities of data that is unlabeled, thus enhancing the learning efficiency of the learning models [10].
- **Model Optimization:** Efficient model architectures are created for streamlining the neural networks, which may need fewer parameters [11] and operations and, hence, result in training. Sophisticated training methods are used for the fine-tuning of the existing data, which results in financial training and a substantial reduction in the usage of resources. The main goal is to decrease the energy used

by the different AI tools. Implementation of models for energy limited resources is done for different mobile devices in the IoT systems [12].

Reliability

Deep Learning models are used to effectively detect and rectify the overall results for transmitting data as compared to the older methods. Extensive datasets are used to predict different patterns in the data and use corrective measures to restore the damaged data; hence, it becomes easy to generate substitute believable data for the integrity of the transmission. All the communication protocols are adjusted through AI-based techniques that guarantee the dependability and efficiency for the uncertain conditions in the system.

Practical Applications

- **5G Networks:** The Generative AI plays a very important role in the implementation and automation of 5G networks. It not only improves the efficiency but also decreases the delay in transmission, increases the efficiency, and boosts the total data that is transmitted, which, therefore, results in faster, more efficient, and dependable mobile communication.
- **Satellite Communication:** Satellite communications are enhanced by AI methods, which help in efficiently allocating the bandwidth, forecasting the weather effects, and rectifying the problems in transmission, which helps enhance the overall dependability as well as data transfer for the satellite connections.
- **Internet of Things (IoT):** IoT systems use AI to handle the data that is present in the systems, which is produced by the interconnected devices. Real-time decision-making, efficient transmission [13], and processing of the data are done in the IoT system.

Security Challenges in Communication Engineering with Generative AI

Generative AI uses artificial intelligence in communicating different text, images, and all other different kinds of media, and hence, forms relationship between Generative AI and communication engineering. There are different kinds of negative implications present in this field. Some of them are discussed below (Fig. 7).

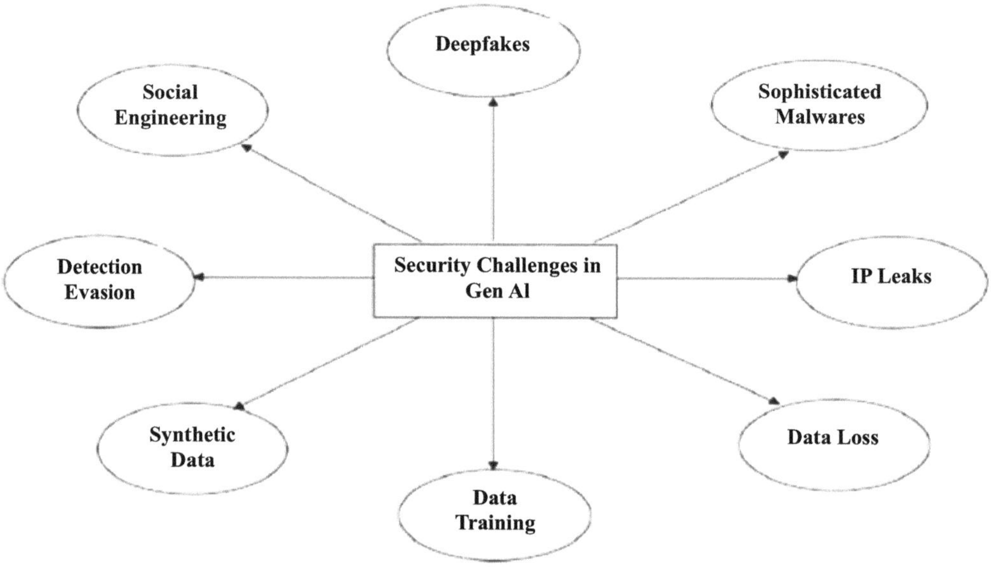

Fig. (7). Security threats in Generative AI.

Social Engineering

AI generation of content has the potential of attracting different phishing attacks in the form of emails, websites, messages, or even plain text or images, which acts as a challenge to the users using different AI generation software and, in turn, becomes part of malicious communications. There are advanced leverages that allow algorithms to generate high-granularity content and give the software the capability to produce human-like data. AI these days can generate fake emails as trusted ones, replicate websites as the original ones, and use different social engineering methods effectively and efficiently. This AI-generated content provides a level of sophistication that undermines the originality of the trusted sources and websites. This whole ordeal makes it challenging for individuals to know which data is resourceful and from a trusted source or party. Hence, there is a need to make a robust and enhanced structure of the AI-generated technologies so that it can mitigate the risks that are associated with this AI-generated content. There are cybersecurity issues, authentication issues, *etc.*, that need to be taken care of.

Text generated through AI has high potential and the ability to create convincing data as well as images and videos than the ones produced by human beings. These AI systems have remarkable skills to adapt according to the given input and the environment provided. Specific situations are present in order to provide the best outputs possible according to the given specific situations. Different tools are used to enhance the effectiveness of social engineering, which is a category of cybersecurity that may attack human emotions in one way or another, such as curiosity, happiness, sadness, or greediness, in such a way that this software can manipulate the human emotions too by divulging into the private data of different individuals.

Research studies have shown a significant increase in communication engineering attacks, and a trend is noticed that the rate of increase of attacks has become exponential in the past few years, which utilize AI generative technologies. Different kinds of voice scams are there where the attackers mimic the voice of an individual's relatives, friends, or acquaintances and then attack the individual. Replicating a voice has become very easy for AI these days due to the advances in technology.

It is not easy to detect a social engineering attack as perceived by some people; rather, it is very difficult to do that, and a very different procedure is followed. It is seen in research that 98% of cyberattacks are done with the help of social engineering tactics, and around 90% of data breaches are because of some kind of human error in which illegal access is given by an individual to the attackers who steal valuable information. Hence, there is a need for cybersecurity awareness programs that may help in employing robust defenses in order to combat threats involved with AI generation.

Deepfakes

Deepfakes in the AI generation present a significant and important privacy concern for the users, which extends to the cybersecurity level. Deepfake is fabricated content or media that is basically generated by AI and has the capability to impersonate human identity and present itself as a malicious actor gathering confidential information. These fabricated materials can easily deceive the biometric machines and devices and different kinds of fingerprint and facial recognition software that are designed solely for the security of the people. Hence, deepfakes pose a significant threat in the field of authentication, and they disseminate misinformation and thus breach privacy and security safeguards [14].

Hence, the emergence of deepfakes has posed a larger security threat to users using security standards and security machines and devices. There is a need for vigilance and different types of innovative countermeasures in order to deal with the multifaceted risks that arise due to Generative AI text and content. This AI-generated text has the capacity to disrupt the normal functioning of the devices and disrupt the societal trust in the devices and, hence, compromise the integrity of the data as well as the digital identity of different verification systems.

Sophisticated Malware

Generative AI has basically advanced utilities and capabilities to generate enhanced and synthesized data that can become the most basic threat in cybersecurity. This technology can be used to harness and attract new kinds of security malware threats and, hence, pushes the boundaries for the generation of new kinds of threats. Hence, Generative AI models can become easy targets for attackers [15]. Generative AI should be used in order to deal with several security threats and different kinds of sophisticated malware threats. Malicious code for the models can be made easily with the help of adversarial actors, which can be a pretty challenging aspect for traditional cybersecurity methods and tools.

The process of conversion of Generative AI into malware poses a major threat to the cybersecurity community. The adaptive and dynamic nature of the Generative AI helps the malicious code to be executed very easily as compared to other technologies. It becomes difficult to neutralize cyberattacks in traditional methods and algorithms. It becomes important for security professionals to develop different innovative and adaptive security strategies that will combat security threats.

Detection Evasion

With the advancements in Generative AI and its ability to detect any threat these days, there has been a growing challenge for cybersecurity systems. Generative models are sophisticated models that are trained meticulously so that they intentionally go beyond the security measures of a device. As this content is so evasive in nature, security standards are not able to protect devices and no security measures will help them to be saved from such malicious Generative AI. Subtle manipulations are done by the adversarial actors, which cause the security systems to wrongly detect the threats, and this whole process gives leverage in controlling the decision-making process of the victim system. In this way, the victim system inaccurately detects the level of threat that is attacking it and hence, causing manipulation.

Generative AI is becoming smarter and better at detecting threat evasion of any form. Different models can be developed using generative models that can help in the evasion of different threats attacking a particular system. AI-based security mechanisms are made to exploit the vulnerabilities of adversarial attacks that may lead to any type of misclassification or some false negatives. The ever-evolving Generative AI systems require evolving and adaptive security systems, which not only enhance security but also provide countermeasures when required or when the system is under attack.

IP Leaks

Internet Protocol is where the user's IP address is disclosed without their intention, which can potentially compromise the security and the privacy of the user. An IP address is basically a unique identifier that is assigned to a device whenever that device is connected to the internet. The information that is revealed through an IP address is the geographical location, the identity of the user, and various other factors. Different factors are there through which an IP address can be leaked. Some of them are discussed below:

- A generative model interacts with another server with the help of API (Application Programming Interface) when on the internet and has an IP address. If this API is not secured, then the information can be exposed.
- Generative AI models depend on different external services or libraries, and if these external services are not secured in a proper way, then again, a potential IP leakage can come up. Therefore, external dependencies are needed to be secured.
- Multiple requests are made by users to the Generative AI models, which rely on metadata as these requests contain metadata, and if this data is not properly secured, then there will again be a potential IP leak if the information is not handled properly.
- Malicious scripts are used on different websites and with different Generative AI applications, which basically transmit the user's IP address without their knowledge.
- Web-based real-time communication enables web browsers to communicate with each other. If there are some vulnerabilities in this communication, then this may enable the leakage of the user's IP address, especially when the communication is a type of peer-to-peer connection.

Data Loss

The disclosure of personal information is done whenever the employees of a particular organization use the Generative AI models to perform their daily tasks over the internet, hence, personal information is shared, and it becomes valuable information for the attackers to steal. A survey report was generated in 2023, which shows that one-third of the people working in organizations take the help of Generative AI on a day-to-day basis to perform normal tasks. Around 22% of them said that they use specific tools over the internet to perform their work.

One of the most basic tools used is ChatGPT, and its popularity is so great that the attackers also attack the individuals who use this software and then uncover sensitive information of various individuals associated with different organizations. Examples of sensitive information can be trade secrets of a company, customer data, classified information of the organization, and intellectual property. This has happened to some renowned companies where the source code of one of the products got uploaded on ChatGPT to get newer solutions, which resulted in banning the use of ChatGPT from that company's workplace in order to prevent any kind of data leakage.

Synthetic Data

Synthetic data is a valuable tool that can be used for Generative AI, and there are a lot of security threats that are associated with text generation. Synthetic data is the data that is artificially generated and mimics the characteristics as it is being generated by a user or it behaves like real data. This kind of data captures certain patterns and relationships in data that may leak confidential data or sensitive information. In this way, the synthetic data contains confidential information but does not directly reveal the original data.

Membership inference attacks are employed by different adversaries, which see to it whether an instance is a part of the original data that is used to generate AI text or synthetic text. Privacy implications are imposed on users that represent the different synthetic datasets. There is a need to implement different security precautions while treating confidential data in order to mitigate the risks. Careful consideration and proactive measures should be taken to ensure the security of the synthetic data in the context of AI-generated text.

Data Training

Data training is an important aspect of synthetic data generation that involves training large datasets in order to model and generate new content such as text, images, graphics, and other media. The training of data is important for the development of accurate and powerful AI generative models. Along with this, there are potential security threats that emerge while dealing with confidential and sensitive information.

Users learn and improve their data with the help of Generative AI, and hence, attackers can reverse-engineer or reconstruct different parts of training data by easily analyzing the generated content. Information about the individuals can be extracted through this process in the training dataset. Model inversion attacks are used to extract useful information from the training data by using some specific queries and seeing the responses for the same. Carefully curated methods are used to remove any kind of personal data of an individual.

Research Contributions

The following section discusses major research fields in the field of Generative AI (Fig. **8**). Research contributions are discussed in detail.

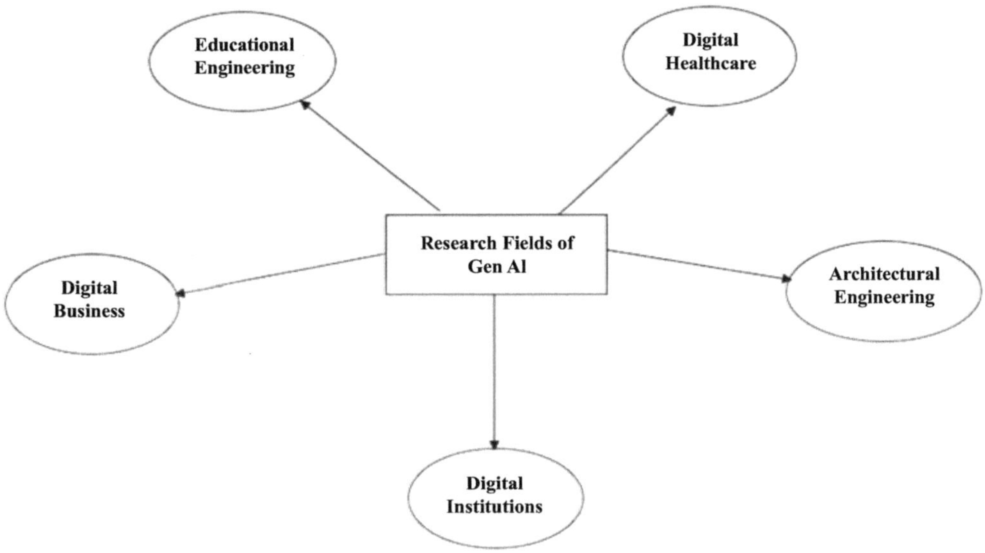

Fig. (8). Major research fields in Generative AI.

Education Engineering

Education engineering helps students to learn about necessary skills that are required for the fast-paced world. The latest advancements will be included in the students' curriculum, which can be challenging for different educators. Some curricular and co-curricular activities should be there in order to train students to become better in all activities and help them make better engineers with multidimensional qualities. Fast changes in technology need to be adapted. Educators need new adaptive and creative ways to use Generative AI and help students focus on it. Professional ethics are also important for educators in this field. Generative AI plays an important part in revolutionizing the design of engineering education, and there are specific examples where students learn from this technology.

Hence, Generative AI is able to revolutionize engineering education by providing all the relative updates and interactive content for students and educators and keeping everything up-to-date. Educators can provide a good learning experience to students with the help of Generative AI and align their ideologies with the industrial demands as well as technological advancements. Creating design scenarios, dynamic simulations are tailored in such a way that students can have theoretical knowledge that they can apply practically through different skills in the real world. Generative AI can help streamline the curriculum design and syllabus; assessments are given to students, with areas for continuous improvements for students and facilitating the evidence-based programs.

Digital Healthcare

Digital healthcare created ChatGPT in order to support patient engagement with healthcare professionals and for commercial purposes. After that, ChatGPT became a Personalized Automatic Messaging System (PAMS) [6]. The performance, capacity, limitations, and advantages are all studied for ChatGPT to get help in product ideation, content development, conceptualization, and software engineering processes that include requirement generation, code production of the design, and the software design for the same. Generative AI has played an important social role in order to help the healthcare industry in so many different ways. Computational tools developed by Generative AI, which are flexible, usable, durable, scalable, extensible, *etc.*, form the standards of Generative AI. Different prompts are included in the framework along with intervention conceptualization as well as the software development process. Fig. (9) shows how AI knowledge is constructed using different prompts in various healthcare applications.

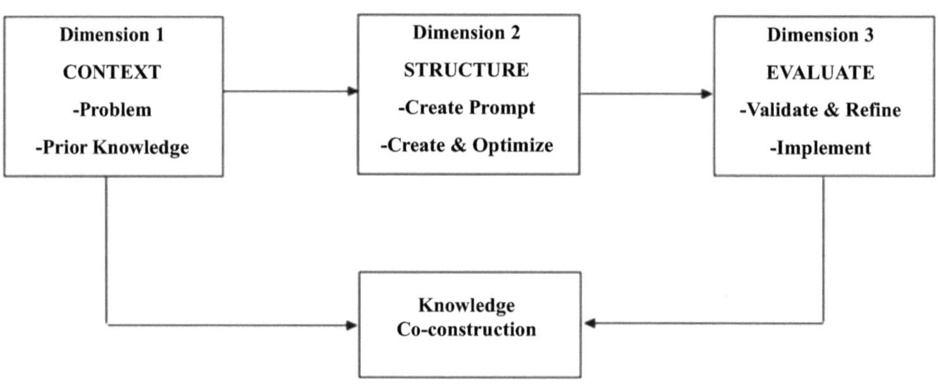

Fig. (9). Co-constructed AI Knowledge.

ChatGPT is able to create a novel digital behavior machine, which is being developed with the help of patient engagement and healthcare commercialization. The capacity and the limitations of ChatGPT in the field of healthcare and software development make it feasible, resource-saving, and time-efficient and provids support to the research teams that make products and technologies for the healthcare of patients. There are different gaps in the outputs in ChatGPT that may limit the effectiveness of this advanced technology developer and this may also affect the completeness of the outputs. The development of more targeted AI-based tools that support the healthcare business and the healthcare researchers is necessary. All levels of software engineering skills are to be covered along with the development of tools that objectively analyze the Generative AI outputs.

Digital Business

Generative AI, including AI-based generative models and ChatGPT, has become popular with business practitioners, and this technology has given them the ability to systematically change what is going on these days and what can come in the next few years. AI tools augment human-like nature and behavior. Effective implementation is required in order to develop one's skills efficiently and effectively. Impactful and appropriate prompts are developed for meaningful engagement of generated content and the users dealing and engaging with it. This helps in optimizing the learning process. Prompts become an important and necessary skill that needs to be harnessed up to its full potential. Constructivist theory is used here, and with its principles, individuals assimilate a lot of knowledge with their existing understanding of the same knowledge. This engagement of AI and humans is co-constructed with the help of Generative AI. Fig. (**10**) shows an enhanced prompt structure that describes how prompts are generated with different stages in a simple ChatGPT structure.

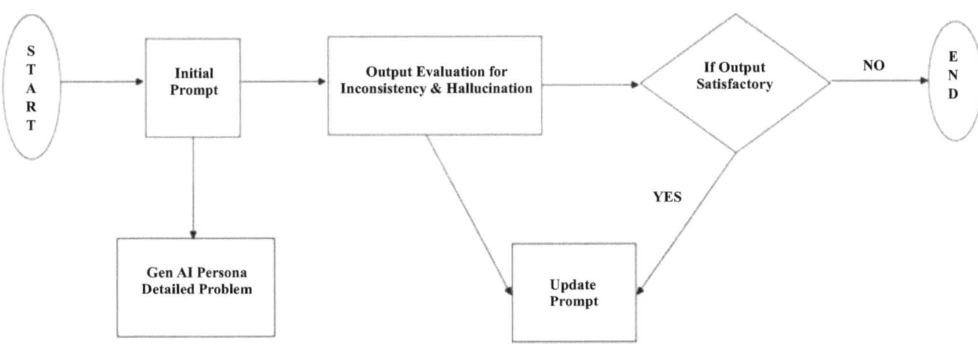

Fig. (10). ChatGPT prompt structure.

The goal of Generative AI is to empower the business teams to make different types of AI prompts that validate the responses, enhance the user interaction, and optimize the workflow, hence maximizing the outputs and performances. With the inclusion of the constructivism theory, Generative AI technologies like ChatGPT and different tools have enhanced knowledge acquisition practices significantly. With the help of AI tools, this Generative AI can generate creative and comprehensive content regularly with a slip of a second. The only disability they currently have is to generate contextual information and provide the information based on the outputs solely based on any given input or prompt. Further studies on this can focus on the conceptualization of context by enhancing the AI's ability for the same, and it can prove as an exciting research field.

Architectural Engineering

Multiple facets of architectural engineering are incorporated with Generative AI, and hence, technologies like ChatGPT play a major role in reshaping the diversifying aspects of architectural engineering. There is a profound influence of Generative AI on structural and architectural engineering, electrical engineering, fire protection engineering, green building design, urban planning and engineering, project engineering: development and management, building information modeling and simulation, *etc.* ChatGPT is able to analyze all the extensive datasets, and it can simulate different intricate data structures with the help of the design process, ensuring structural integrity and optimizing the costs. Energy-efficient systems, such as climate control systems, sustainable building systems, *etc.*, are used in HVAC engineering. AI's capabilities have reached new heights in designing and the optimization of electrical systems that ensure safety as well as the reliability of electrical systems.

In fire protection engineering, ChatGPT helps in creating very inclusive and efficient design layouts of plumbing as well as fire suppression systems that not only ensure compliance but also see to it that everything is done under regulations. Advanced sustainability and green building designs are made by different Generative AI software in the field of environment engineering. By evaluating all the environmental factors and looking into all the eco-friendly materials, designs are made for responsible and efficient structures. Data security, ethical concerns, and the necessity of very skilled professionals are a few challenges that AI and architectural engineering face. These challenges potentially deplete the performance of Generative AI and hence, it becomes very important for these technologies to transform and overcome these challenges.

Digital Institutions

Institution performance and how Generative AI can help in improving productivity and overall work performance have become the talk of the town. In this research, different sectors have been studied, such as technologies used, architecture design, communications, government, academia, agriculture, research methodologies implemented, business opportunities, *etc.* A detailed content analysis has been done in such a way that all the analytical and social domains and the future results have been covered for the same. An analytical and robust trend has been seen in the field of Generative AI that can provide research directions and impact user experiences over a given time and in various professional fields. The integration of Generative AI with different organizations helps increase the productivity and accuracy of the technical reports given. After all the benefits and the application of Generative AI in all fields, there are still cultural and social implications that can prove to be the major challenges in this field.

An in-depth review analysis is done for the applications of Generative AI in different fields like communications, research engineering, academia, agricultural sciences, public administration, *etc.* A comprehensive content analysis is done, which reveals noteworthy findings for different Generative AI applications, which provide various difficulties and challenges for the same. Generative AI promotes emphasis on educational governance, academia, and information exchange, and the main emphasis is on safety, error detection, increased efficiency, *etc.* All the technologies integrated with Generative AI try to improve the user experience as well as the communication and reputation of different associated companies.

In the healthcare industry, the role of chatbots comes into play for medical tasks, and the emphasis is on privacy and practices for medical healthcare professionals. The government uses Generative AI in the agricultural industry in order to boost production and overcome any obstacles faced by the stakeholders, as well as the issues with data and the security and confidentiality of data. The role of Generative AI in the business management field helps in the growth of associated companies, again emphasizing data security and the balance of human aspects. Hence, computer science research helps in examining and predicting performance while addressing different societal and ethical issues.

CONCLUSION

The exploration of opportunities and security challenges in communication engineering through Generative AI reveals a dynamic and transformative potential in the field. Generative models have the capability to deal with security concerns and, hence, enhance efficiency and accuracy. Optimized network performances, complex automation, and the creation of advanced network models lead to a technical revolution in the field of communication models.

Significant security challenges exist in the integration of Generative AI into the communication models, which may lead to the malicious exploitation of the data. Assurance of security and integrity is very necessary for AI-driven systems as real-time threat detection may occur, which includes advanced encryption details and different security-based strategies. Multi-disciplinary approaches are used to deal with security standards in Generative AI for cybersecurity in communication engineering. Hence, substantial advancements are required along with rigorous security protocols to harness the full potential levels of Generative AI that pave the way to a safer landscape.

REFERENCES

[1] S. Feuerriegel, J. Hartmann, C. Janiesch, and P. Zschech, "Generative AI", *Bus. Inf. Syst. Eng.,* vol. 66, no. 1, pp. 111-126, 2024.
[http://dx.doi.org/10.1007/s12599-023-00834-7]

[2] Z. Epstein, A. Hertzmann, M. Akten, H. Farid, J. Fjeld, M.R. Frank, M. Groh, L. Herman, N. Leach, R. Mahari, A.S. Pentland, O. Russakovsky, H. Schroeder, and A. Smith, "Art and the science of Generative AI", *Science,* vol. 380, no. 6650, pp. 1110-1111, 2023.
[http://dx.doi.org/10.1126/science.adh4451] [PMID: 37319193]

[3] A. Bandi, P.V.S.R. Adapa, and Y.E.V.P.K. Kuchi, "The power of Generative AI: A review of requirements, models, input–output formats, evaluation metrics, and challenges", *Future Internet,* vol. 15, no. 8, p. 260, 2023.
[http://dx.doi.org/10.3390/fi15080260]

[4] E. Brynjolfsson, D. Li, and L. R. Raymond, "Generative AI at work," *National Bureau of Economic Research*, Working Paper No. w31161, 2023.

[5] K. Kenthapadi, H. Lakkaraju, and N. Rajani, "Generative AI meets responsible AI: Practical challenges and opportunities", *Proceedings of the 29th ACM SIGKDD Conference on Knowledge Discovery and Data Mining,* pp. 5805-5806, 2023.

[6] R. Michel-Villarreal, E. Vilalta-Perdomo, D.E. Salinas-Navarro, R. Thierry-Aguilera, and F.S. Gerardou, "Challenges and opportunities of Generative AI for higher education as explained by ChatGPT," *", *Educ. Sci. (Basel),* vol. 13, no. 9, p. 856, 2023.
[http://dx.doi.org/10.3390/educsci13090856]

[7] R. Yelamarthi, R. Dandu, M. Rao, V. P. Yanambaka, and S. Mahajan, "Exploring the potential of Generative AI in shaping engineering education: Opportunities and challenges," *J. Eng. Educ. Transform.* , 2024, 37, 439–445.

[8] D.V. Rodriguez, K. Lawrence, J. Gonzalez, B. Brandfield-Harvey, L. Xu, S. Tasneem, D.L. Levine, and D. Mann, "Leveraging Generative AI tools to support the development of digital solutions in health care research: Case study", *JMIR Human Factors,* vol. 11, p. e52885, 2024.
[http://dx.doi.org/10.2196/52885] [PMID: 38446539]

[9] J. Robertson, C. Ferreira, E. Botha, and K. Oosthuizen, "Game changers: A Generative AI prompt protocol to enhance human-AI knowledge co-construction," *Bus. Horiz.* 2021, 67, 5, pp. 499-510.
[http://dx.doi.org/10.1016/j.bushor.2024.04.008]

[10] N. Rane, "Potential role and challenges of ChatGPT and similar generative artificial intelligence in architectural engineering," *Int. J. Artif. Intell. Mach. Learn.* 2024.
[http://dx.doi.org/10.51483/IJAIML.4.1.2024.22-47]

[11] H. Al Naqbi, Z. Bahroun, and V. Ahmed, "Enhancing work productivity through generative artificial intelligence: A comprehensive literature review", *Sustainability (Basel),* vol. 16, no. 3, p. 1166, 2024.
[http://dx.doi.org/10.3390/su16031166]

[12] U. Kant, and V. Kumar, "“IoT network used in fog and cloud computing,” in Internet of Things: Security and Privacy in Cyberspace, Singapore: Springer", *Nat. Singap.,* pp. 165-187, 2022.

[13] F. Fui-Hoon Nah, R. Zheng, J. Cai, K. Siau, and L. Chen, "Generative AI and ChatGPT: Applications, challenges, and AI-human collaboration", *J. Inf. Technol. Case Appl. Res.* , vol. 25, no. 3, pp. 277-304, 2023.
[http://dx.doi.org/10.1080/15228053.2023.2233814]

[14] A. Golda, K. Mekonen, A. Pandey, A. Singh, V. Hassija, V. Chamola, and B. Sikdar, "Privacy and security concerns in Generative AI: A comprehensive survey", *IEEE Access,* vol. 12, pp. 48126-48144, 2024.
[http://dx.doi.org/10.1109/ACCESS.2024.3381611]

[15] Y. Chen, and P. Esmaeilzadeh, "Generative AI in medical practice: In-depth exploration of privacy and security challenges", *J. Med. Internet Res.,* vol. 26, p. e53008, 2024.
[http://dx.doi.org/10.2196/53008] [PMID: 38457208]

SUBJECT INDEX

A

B

C

D

Shelly Gupta, Sapna Juneja & Sandeep Kautish (Eds.)
All rights reserved-© 2025 Bentham Science Publishers

M

N

O

P

Q

R

S

T

U

V

W

Y

www.ingramcontent.com/pod-product-compliance
Lightning Source LLC
LaVergne TN
LVHW070950210926
848482LV00002B/168